IMAGES
of America

ROCHESTER

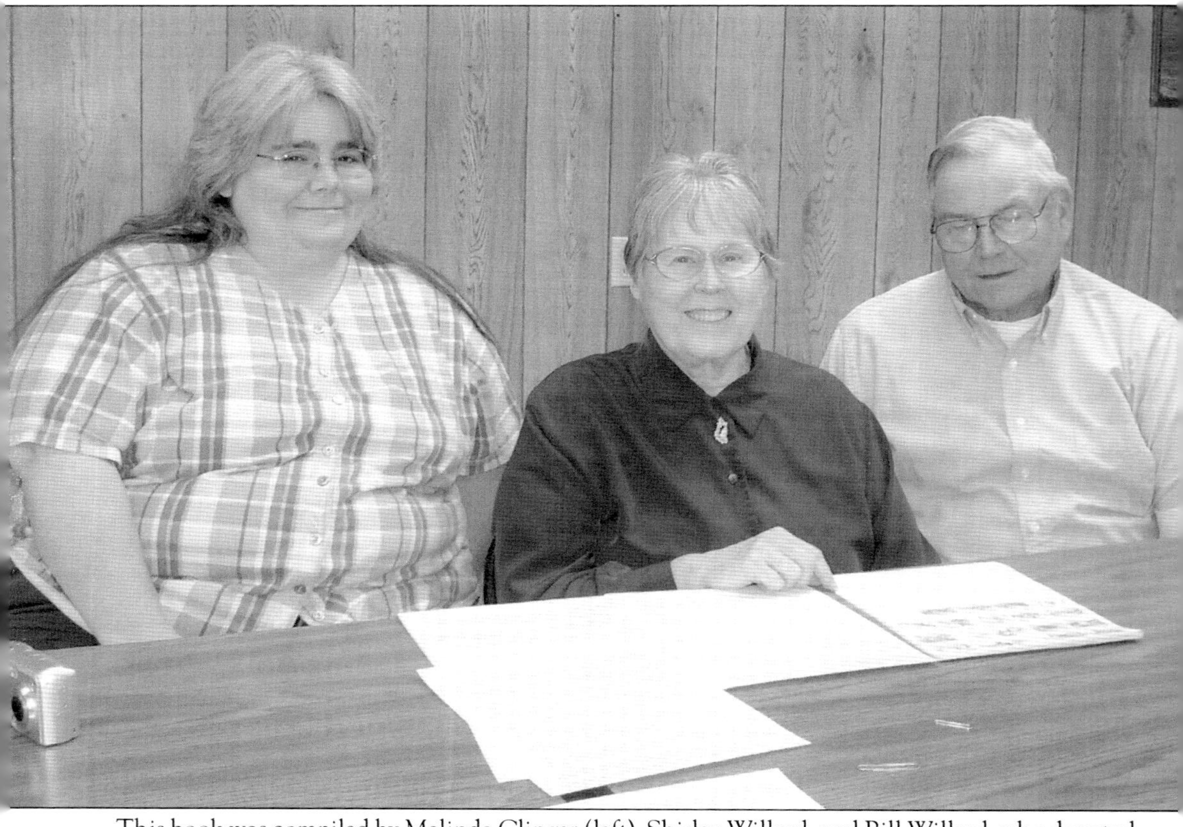

This book was compiled by Melinda Clinger (left), Shirley Willard, and Bill Willard, who donated their time to do the work of putting it together. Bill and Melinda scanned the photographs. Shirley wrote the captions and did the organizing. (Courtesy of the Fulton County Museum.)

On the Cover: William Jennings Bryan attracted an estimated 25,000 to hear his speech as the Democratic candidate for president. In 1896, the "silver-tongued orator" from Nebraska came to Rochester's brand new courthouse. Bryan was defeated in November by Republican William McKinley. This photograph was taken by photographer George Moore, who had a studio on the second floor across Main Street from the courthouse. The lines across the photograph are utility wires. (Courtesy of the Fulton County Museum.)

IMAGES
of America

ROCHESTER

Shirley Willard with the
Fulton County Historical Society

ARCADIA
PUBLISHING

ISBN 978-0-7385-6177-6

Published by Arcadia Publishing
Charleston, South Carolina

Printed in the United States of America

Library of Congress Control Number: 2008926312

For all general information contact Arcadia Publishing at:
Telephone 843-853-2070
Fax 843-853-0044
E-mail sales@arcadiapublishing.com
For customer service and orders:
Toll-Free 1-888-313-2665

Visit us on the Internet at www.arcadiapublishing.com

We dedicate this book to Jack K. Overmyer, who founded the Fulton County Historical Society in 1963. We also dedicate this to all present and past residents of Rochester, Indiana, who lived here and loved history, supported its preservation, and worked toward the future of the Fulton County Museum, which supplied most of the photographs in this book. We thank all of you and sincerely hope you enjoy and treasure this book.

Contents

ACKNOWLEDGMENTS

This is a sample of the thousands of pictures preserved in the Fulton County Museum. Thanks to its diligent museum director, Melinda Clinger, for helping me select and scan the photographs in this book. Annette Wise, Peggy Van Meter, and Lola Riddle helped with research to be sure that the captions are accurate. I spent many hours searching for dates and information for the captions, including the city council books at city hall. Thanks to Wendell Tombaugh's books of indexes and newspaper excerpts, obituaries, and handbooks, enabling us to find the data for this book. Without his books, this research would have taken so much time as to make it impossible.

Without the museum, Rochester's history would be scattered in many homes and attics or lost entirely. We greatly appreciate this special treasure, the Fulton County Museum, which was made possible by donations from hundreds of individuals, clubs, and businesses.

Thanks to my patient husband, Bill Willard, for scanning pictures and helping me with the computer, which at times was very frustrating.

Thanks for contributing pictures go to the *Rochester Sentinel*, Rochester schools, Fincher's DeBruler Studio, and various members of the public. We are very grateful to them. Photographs without courtesy lines are from the Fulton County Museum; others are acknowledged with a courtesy line. I wish we could have included all the photographs and materials that were offered, but this book has a specific number of pictures and pages. Thank you to all those who helped with history, photographs, memories, and history.

A few of the photographs were taken by me in 2009. This book has old photographs and new photographs, a sample of life in Rochester, Indiana, from A to Z, Arlington Hotel to Zac DeBois. We tried to include the various aspects of life, including schools and businesses, young and old, fun and work. We hope you enjoy this book and also use it for a reference when questions of history come up.

—Shirley Willard
President Emerita
Fulton County Historical Society

INTRODUCTION

There are more than 12 towns or cities named Rochester in the United States. The name comes from England, which has two Rochesters: one near London (where Charles Dickens lived) and one in northern England. Any English place name that ends in –chester is a former Roman military settlement. The term means "Rock-chester" or "the fort near (or on) a rock." A Canadian town near Edmonton, Alberta, bears the name of Rochester. Australia has a Rochester in Victoria. These four are the only Rochesters outside the United States. The states that boast of having a town or city named Rochester include Massachusetts—its Rochester was founded 1686—New Hampshire (1722), Vermont (1781), New York (1803), Kentucky (1786), Pennsylvania (1806), Illinois (1818), Indiana (1835), Wisconsin (1838), Minnesota (1855), Washington (1890), and Texas (1906). Two other Rochesters once existed in Oklahoma and Nevada. In addition, there are many Rochester townships and other entities, plus several variations on the name, such as Rochester Junction, Michigan; Rochester Mills, Pennsylvania; and Rochester Place, Ohio.

Rochester, Indiana, is not a big, well-known place like Rochester, New York, which is famous as the birthplace of the Eastman-Kodak Company; or Rochester, Minnesota, famed for its Mayo Clinic. Farming and agribusiness provide the major portion of the Hoosier Rochester's landscape. Lake Manitou and the Tippecanoe River provide recreation, and this little Rochester has many outstanding features and qualities that make it unusual.

There must be something in the drinking water that produced so many famous people from this one small town, which today has a population of 6,500. The first white settler, William Polke, fought in the 1794 Battle of Fallen Timbers and the 1811 Battle of Tippecanoe, was elected Indiana Territorial representative, and served on the Constitutional Convention of 1816, as surveyor of the Michigan Road 1830, and then as commissioner to sell Michigan road lands. He was the federal conductor on the Potawatomi "Trail of Death" from Indiana to Kansas in 1838.

Following him are many other famous people from the area including, Elmo Lincoln (the big screen's first Tarzan); Clyde Beatty (circus lion and tiger trainer); and Dr. Otis Bowen (Indiana governor from 1973 to 1981 and secretary of Health and Human Services under Pres. Ronald Reagan). Other famous people who lived in Rochester or Rochester Township include Oliver "The Pacing Farmer" Powell (who won horse races from 1895 to 1953, setting six world records); Jorgen Christiansen (circus horse trainer who trained the first Liberty Horse act in 1924); Zoppe-Zavatta (a family of circus performers with horses, dogs, unsupported ladders, clowns, juggling, and more from 1920s to the present); the Great Gretonas (high wire performers); Floyd J. "Jack" Mattice (first in nation to broadcast a sports event in 1903); Col. Isaac Washington Brown (the "Bird and Bee Man," who traveled the United States giving speeches to save birds); Marguerite Miller (popular Chautauqua speaker in 1920s as well as editor and author); the King's Jesters (radio singers from the 1920s until the 1960s); and others. Even Rochester's livestock has made headlines: Ellen, a local Holstein cow, was a world-champion milk producer whose record stood from 1975 to 1992.

Rochester, though small, has more important history and truly famous individuals than most towns of its size. (Unfortunately, we could not find good clear photographs of all of them.) Three events of especial historic importance took place in or near the town: on September 4, 1838, nearly 900 Potawatomi Indians were marched single file down Rochester's Main Street on the infamous Trail of Death from Indiana to eastern Kansas. Realizing the unjustness of this event, the Fulton County Historical Society (FCHS) began the annual Trail of Courage Living History Festival in 1976 to commemorate and honor the Potawatomi. In 1988, for the 150th anniversary of the march, the FCHS began work with 25 other counties to help erect 78 Trail of Death historical markers, establish a commemorative caravan held every five years to travel the 660-mile route, and place historic highway signs at each turn to mark the trail's route. The Potawatomi Trail of Death Association, a branch of FCHS, created a Web site (www.potawatomi-tda.org) that shows pictures of all the markers, GPS locations, driving directions, Polke's 1838 diary, and histories of Chief Menominee, Fr. Benjamin Petit, and St. Philippine Duchesne. (The Fulton County Historical Society has three other branches: Genealogy, Blacksmiths, and Historical Power.)

The second event of national import was the building of round barns in the area from 1910 to 1924. The annual Round Barn Festival is held in downtown Rochester because Fulton County has more round barns than any other county in Indiana, and Indiana has more round barns than any other state. The Rochester Chamber of Commerce sponsors the Round Barn Festival in June.

A third item of great historic importance was the discovery of Rochester's giant short-faced bear skeleton in 1967. The largest giant short-faced bear discovered in the continental United States and the only one in Indiana, it can now be viewed at the new Indiana State Museum in Indianapolis.

Rochester was founded in 1835, organized as a town in 1853, and incorporated as a city in 1910. It is a dynamic thriving town today and keeps up with the very latest developments. For example, Rochester High School adopted New Tech High (computer project-based teaching) in 2007 and is hailed as one of the Midwest's most outstanding schools. An addition to the public library in 2007 doubled its size. The Fulton County Tourism Commission has a Web site (www.rochestertourism.org) that includes bicycling routes on public roads. Rochester's airport is one of the best in the area, even through some neighboring counties have a bigger population. The Fulton County Recycling Center, located on Wentzel Street, not only recycles but also has a compost area. Rochester Telephone Company offers internet, email, and cable television. Rochester still has a daily newspaper whose Web site offers videos of interviews and local events. WROI is Rochester's own radio station.

According to the Indiana Historical Society, the Fulton County Historical Society is one of the five most active and outstanding historical societies in the state. FCHS is often cited as an example of what a small community can do without a lot of money. FCHS bought 35 acres in 1985 with money saved from producing the annual Trail of Courage. The Fulton County Museum was built in 1986–1988 with donations. The Leedy/Partridge/Paxton round barn was moved and restored in 1990–1991. The William Polke 1832 house and stagecoach inn was donated by Airvac and moved in 1993. At that point FCHS decided to create a Living History Village to portray the years 1900–1925 and call it Loyal, Indiana, for a tiny village that once existed 4 miles west of the museum. This village was originally called Germany but changed its name during World War I to Loyal. The buildings in the Living History Village include a print shop, blacksmith shop, 1876 depot, round brooder house, 1920s general store (donated by Rochester Telephone Company), 1912 Kewanna jail, log cabin, old-time doctors and dentists office, Athens cider mill, and octagonal corncrib. The village also includes 160 feet of railroad track, a caboose, boxcar, railcar garage, windmill, and Rochester Bridge Company bridge.

The Fulton County Historical Society preserves Rochester's history and all of the county's history at its museum. FCHS festivals range from frontier life (Redbud Trail Rendezvous in April and the Trail of Courage in September) to modern antiques (Historical Power Show in June). See FCHS Web site at www.fultoncountyhistory.org.

One

Horse and Buggy Days

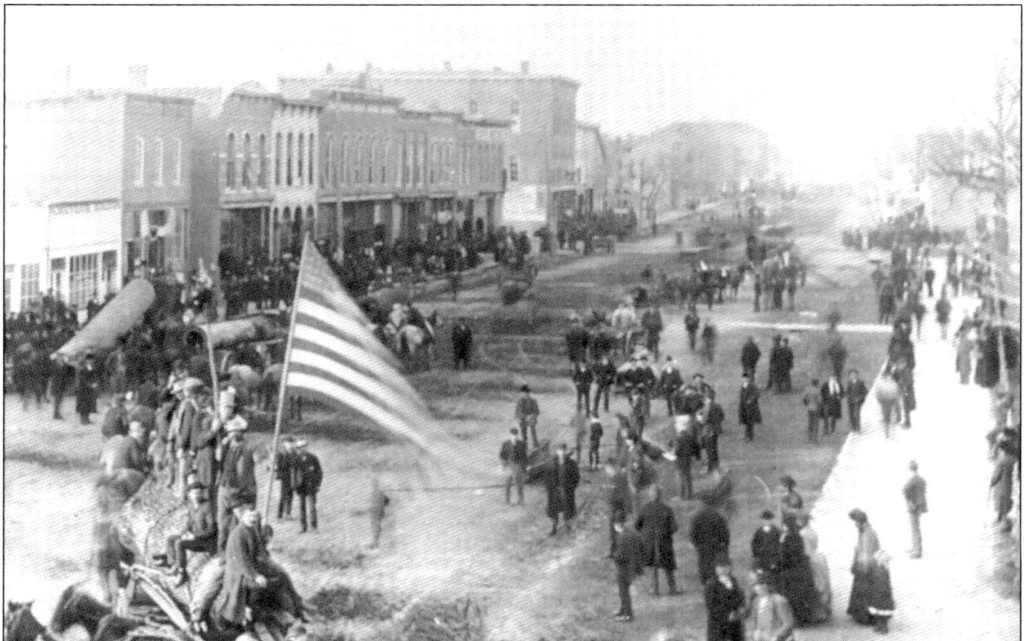

Gum logs were burned to celebrate elections, the Fourth of July, and other events. In November 1888, Indiana Republican Benjamin Harrison won the presidency. When the news arrived by telegraph, local Republicans staged a big celebration with gum burning, parade, speeches, and fireworks. This scene is in front of the courthouse looking north. Notice the wooden buildings at left. They were soon replaced by brick buildings.

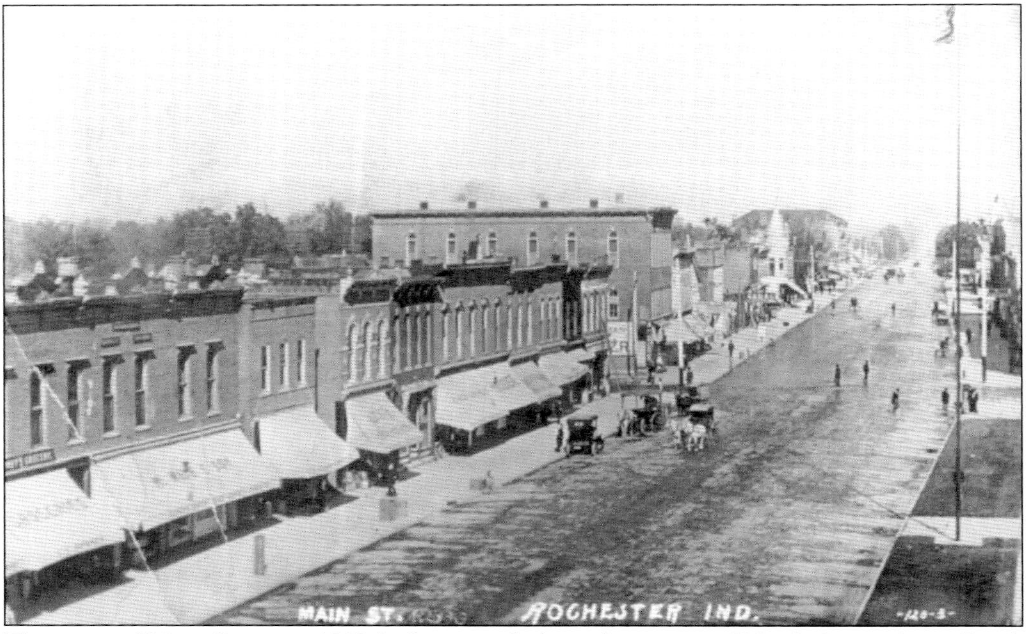

This view of Main Street in 1909 looking north from the corner of Ninth Street shows Frank Marsh Grocery, Wile's Clothing, Cy Davis Variety, Meier Levi Dry Goods, Dave Shaw Cigar Store, and Hoosier Shoe Store. The three-story building on the corner was built by the Masonic lodge and had the First National Bank downstairs from 1914 to 1972. The three-story building at the end of town was the opera house. (Courtesy of Stephen Coleman.)

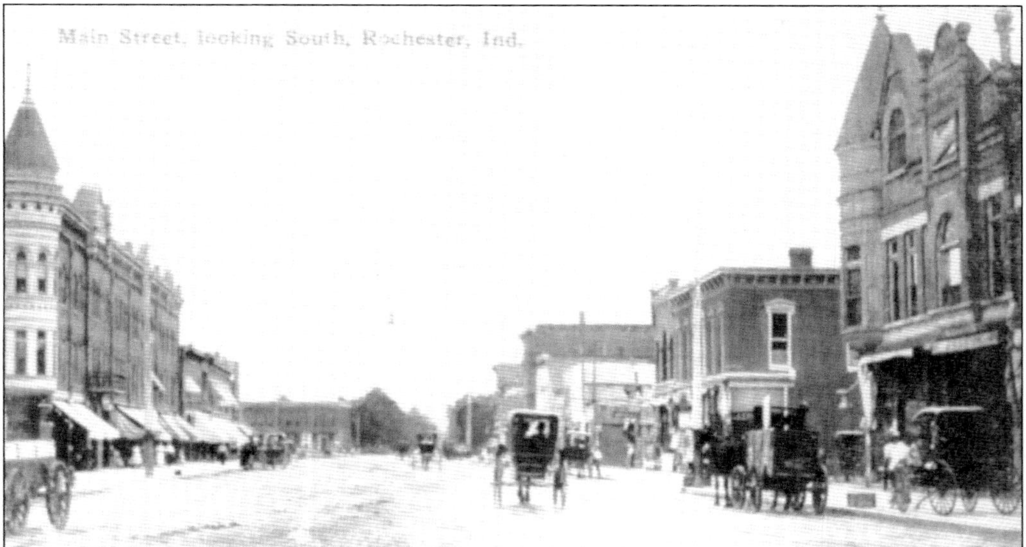

Main Street in 1912 had two buildings with turrets on the corners of Main and Seventh Street. On the east side was the Arlington Hotel (left), and on the west was Newby's Drug Store, which operated from 1911 to 1916. It was Gilbert's Drug Store in the 1930s, a popular hangout for high school students after school. Seldon Brown had his office in the corner tower, which was removed before the building became a furniture store in 1950.

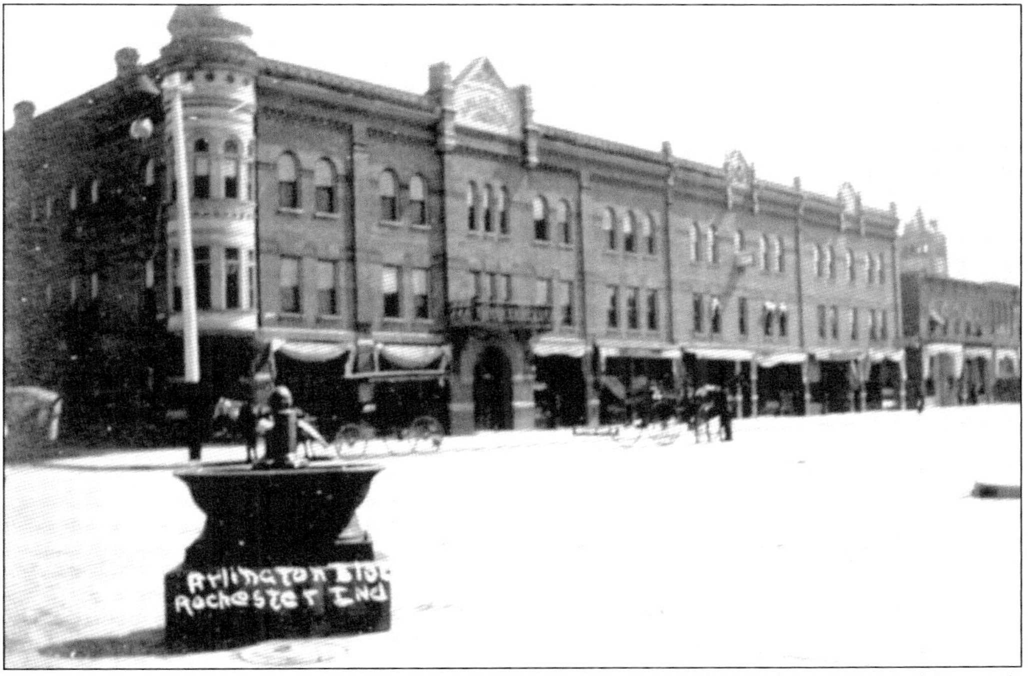

Arlington Block contained the Arlington (also known as Barrett) Hotel at Main and Seventh Streets. The hotel operated from 1890 to 1962. In the foreground is a circular horse trough, several of which stood on street corners. A horse-drawn hack stands in front of the hotel to transport guests to the depot. The courthouse tower can be seen at the upper right. (Courtesy of *Rochester Sentinel.*)

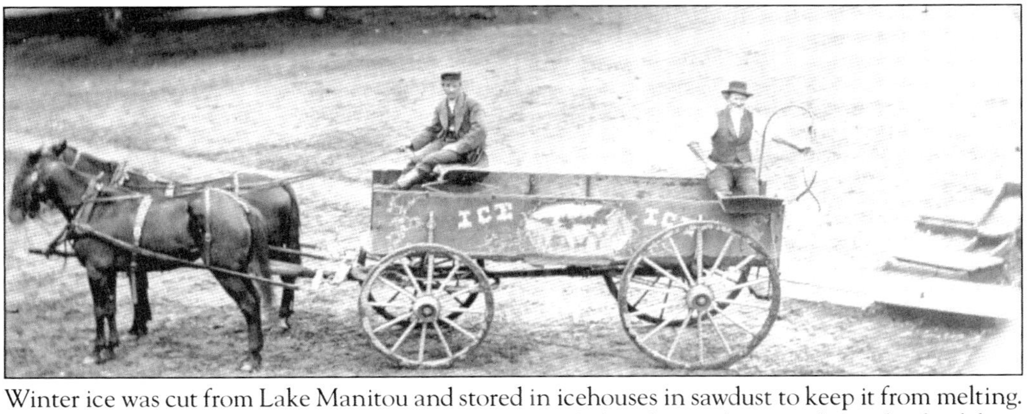

Winter ice was cut from Lake Manitou and stored in icehouses in sawdust to keep it from melting. In summer, blocks of ice were delivered to houses and placed in iceboxes to keep the food from spoiling. William Carter is shown seated at the rear of his ice wagon, with a chunk of ice suspended from the scales. (Courtesy of *Rochester Sentinel.*)

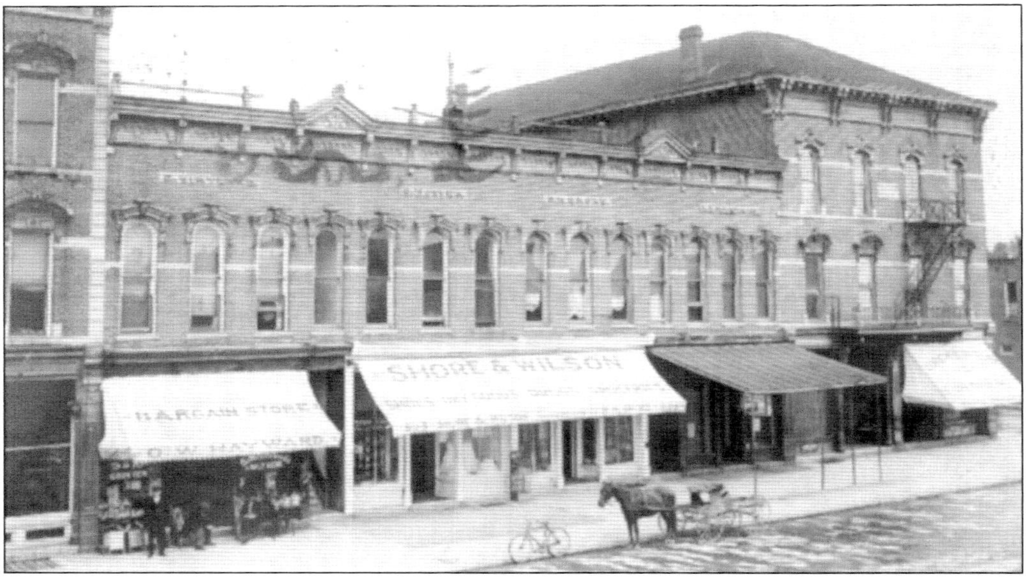

Old Cap the delivery horse stands waiting in front of Shore and Wilson Grocery at 506–508 Main Street in 1911. To the left is Hayward's Bargain Store, and at right is the opera house or Academy of Music, built by William H. Davidson in 1876. The awning says "Balms Groceries and Dishes." Names at the top of the buildings are E. Kirkland, C. Hoover, P. M. Shore, and V. Zimmerman. A bicycle stands at the high curb.

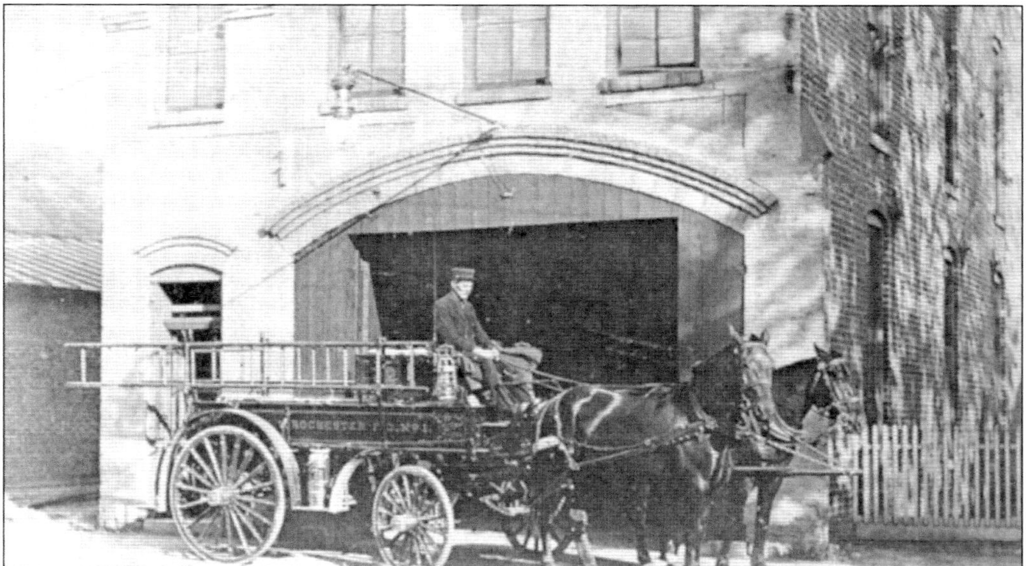

Joe Bibler is driving the new hook and ladder wagon, purchased in 1908. Rochester Fire Station on East Seventh Street was built in 1878. A volunteer company of fire fighters called Protection Hook and Ladder Company was mentioned as early as 1859. Now located in a new fire station on State Road 14, they still own the 1908 fire wagon (with "1910" painted on it). (Courtesy of *Rochester Sentinel.*)

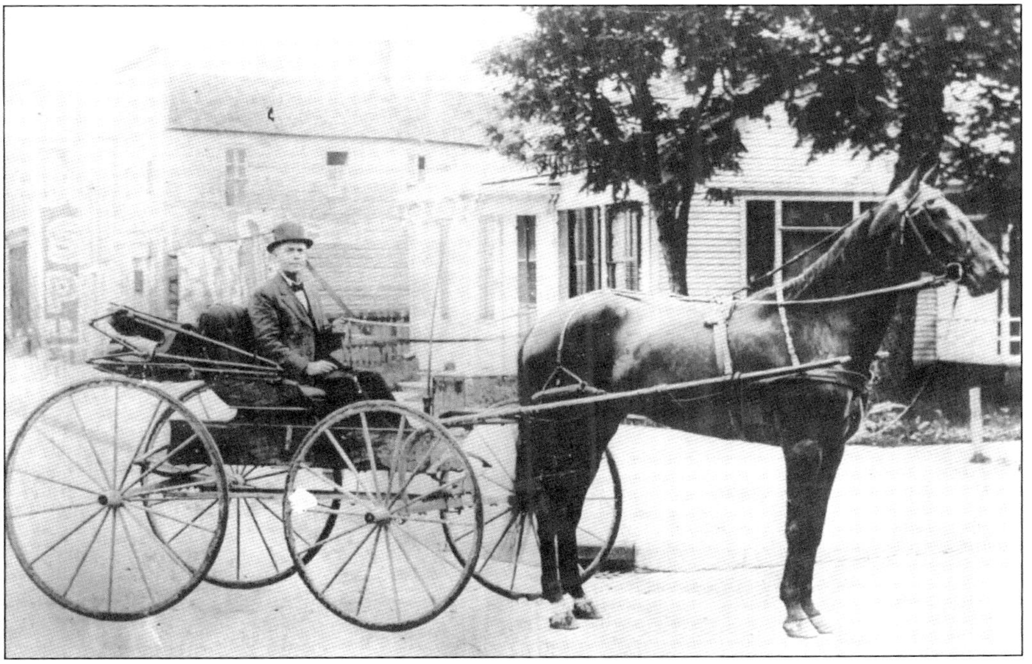

Above, Dr. Isaac L. Babcock shows off his fancy horse and rig in 1908 at the corner of Main and Sixth Streets. The house on the corner was moved to West Ninth Street when Louderback's Garage was built. Babcock liked to race horses. He was elected a member of Rochester's first city council in 1910. He died at Woodlawn Hospital in 1912.

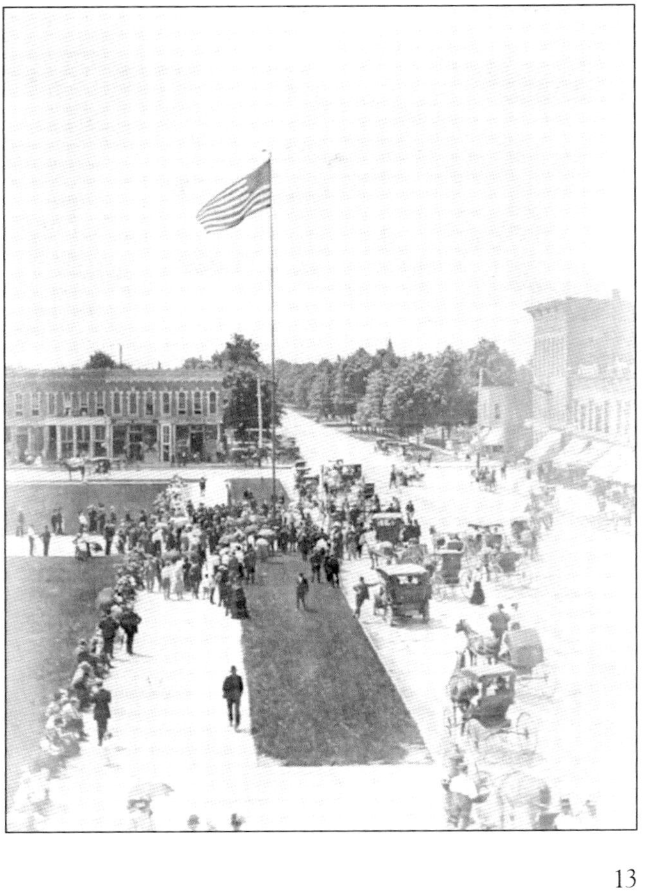

A ceremony on May 30, 1908, dedicated the first flagpole erected in front of the courthouse. A Civil War veterans group, the McClung Post Grand Army of the Republic, paid for the flagpole. A band plays from a stand, and spectators seek shade under parasols. The flagpole was moved 60 feet east, and the pole was shortened 8 feet on August 14, 1974, when Main Street was widened. (Courtesy of *Rochester Sentinel*.)

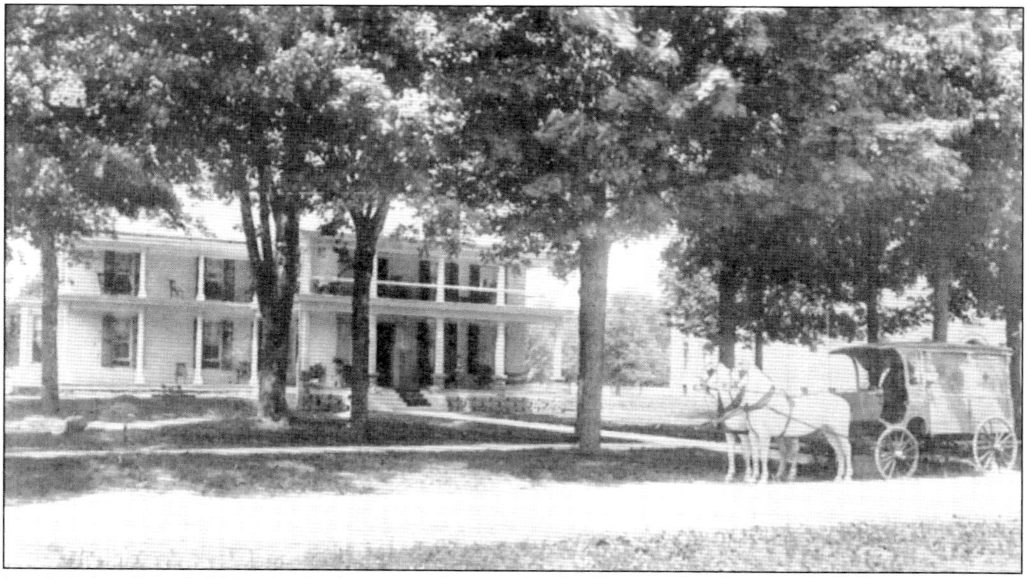

In 1905, Dr. Winfield S. Shafer founded a hospital in his home at Seventh and Pontiac Streets. In this 1910 photograph, Val Zimmerman's ambulance (also used as a hearse) waits to make a call. The matched white horses were kept at Ward and Huffer livery barn. This house was demolished in 1936 and replaced with the first part of the brick hospital at this site.

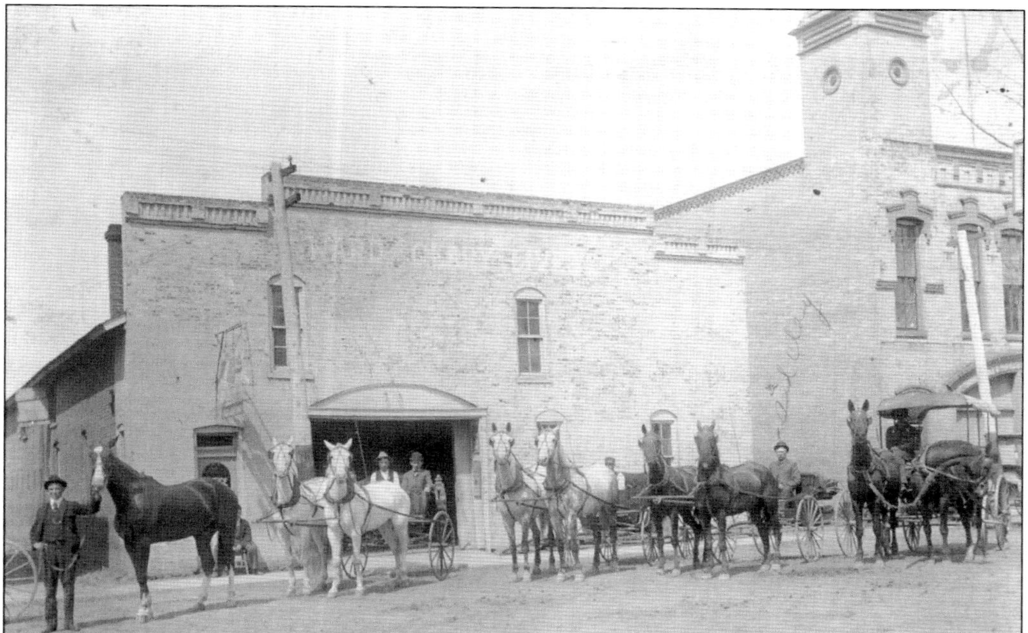

William "Uncle Del" Ward and Elbert Clary's livery stable (formerly Ward and Huffer) was located east of Arlington Hotel on East Seventh Street. Ward had moved to Rochester as a child in 1832 and saw the Potawatomi march through town on their way to Kansas in 1838. He operated the livery stables from 1855 to 1895. After Ward retired, the business was called Clary and Shobe Livery, then Clary and Onstott Livery. (Courtesy of *Rochester Sentinel*.)

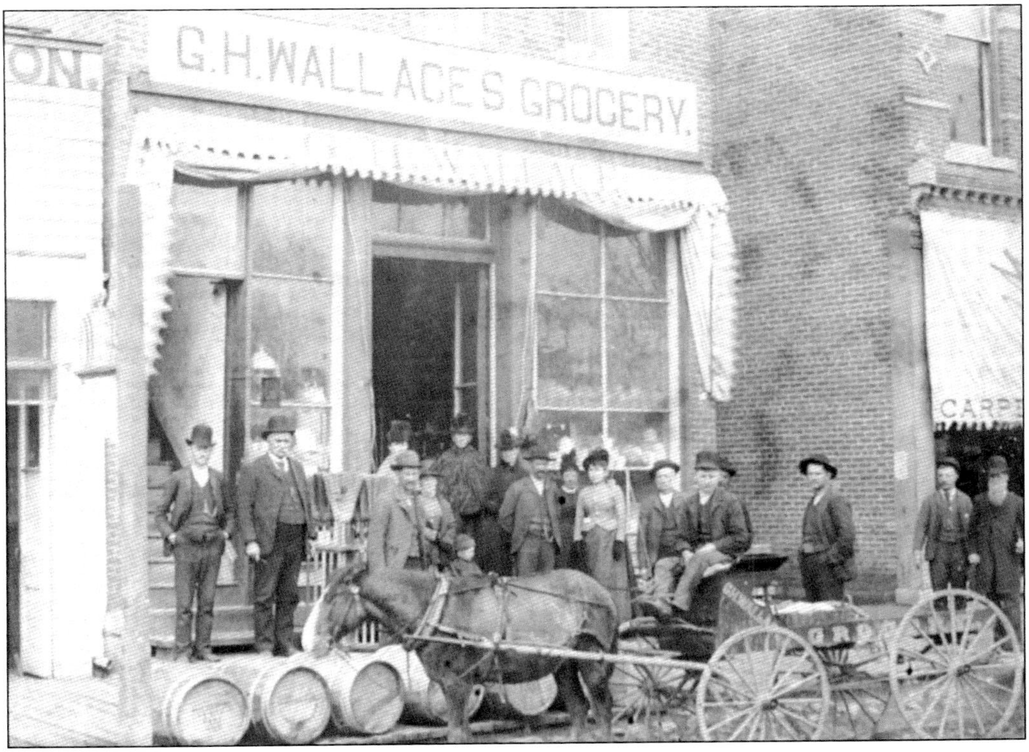

G. H. Wallace's Groceries was on the south side of the alley at 816 Main Street. George Wallace also sold clothing, dry goods, shoes, and carpets. Beginning in 1858, he was in the general merchandising and produce business for 45 years and had business locations in practically every block in downtown Rochester. Coal oil lamps were the only lighting in his store.

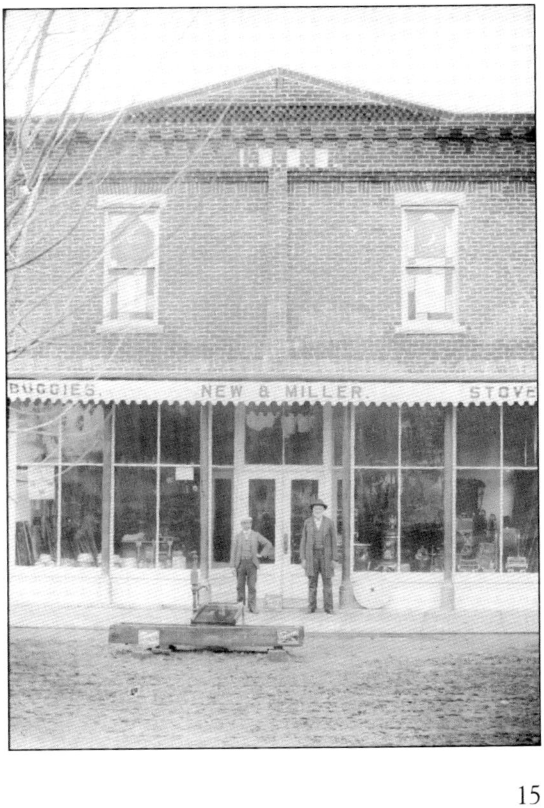

A pair of men pose outside the store of New B. Miller at 625 Main Street. According to the slate on the ground between the men, it is November 17, 1902. Notice the dirt street and the hand pump and horse watering trough at the curb. Cows and pigs sometimes wandered the streets at the turn of the century. A runaway horse and buggy caused lots of excitement. Buggy and wagon manufacturers operated in Rochester, but Miller was probably a buggy salesman, and sold stoves as well. It is believed his full first name was "Newton."

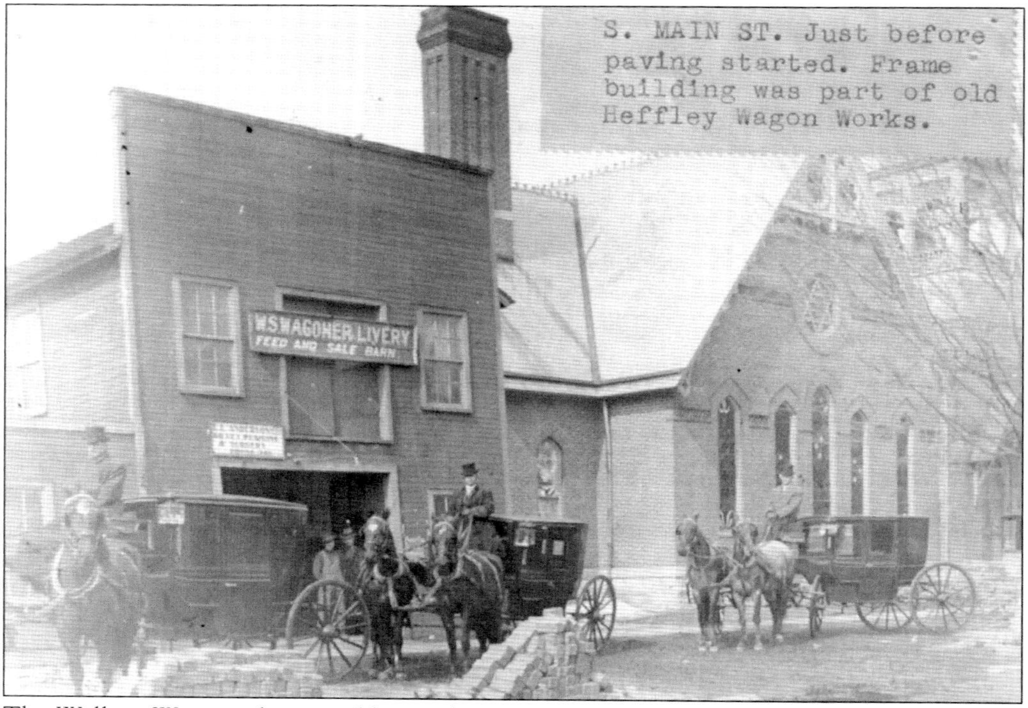

The Wallace Wagoner livery stable stood on South Main Street in 1904, next to the Baptist church. A stack of paving bricks is seen in the foreground, ready for the street to be bricked. The livery building had been part of the Heffley Carriage and Wagon Works, which later became the John F. Hill Company, manufacturer of wagons. (Courtesy of *Rochester Sentinel*.)

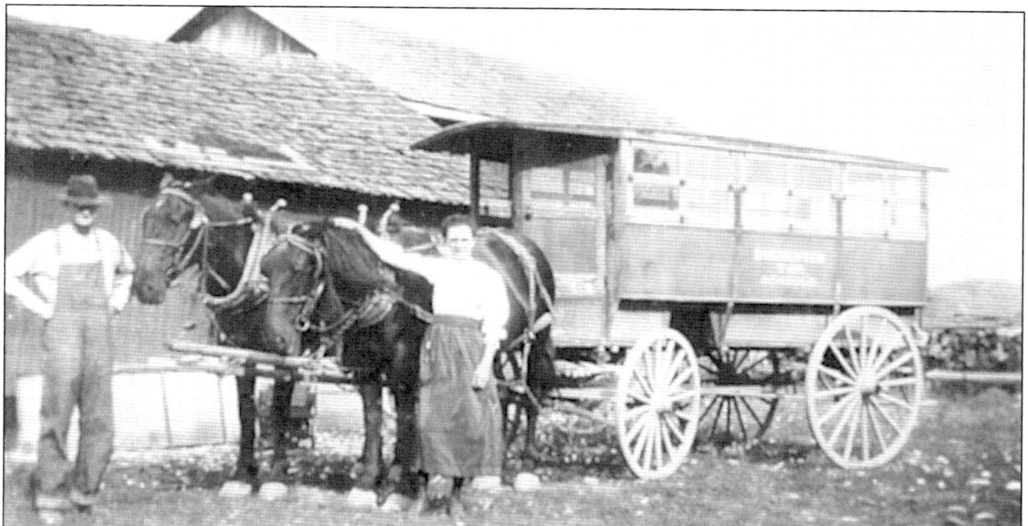

Merley and Elma Dawson pose by the hack he drove to transport students to Woodrow School in 1922. Woodrow was a consolidation of several one-room schools: Ebenezer, Union, Green, School 16 (or Mount Tabor), Mudsock, Sawmill, Mount Zion, Sprinkleburg, and later McKinley (a four-room school). Woodrow School's name was actually Woodrow Wilson School, built in 1917. The first motorized school bus was purchased by Stacy Tobey in 1927.

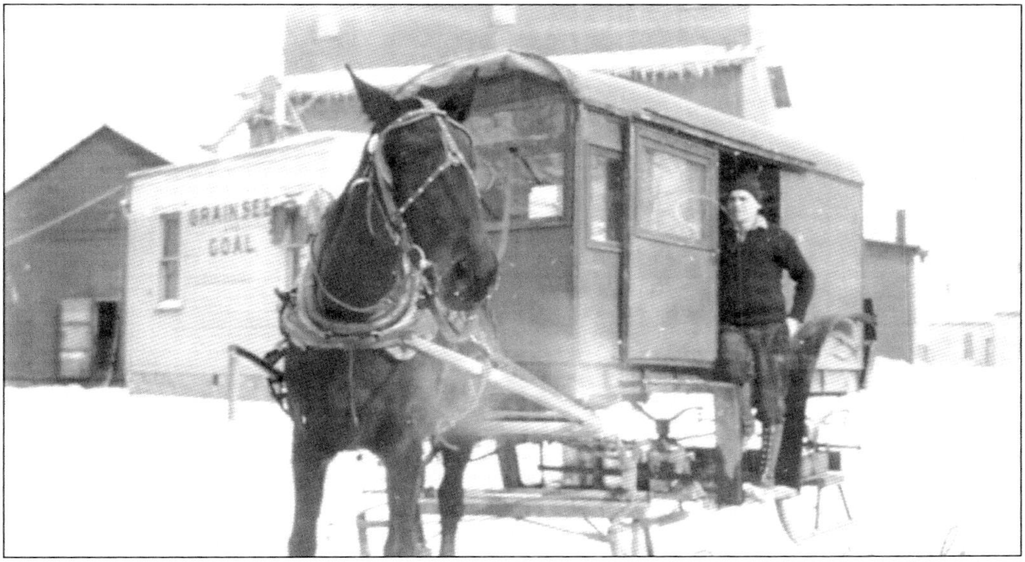

Harvey Clary delivered merchandise and groceries with his horses and used a sled in winter instead of wheels. Behind him is the grain elevator on East Ninth Street, first owned by William Deniston, and owned by the Wilsons since 1933. Clary also had a livery stable in partnership with Ward. (Courtesy of *Rochester Sentinel.*)

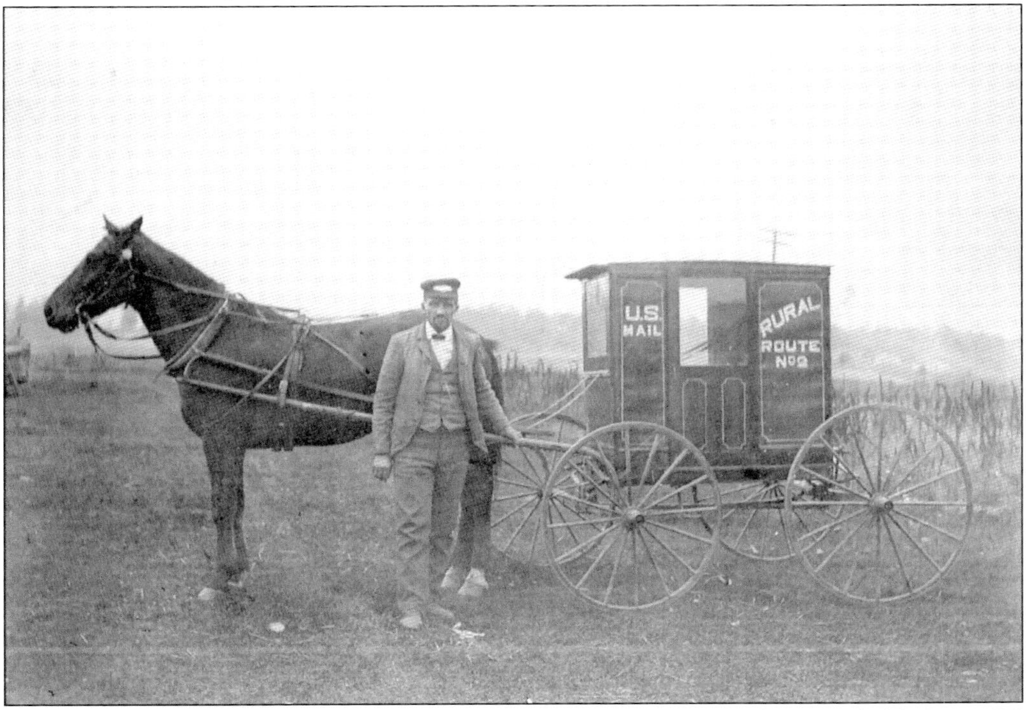

This rural mailman with his horse and mail wagon served Route 2. This is probably James W. Wilder, one of the first rural mail carriers. A Civil War veteran, he was a member of the Grand Army of the Republic (GAR). He entered the postal service on January 1, 1902, carrying a rural mail route out of Rochester until he retired on pension on September 20, 1920.

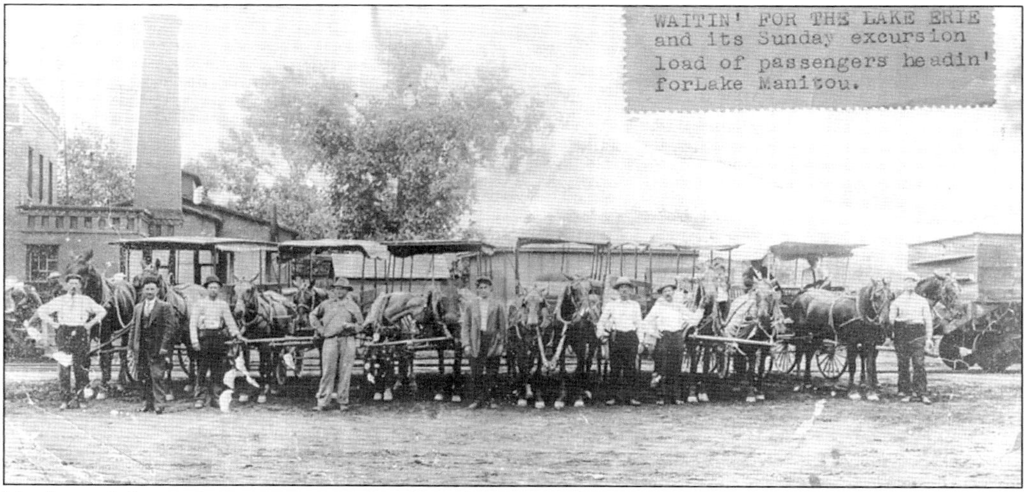

Hacks and drivers line up waiting for the Lake Erie and Western train from Indianapolis in 1910. The fare to transport passengers to Lake Manitou was 10¢. Seen here from left to right are Hank Entsminger, Charlie Knight, Fred Yeazel, Charles Kilmer, Joe Castle, Nick Robbins, Bert Mow, and Viv Essick. Behind them stands the Ross Foundry chimney. The depot was on the corner of Eighth and Franklin Streets. (Courtesy of *Rochester Sentinel.*)

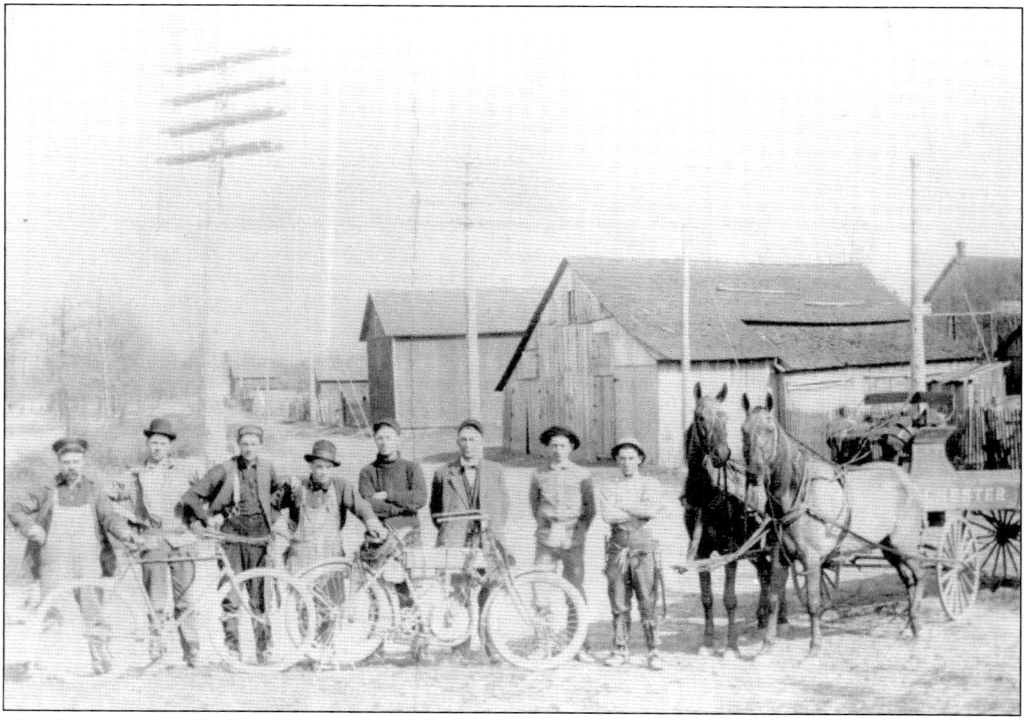

The Rochester Telephone Company (RTC) plant crew in 1903 used horses and bicycles. From left to right are John Kepler, Rube Carr, Harry "Mike" Brickle, Jack Merchant, Fred Carr, Tully Pontious, John Nungesser, Ray Cook, and horses Blackie and Mingo. The Harley Davidson motorcycle was the first gasoline-propelled vehicle owned by the RTC and was used by Pontious, the foreman. This photograph was taken looking east on Race Street. (Courtesy of RTC.)

Two

Cars, Trains, and Airplanes

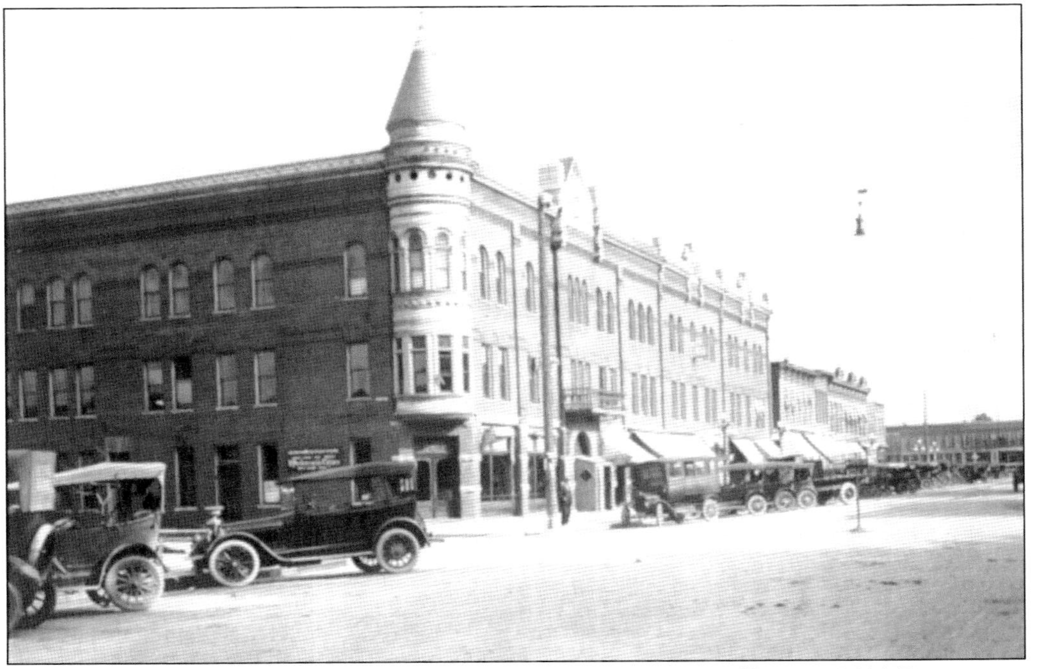

Arlington Hotel was Rochester's grandest hotel until it closed in 1962 and became Wile's Department Store. Built by Lyman Brackett and Abner Barrett in 1890, it was a three-story redbrick Victorian structure on the southeast corner of Main and Seventh Streets. It had 50 guest rooms and a dining room that seated 200. The building burned in 1975 and was replaced by a new building that now contains Jarrety's Place and Taekwondo.

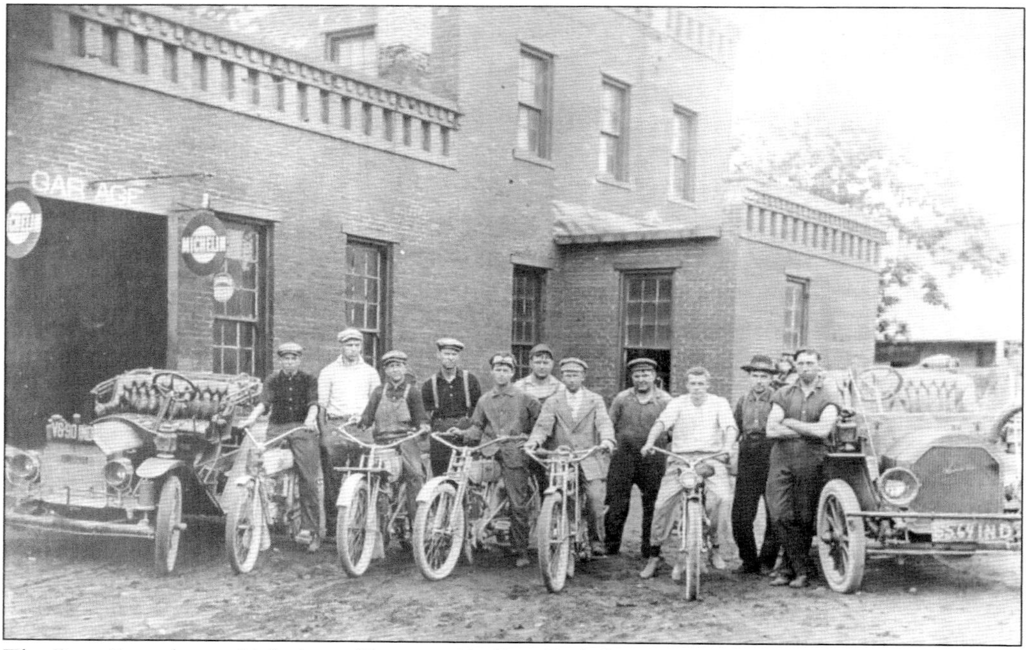

The Ross Foundry and Machine Shop, at 401 East Eighth Street, manufactured bicycles around 1900. It also made iron and brass castings and repaired engines, boilers, pumps, automobiles, and farm machinery. Seen from left to right in this 1911 image are Walter Ross, Hugh Barnhart, Donald Ross, William P. Ross, Walter Overmyer, Loy Ross, Artie Miller, Charles Ross, Robert Shafer, Albert Ross, and John Stanley. The men are posing with a Brush automobile, two Wagner motorcycles, an Excelsior motorcycle, a Pierce motorcycle, and an Auburn motorcar.

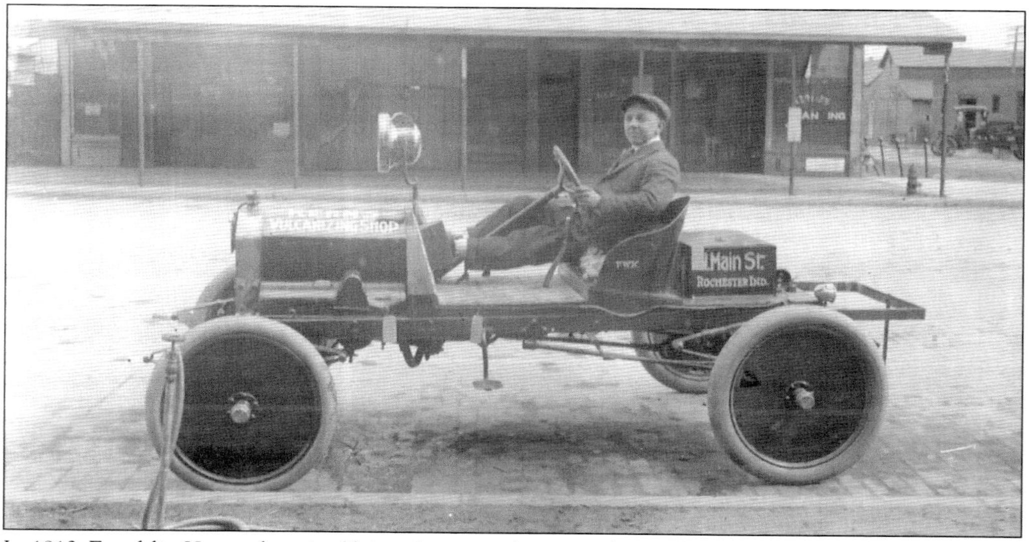

In 1913, Franklin Kern advertised his vulcanizing business, located in the building south of Progress Wholesale Grocery Company, at Fourth and Main Streets. The shop mended and retread tires and patched blowouts and cuts. Frank started the Rochester-Akron Bus Company in 1917 as well as other lines. He worked for the Indiana Motor Bus Company from 1931 to 1936. His younger brother was Bob Kern. (Courtesy of Shirley Kern Needham.)

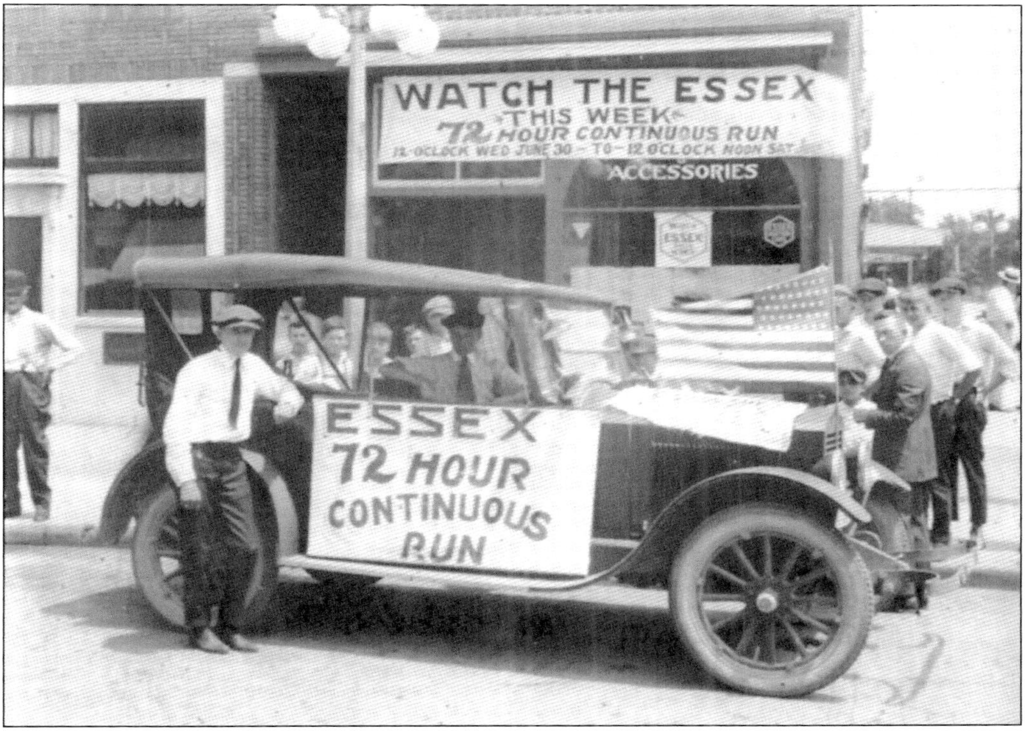

Essex advertised its automobiles by sponsoring a 72-hour continuous run in 1920. This picture was taken in front of the brick building at Eighth and Main Streets. Car dealer L. V. R. Louderback is in the white shirt at left, and his son Harry is behind the steering wheel. Essex cars were made by Hudson Motor Company between 1918 and 1932. Notice the sign for the furniture store on the corner of Eighth and Madison Streets. (Courtesy of Linda Louderback Damas.)

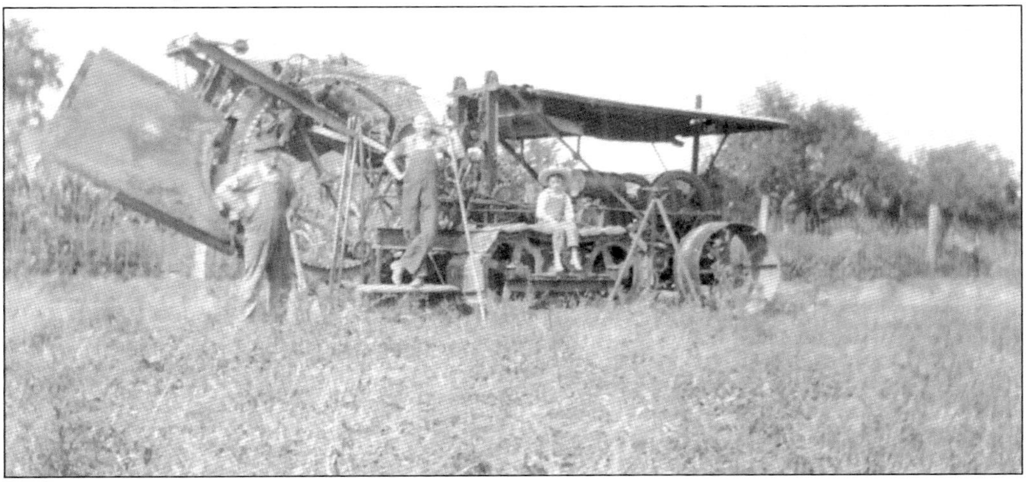

Henry W. Sherrard (center) bought the first caterpillar in Indiana in 1915 for $1,650. This was the third "cat" made by Buckeye Tractor Ditcher Company. Following a stint in World War I, Sherrard dug ditches from 1920 to 1963 in 28 counties across Indiana. He served as Fulton County surveyor in 1934–1935 and 1965–1968. His house at Green Oak had served as a station on the Underground Railroad before the Civil War.

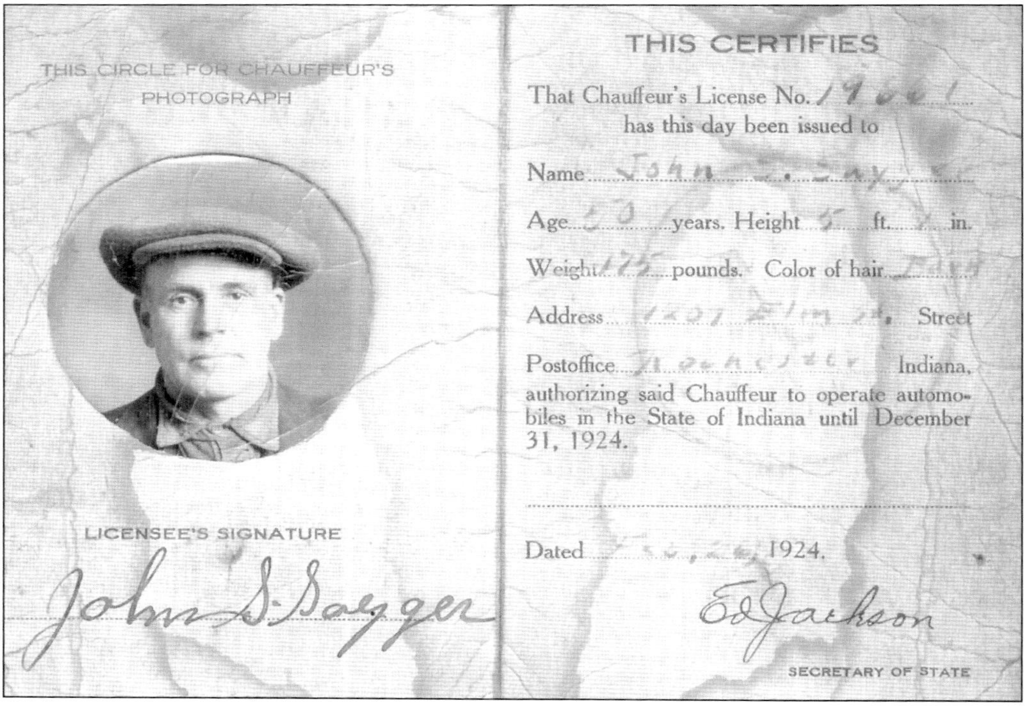

THIS CIRCLE FOR CHAUFFEUR'S PHOTOGRAPH

LICENSEE'S SIGNATURE

John S. Sayger

THIS CERTIFIES

That Chauffeur's License No. .... has this day been issued to

Name ....

Age .... years. Height .... ft. .... in.

Weight .... pounds. Color of hair ....

Address .... Street

Postoffice .... Indiana, authorizing said Chauffeur to operate automobiles in the State of Indiana until December 31, 1924.

Dated .... 1924.

Ed Jackson

SECRETARY OF STATE

Since 1992, commercial driver's licenses (CDLs) are required if transporting 26,000 pounds or 16 passengers, but chauffeur licenses are still used for smaller vehicles. John "Jack" S. Sayger carried this Indiana chauffeur driver's license in 1924. He was born in Athens, Indiana, in 1873 and died in Woodlawn Hospital on April 23, 1949. (Courtesy of Charles Clevenger.)

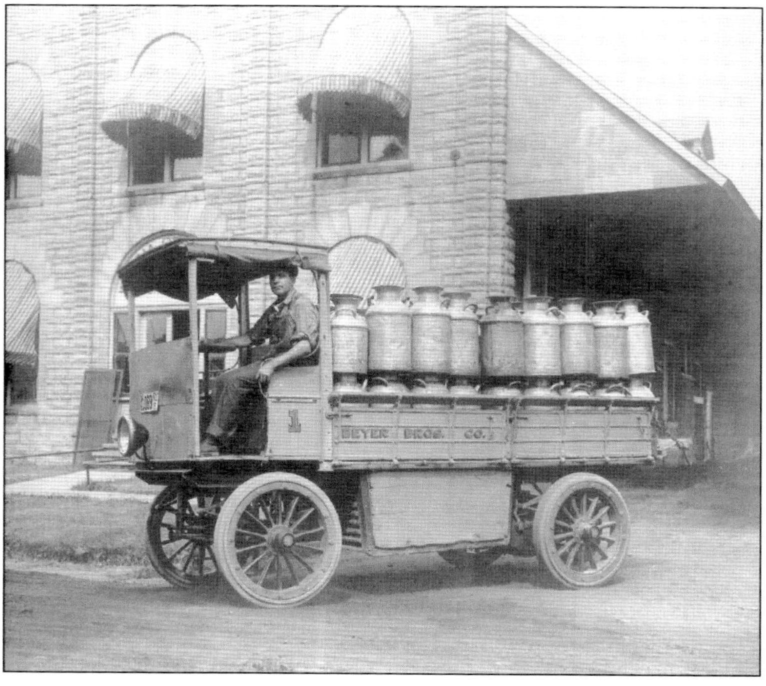

Beyer Brothers' milk truck was driven by John Sayger in 1916. The Beyer Brothers Winona Creamery was located at 619 Madison Street. The words Winona Creamery can be seen above the doorway behind the truck's canopy. The truck had chain drive, solid rubber tires, and was electric with two large batteries. One battery powered the truck while the other battery recharged in Beyer's ice plant. (Courtesy of Charles Clevenger.)

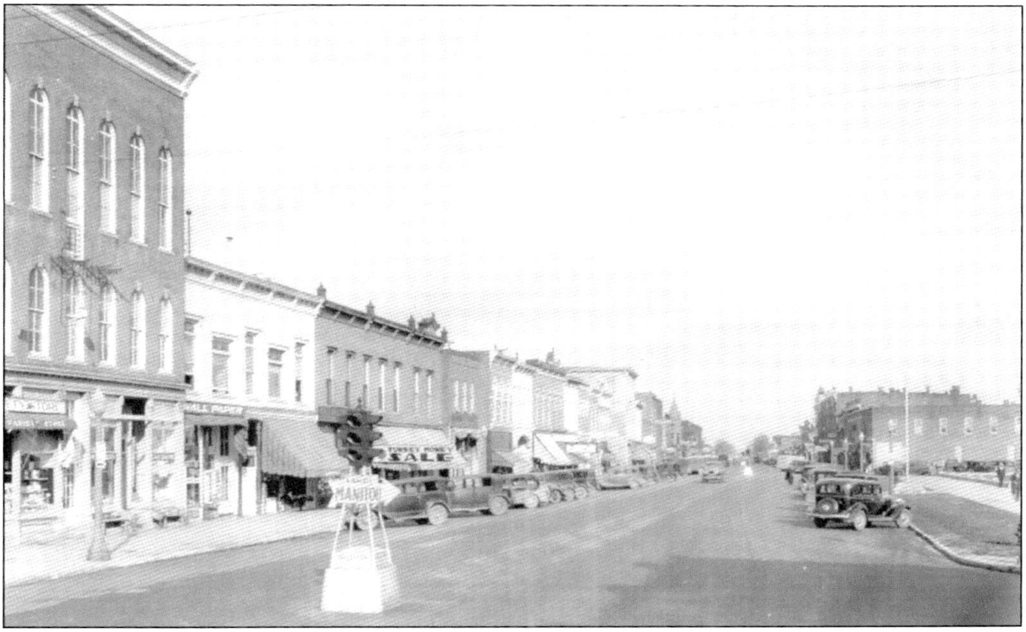

Main Street looking north from Ninth Street shows the traffic light on the Lake Manitou sign standing on the ground in the middle of the intersection. Signs indicate Fristoe Variety Store at left, Wall Paper in Carter's Book Store, and Turkey Money Sale at the Boston Store. Carter's and the Boston Store were destroyed by fire in 1936.

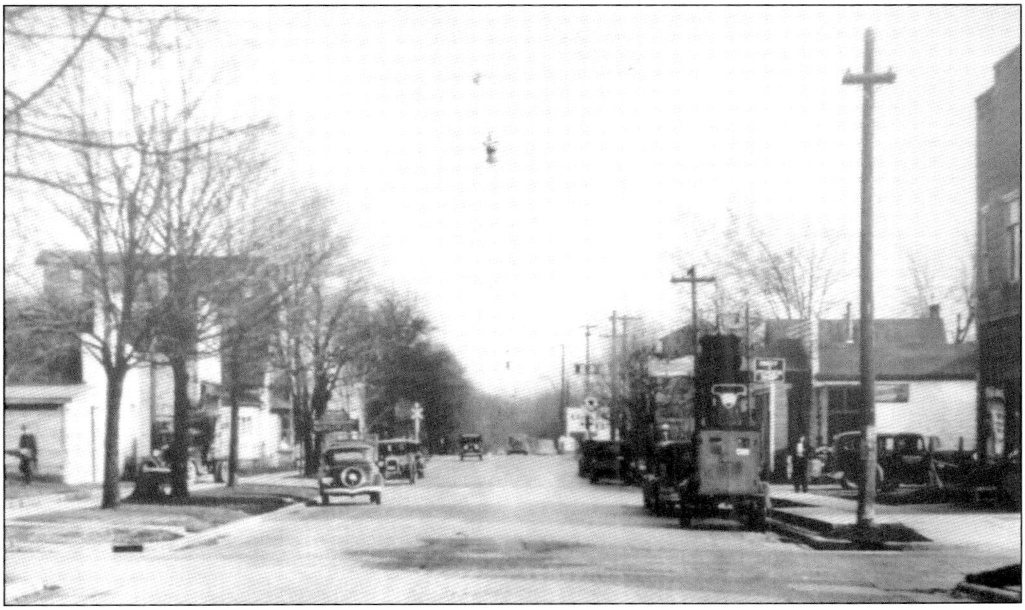

Looking east about 1920 on Ninth Street from Monroe reveals, from front to back on the left (north) side of the street, Claude Johnson's Meat Market, three houses, Snapp's Grocery, and Deniston's elevator by the railroad tracks. On the right (south) side are, from front to back, Ewing Grocery, Miller Brothers Garage, chick hatchery, Manitou Café, Reuben Thrush barbershop, Farm Bureau (white building), and Nickel Plate railroad track.

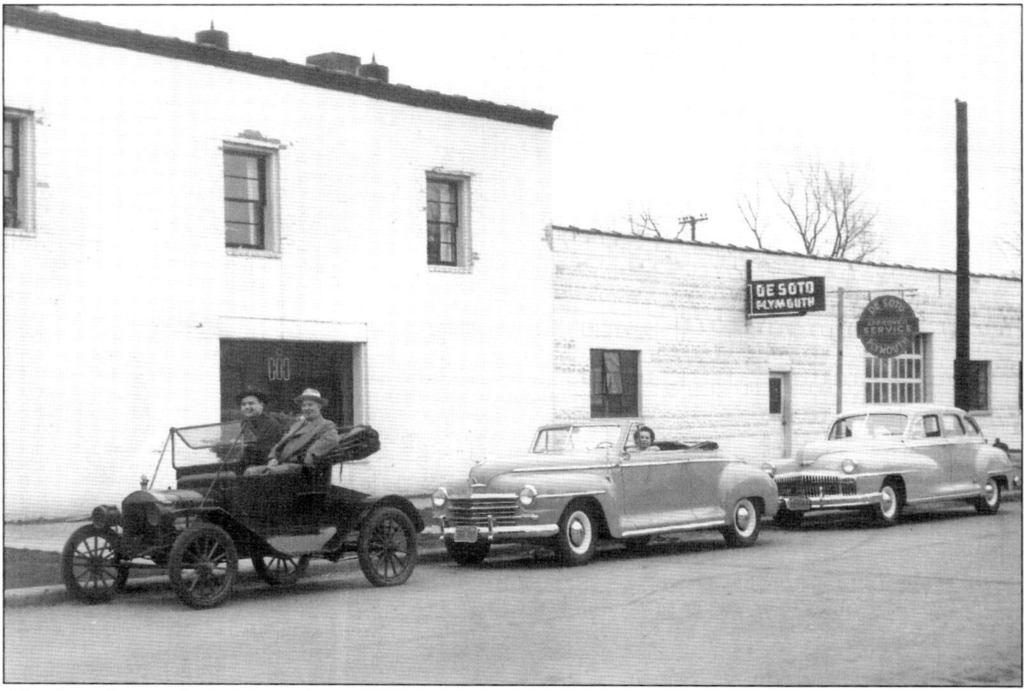

Charles "Casey" Jones owned an International Harvester implement store and DeSoto-Plymouth dealership at 226 East Seventh Street. Pictured here are Jones (left, wearing a black hat) with an unidentified man seated in a pre-1910 Buick or Packard. Behind them is parked a 1946 Plymouth (with an unidentified woman) and a 1946 DeSoto. Before his death in 1970, Casey dropped the car dealership and continued with Farmall tractors. His building had once been a chicken house; the Joneses lived on the second floor. (Courtesy of Pam Jones Loebig.)

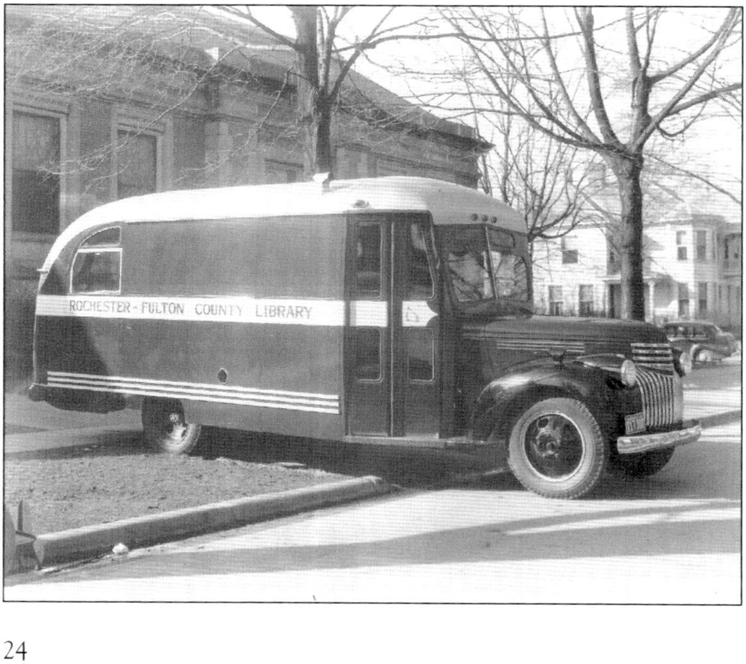

Rochester–Fulton County Library operated this bookmobile in the 1930 and 1940s. The library was constructed on the corner of Eighth and Pontiac Streets in 1907 with grants of $13,000 from Andrew Carnegie and the money raised by the Rochester Women's Club. A new library was built in 1982 at 320 West Seventh Street. The old library is now a residence. (Courtesy of Fulton County Library.)

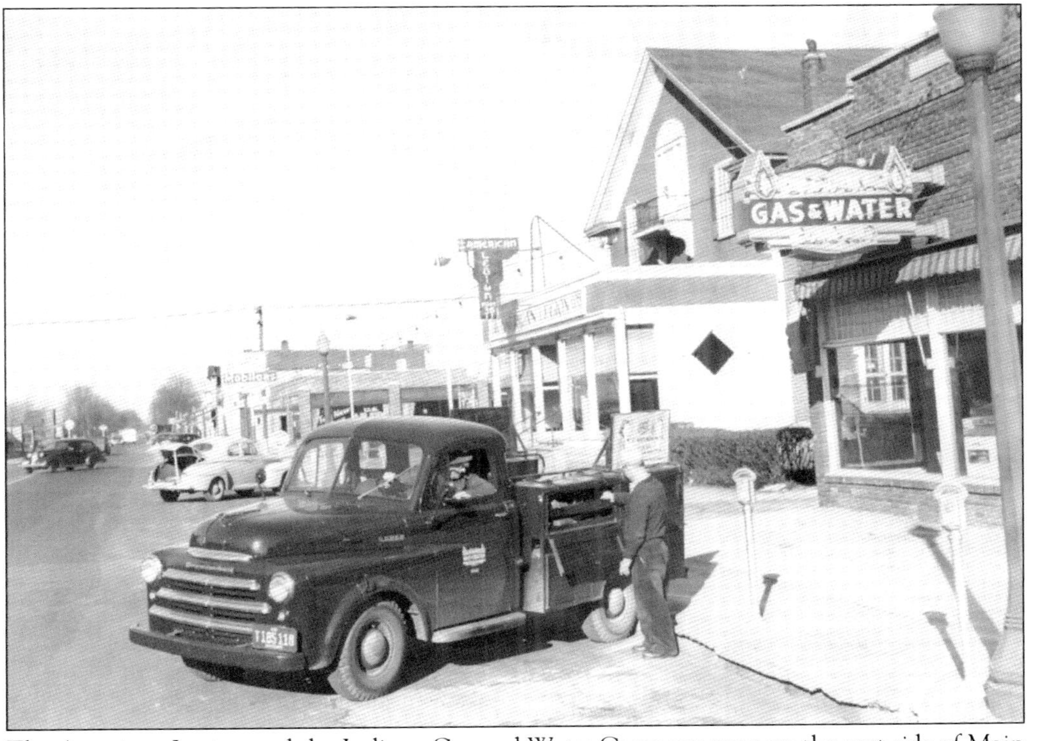

The American Legion and the Indiana Gas and Water Company were on the east side of Main Street in the 500 block in 1951. Notice the parking meters, installed in 1948, charging 1¢, 5¢, or 10¢ for 12 minutes, 60 minutes, or two hours. Farmers hated them. In 1983, at the request of the Rochester merchants, the meters were taken out, according to the city council meeting books in city hall.

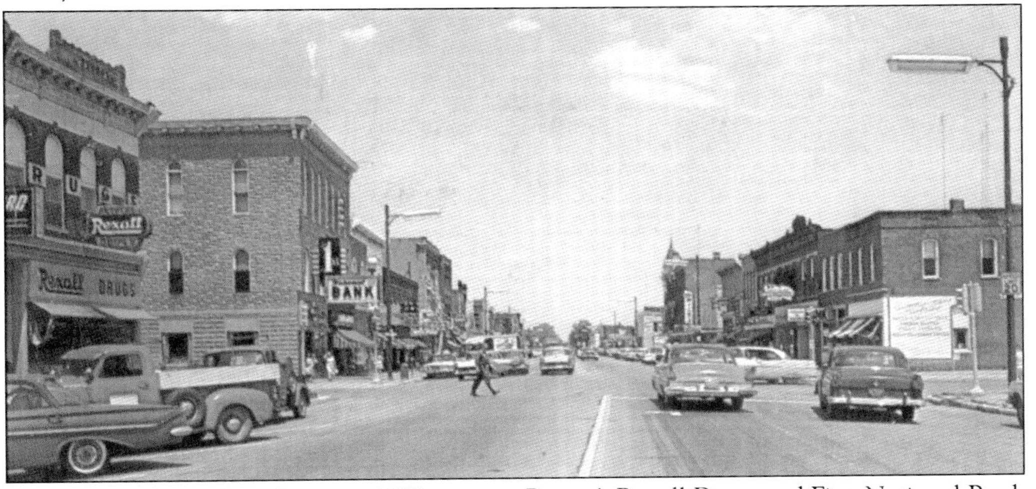

Looking north on Main Street in 1957, one saw Baxter's Rexall Drugs and First National Bank on the left. The bank was founded in 1866 by Arthur C. Copeland as the Rochester Bank and changed to First National Bank in 1872. The bank was owned by his family for four generations. It moved to 125 East Ninth Street in 1972. Elmer Zimmerman's Bakery is on the right on the corner of Main and Eighth Streets.

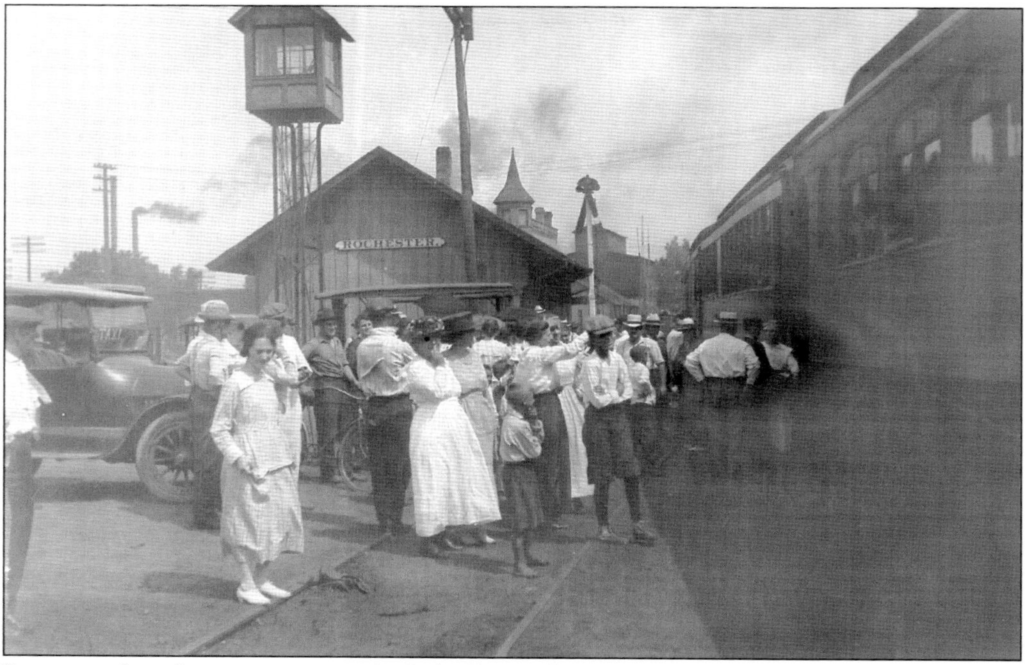

Passengers board a steam train at the Lake Erie and Western depot on East Eighth Street. This was the first railroad built in Fulton County, in 1869, by Indianapolis-Peru and Chicago. In 1887, it became the Lake Erie and Western; in 1923, its name changed to Nickel Plate, and in 1964, it became part of the Norfolk and Western Railroad. Passenger service ceased in 1932. In the background are the turret of H&H Lumberyard and Deniston's elevator (later Wilson's).

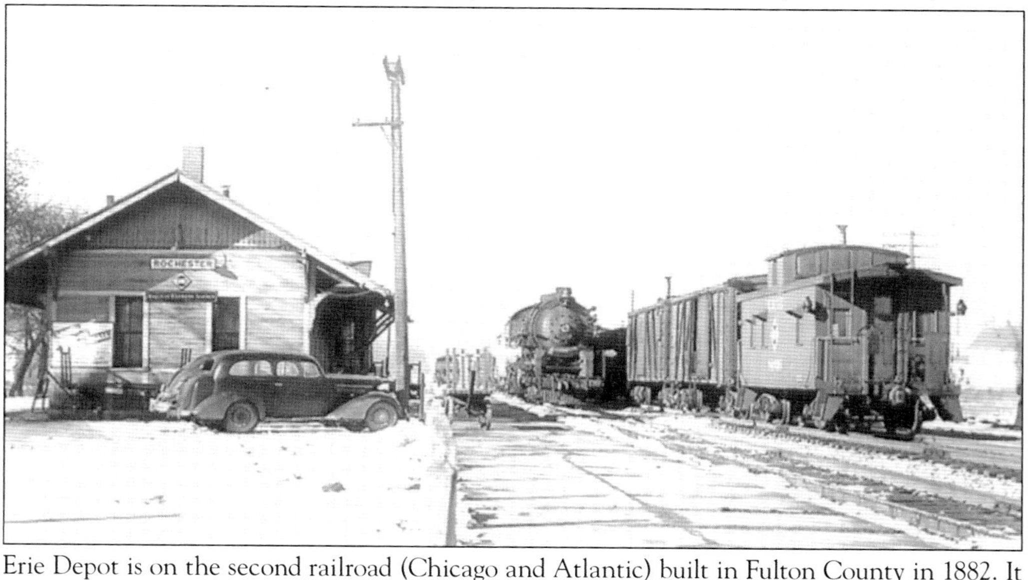

Erie Depot is on the second railroad (Chicago and Atlantic) built in Fulton County in 1882. It became the Erie and was double-tracked in 1912–1914. From this depot, many soldiers left home in Rochester on their way to World Wars I and II and the Korean War. The railroad's name was changed to Erie-Lackawanna in 1960; it went bankrupt in 1976. Afterwards, Wilson Elevator bought the depot and 2 miles of track.

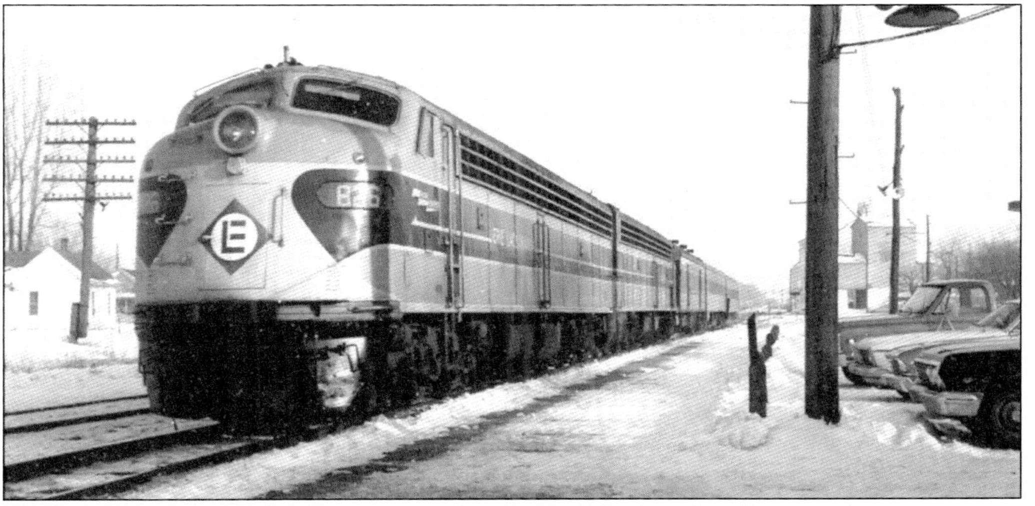

The last passenger train left Rochester on January 6, 1970, from Erie Depot with one passenger, Mike Yates, a Culver Military Academy cadet. Notice the grain elevator in the background. The Erie tracks were removed in 1980, with some rails and ties donated to the Fulton County Historical Society to lay track at the Leiters Ford Depot Museum. The track was moved in 1995 to FCHS grounds for the historical society's Norfolk and Western depot and caboose.

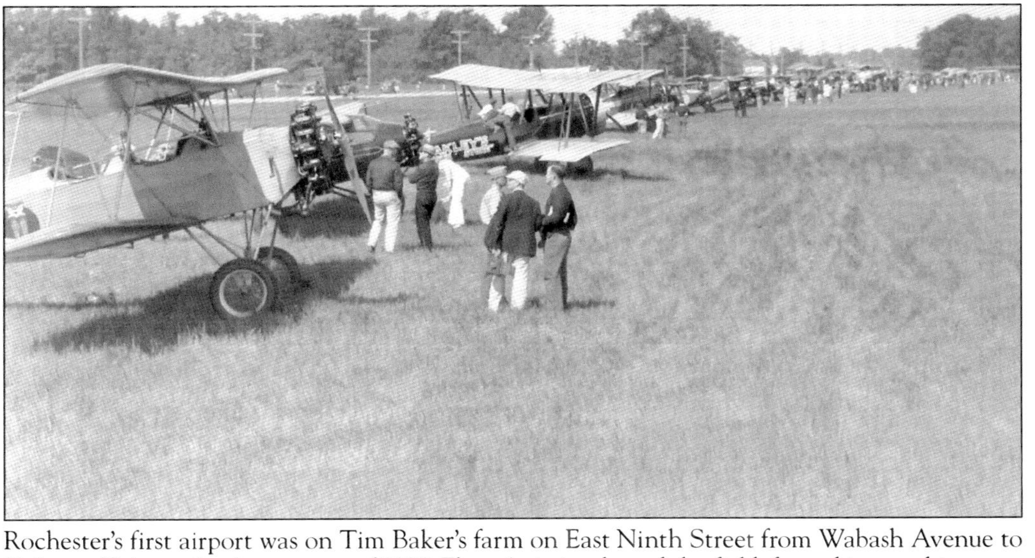

Rochester's first airport was on Tim Baker's farm on East Ninth Street from Wabash Avenue to Oakwood Manor. In the summer of 1929, Flora Aviation leased the field, fenced in a parking area next to the road to Lake Manitou, built a stile over the fence, and constructed outdoor restroom facilities. Lee Eikenberry would carry passengers in his 1929 open-cockpit Waco airplane for $2.50 each. Often other planes used the landing strip as well.

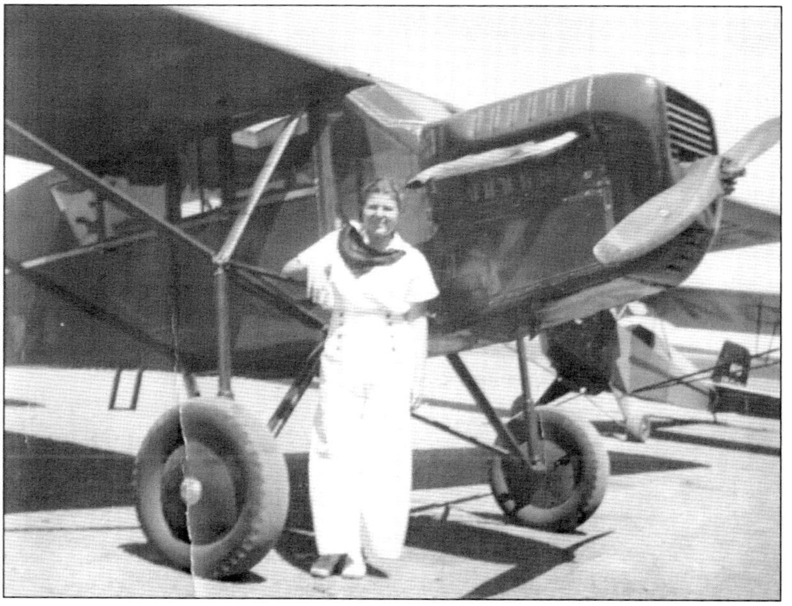

In the 1930s, Helen House was the first Fulton County woman to learn to fly. She taught many local people to fly and gave plane rides to many kids. She operated the Rochester Airport and flying service with her husband, Wayne Outcelt. Helen House Outcelt took many local people for their very first airplane ride. She often took her teddy bear along.

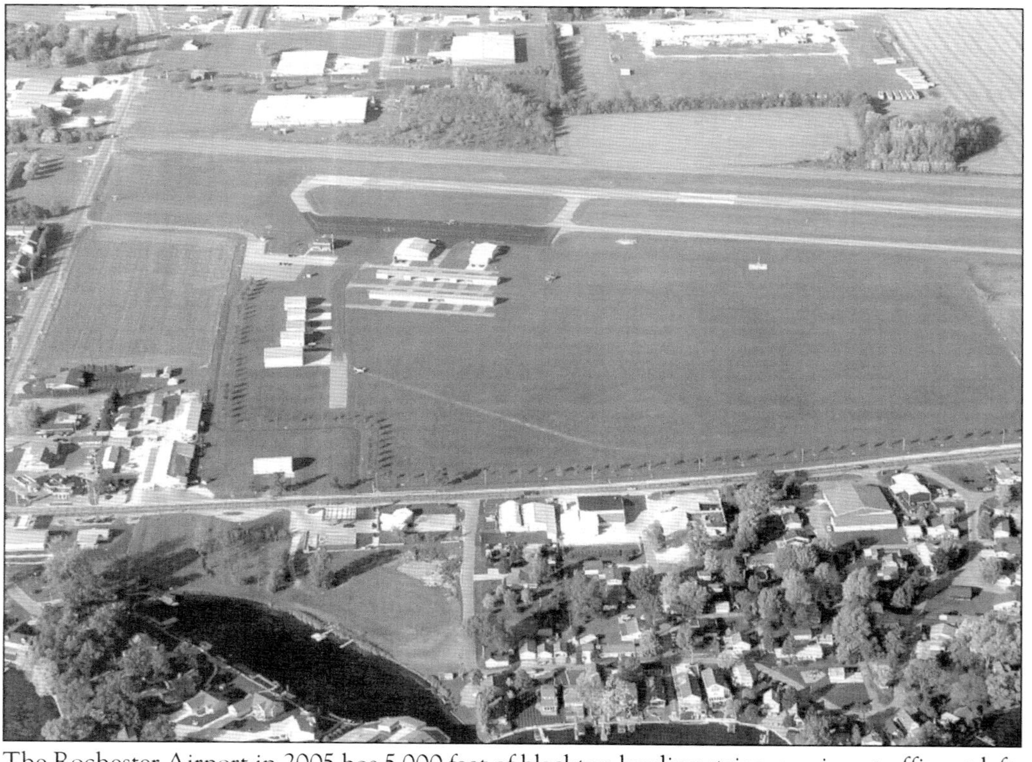

The Rochester Airport in 2005 has 5,000 feet of blacktop landing strips, an airport office at left, a maintenance hangar, a Good Samaritan helicopter hangar, and two rows of "T" hangars for rent. A row of five hangars includes two owned by the Mentone Flying Club. Factories border the airport to the north. Several restaurants, Lake Manitou, and many houses are on the south side of the highway. (Courtesy of Fulton County Airport.)

Three

Public Buildings and Businesses

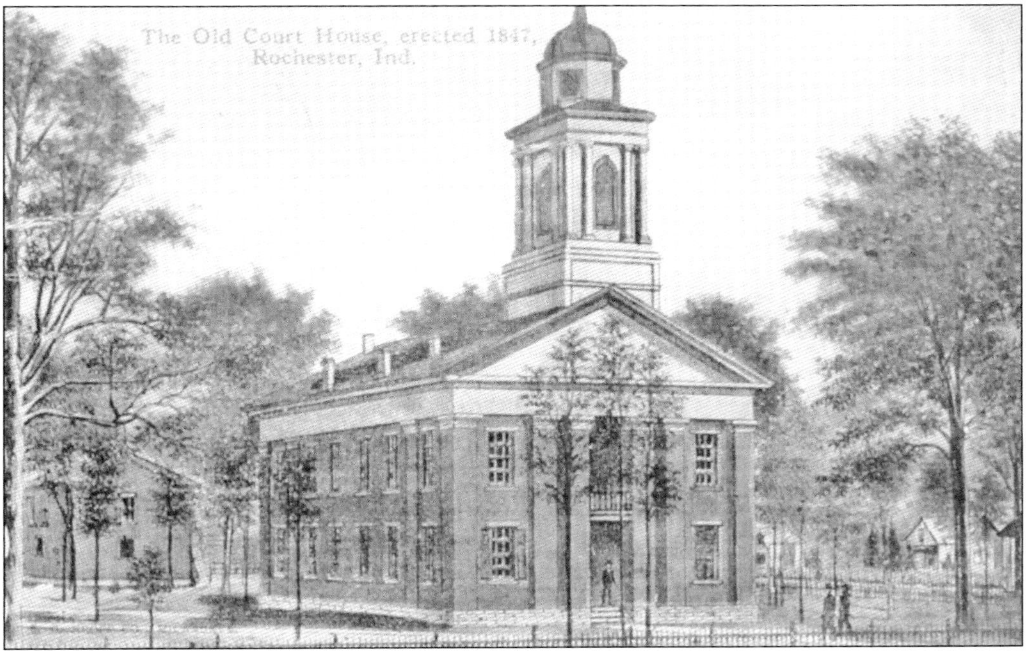

Fulton County's old courthouse, erected 1847, shared the courthouse square with a brick jail (at back, east of the courthouse). There was also a bandstand on the square. The style is classic Greek Revival, popular for official buildings prior to the Civil War. When this courthouse was torn down to make way for the new courthouse in 1895, the ornate iron fence was moved to the Fulton County Poor Farm.

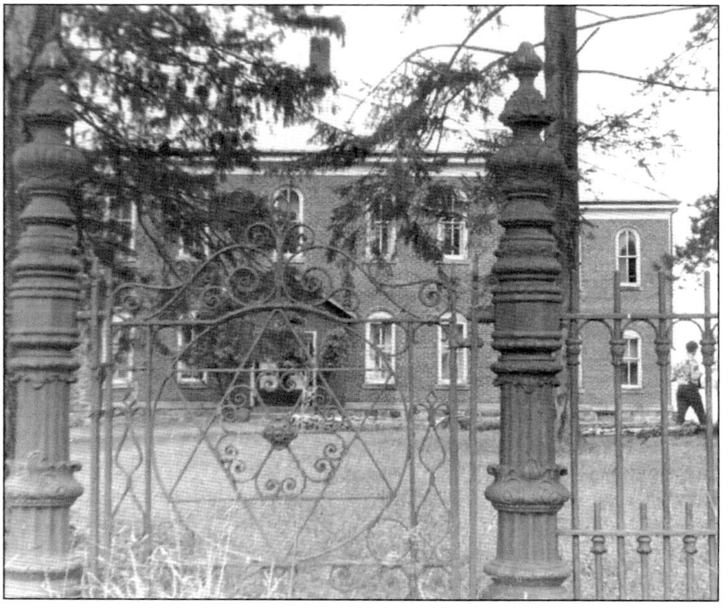

Fulton County Poor Farm was built in 1876 as a home for "indigent, retarded, orphans, and insane." The beautiful wrought iron fence was moved from courthouse to the poor farm in 1895. The poor farm was closed in 1965 and sold to Robert Peterson in 1966. Rochester High School (RHS) photography class students took field trips there to take photographs. The home was falling down and was finally torn down in January 1998.

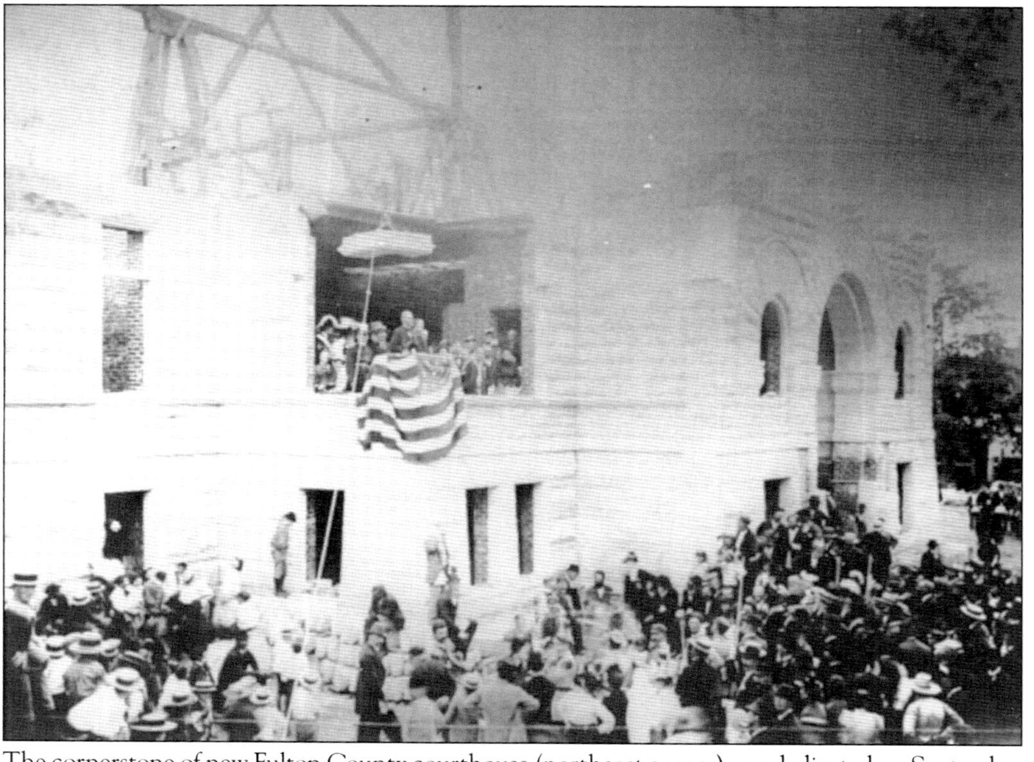

The cornerstone of new Fulton County courthouse (northeast corner) was dedicated on September 19, 1895. The speaker was B. F. Shively. This photograph hangs in the county clerk's office. The cornerstone was opened in 1995 for the 100th anniversary of the courthouse. The items it contained are on display in the first floor of the courthouse today; they include 19th-century Rochester newspapers, coins, a Civil War regiment history book, and other artifacts.

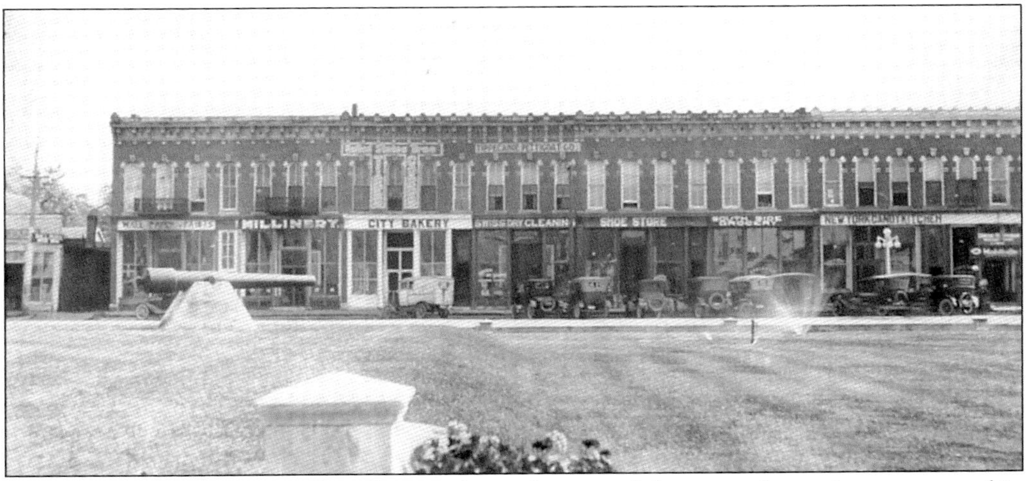

Two Civil War cannons stood on the courthouse lawn until they were donated as scrap metal in 1942 to help win World War II. Fulton County was given two World War II cannons, but they were later moved to the VFW post. Looking south from the courthouse, signs at the tops of buildings in this image are United States Tires and the Tippecanoe Petticoat Company. From left to right are Wallpaper–Paint, Millinery (hats), City Bakery, Swiss Dry Cleaning, Shoe Store, South Side Grocery, and New York Candy Kitchen. The cars are 1920s Ford Model Ts.

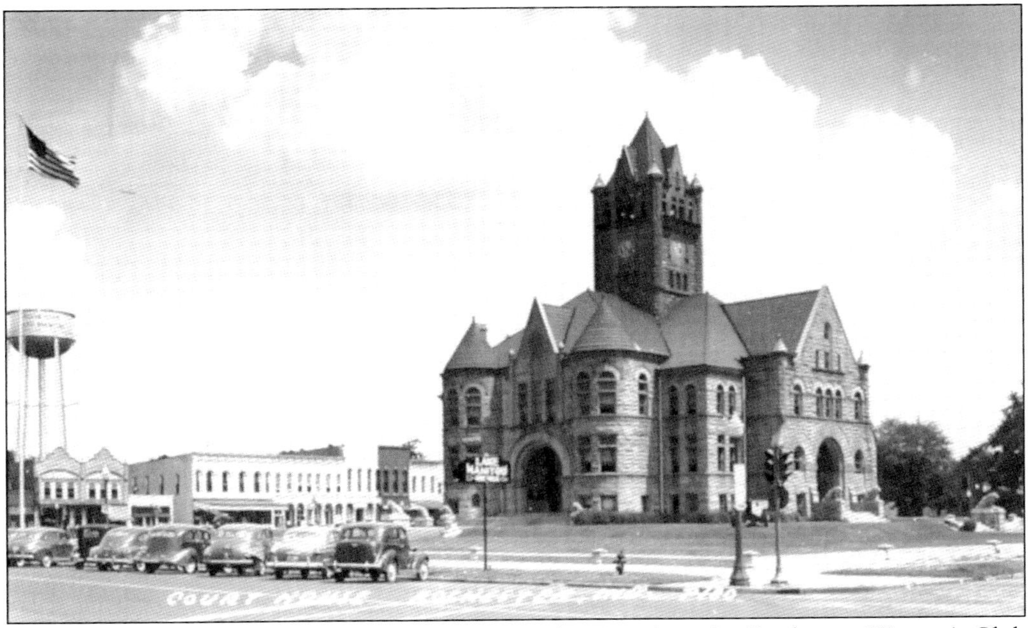

The Fulton County courthouse had no trees until 1962, when the Rochester Women's Club landscaped the courthouse grounds. The previous courthouse had been surrounded by trees, and maybe the many leaves are why the county commissioners refused to allow trees to be planted there. Or maybe they wanted a clear view of the beautiful 1895 courthouse, which cost over $100,000, considered very expensive in that day.

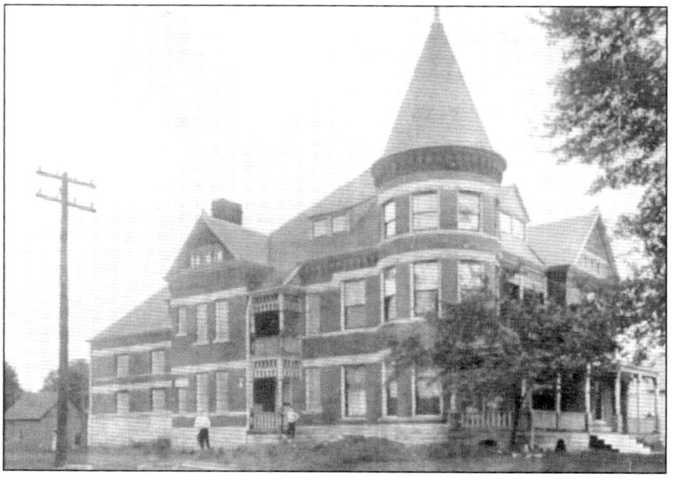

Fulton County was organized in 1836. The very first jail was made of logs for $550 in 1837. This jail was replaced by a brick jail on the courthouse square, which was built for $5,000 in 1851. The Fulton County jail pictured at left was built in 1893 for $25,000 on the corner of Madison and Eighth Streets. The style of architecture is Romanesque Revival, while the courthouse is Richardson Romanesque. It was replaced by a new jail in 1984.

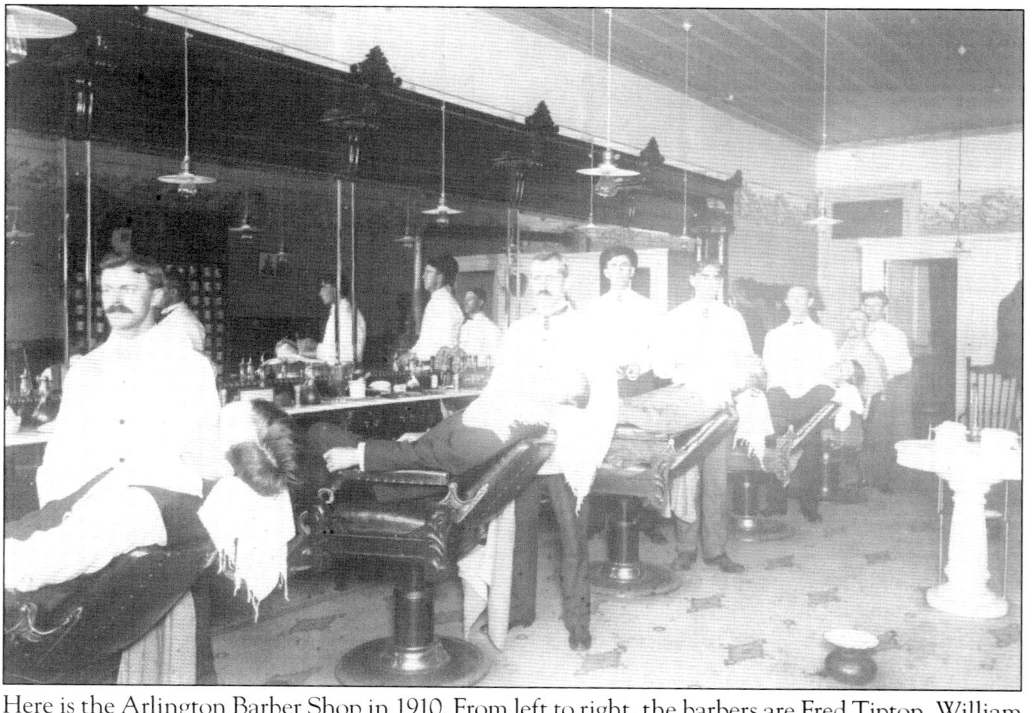

Here is the Arlington Barber Shop in 1910. From left to right, the barbers are Fred Tipton, William Leroy Crabill, Claude Brubaker Sr., Frank Stetson (with cap on), an unidentified man, and Bruce Moerett standing at the back door. The customers are unidentified. Notice the spittoon on the floor. This barber shop was located inside the Arlington Hotel on the northeast corner of Main and Seventh Streets.

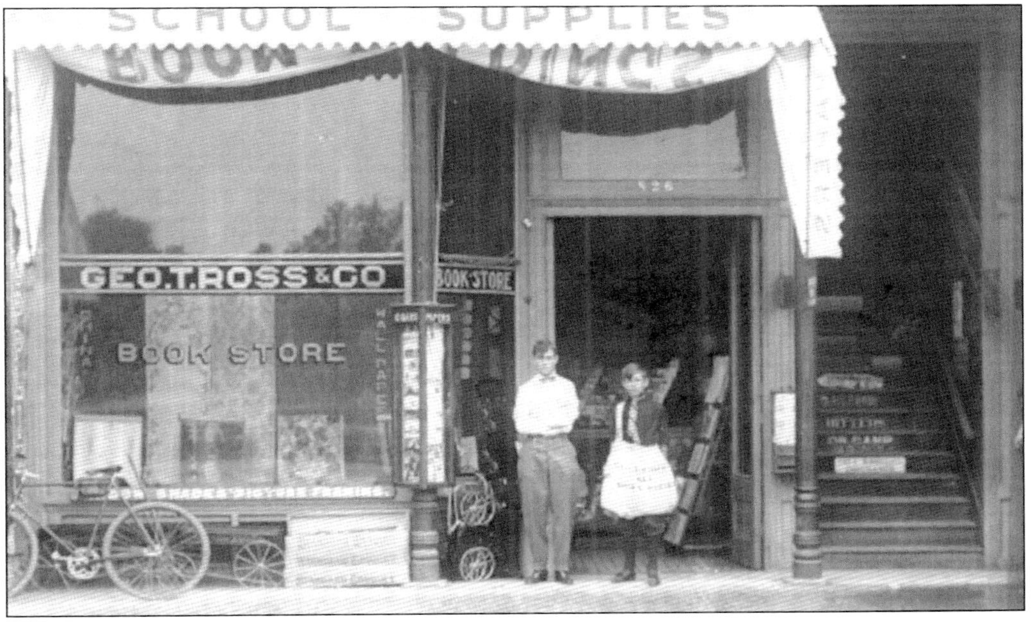

Rannel's Book Store, at 826 Main Street, was purchased by George T. Ross in 1907 and sold to Everett Lichtenwalter in 1944. Founded in 1897, the store sold magazines, stationery, and school books. Jackie Burkett bought it in 1980, adding art and collectibles. Rob and Mary Ellen Lowe bought the store in 1996 and added picture framing. They changed the name to Fine Things in 2005; the store closed in 2009.

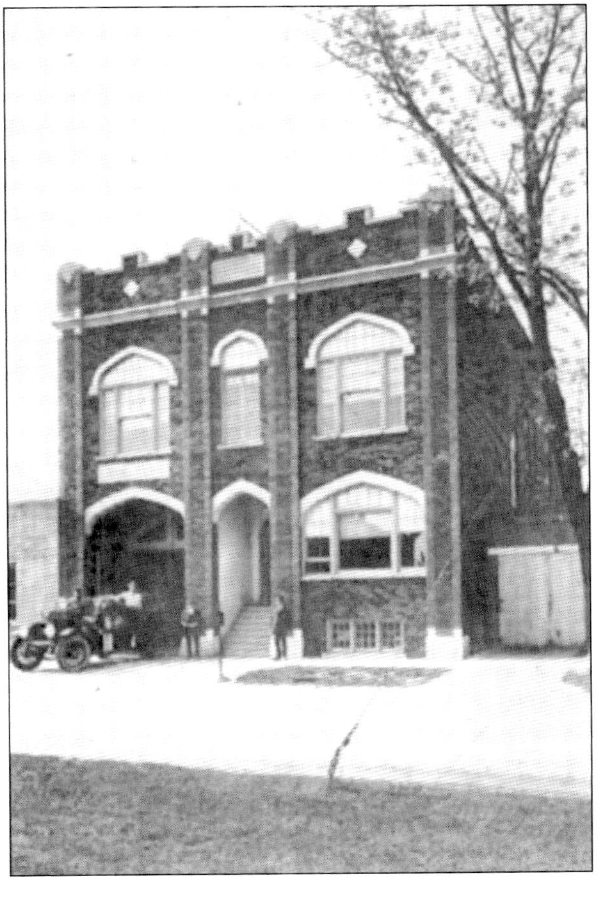

The old engine house was torn down and a new city hall and fire department was built in 1924. The city council met in chambers on the second floor, where city offices were located. Their first "auto fire truck" (shown at right) was purchased in 1917 and was driven by Frank Ross, fire chief. In 1946, the city purchased Miller Garage to the west and built an addition for the fire department and a bay for another fire truck.

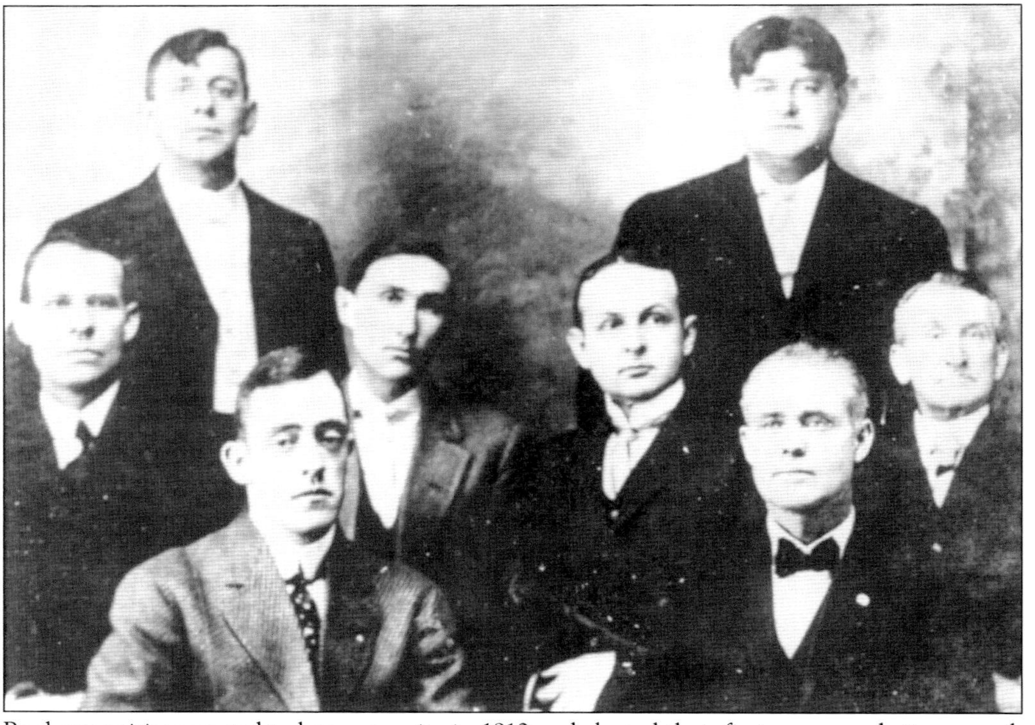

Rochester citizens voted to become a city in 1910 and elected their first mayor and city council. Seen here from left to right are (front row) councilmen A. L. Deniston and Dr. Isaac L. Babcock; (second row) councilman William Ross, clerk Joseph Bibler, Mayor Omar B. Smith, and councilman Perry M. Shore; (third row) councilman William Brinkman and treasurer Roy Shanks. Smith, Deniston, and Shanks were Democrats; the others were Republicans.

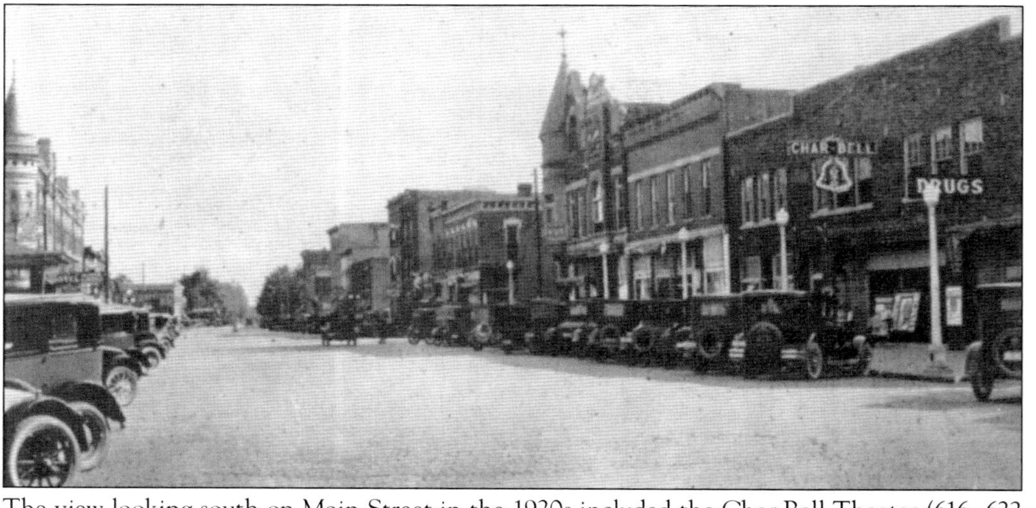

The view looking south on Main Street in the 1920s included the Char-Bell Theater (616–622 Main), owned by Charles and Bell Kreighbaum. It was built in 1924 with bricks salvaged from tearing down Rochester College. The theater had 800 seats and a stage for vaudeville and orchestras. Tickets were 20¢ to 40¢. Sound pictures arrived in 1928. Charles's brother Lisle Kreighbaum bought the theater in 1934, renaming it the Times Theater in 1942. (Courtesy of Steve Coleman.)

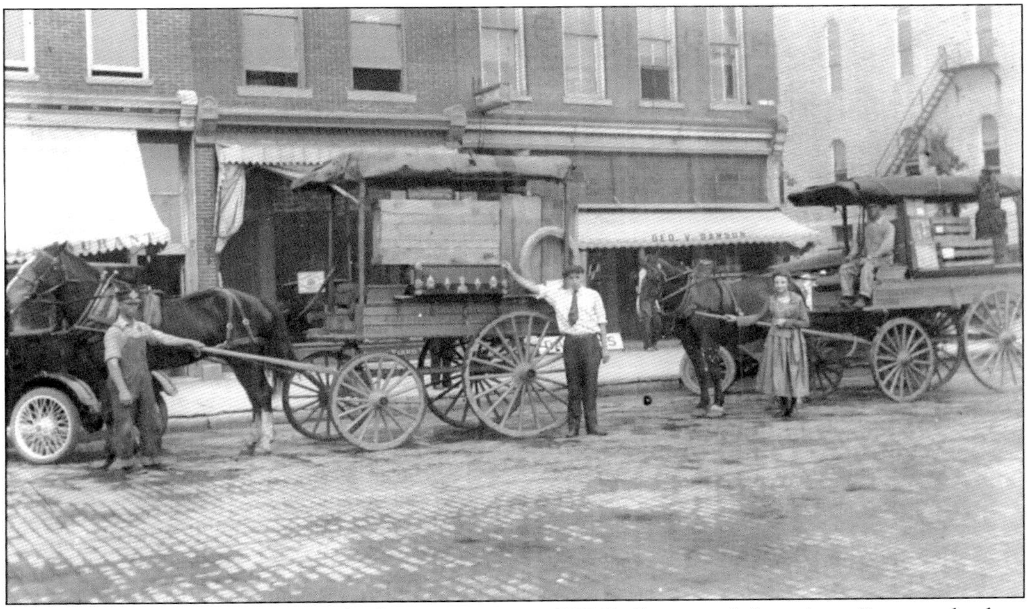

The Railway Express Agency, which was a merger of Wells Fargo and American Express, had an office on Main Street in 1919. Seen here from left to right are driver John Lewis, manager Floyd Christman, clerk Margaret Bitters, and driver William Brown. Businesses visible in this image include True's Restaurant, the American Express office, and Dawson's Drug Store on the corner of Eighth and Main Street. Above the express office was Dr. C. J. Loring's office.

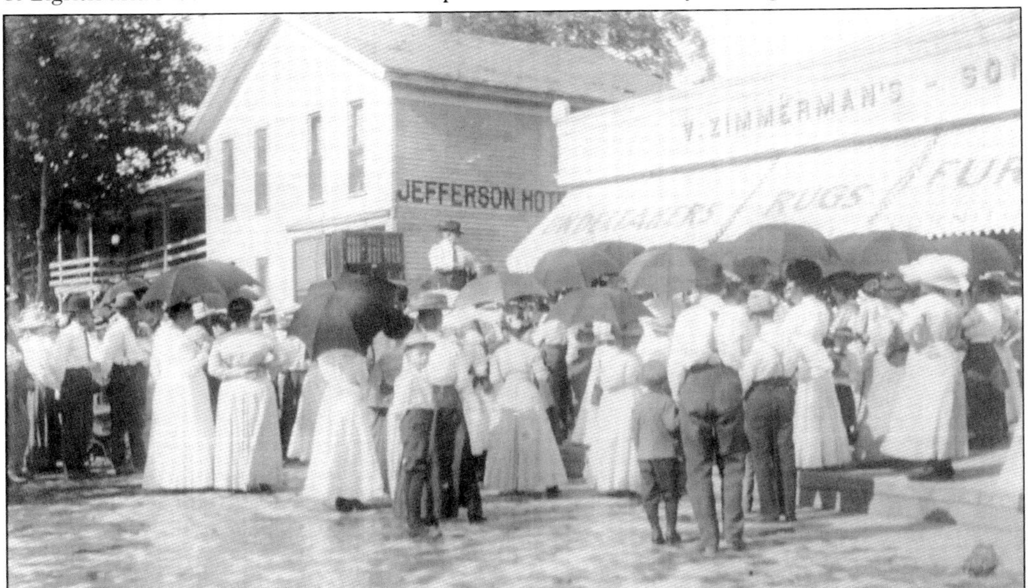

Jefferson Hotel, at 601 Main Street, stood next to Zimmerman and Sons Funeral Home on the west side of the street. Jefferson Hotel was built in 1865 as Central House. Val Zimmerman remodeled it and named it Jefferson Hotel in 1897. After changing owners several times, it was torn down in 1913. Apparently the crowd is attending a funeral in the rain. (Courtesy of Darin Beeker, owner of Zimmerman Funeral Home.)

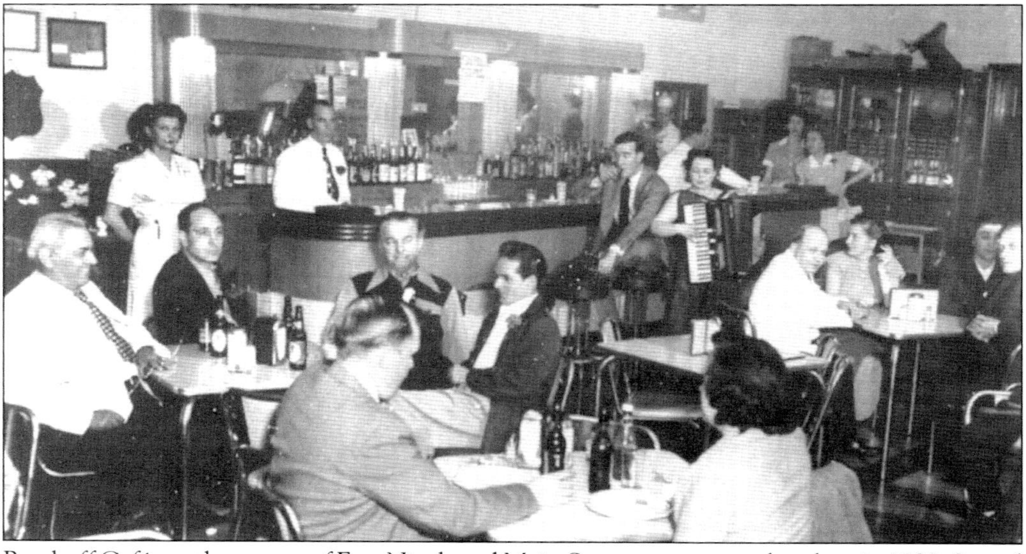

Berghoff Café, on the corner of East Ninth and Main Streets, was a popular place in 1938. Seated at the table at left are Louis Ninios, Johnny Zoppe, Otto Gretona, and Willie Lamberti. Clyde Beatty–Cole Brothers Circus performers hung out at the Berghoff. Mary Whittenberger plays accordion in the background. Bing Crosby sang there one time in 1945.

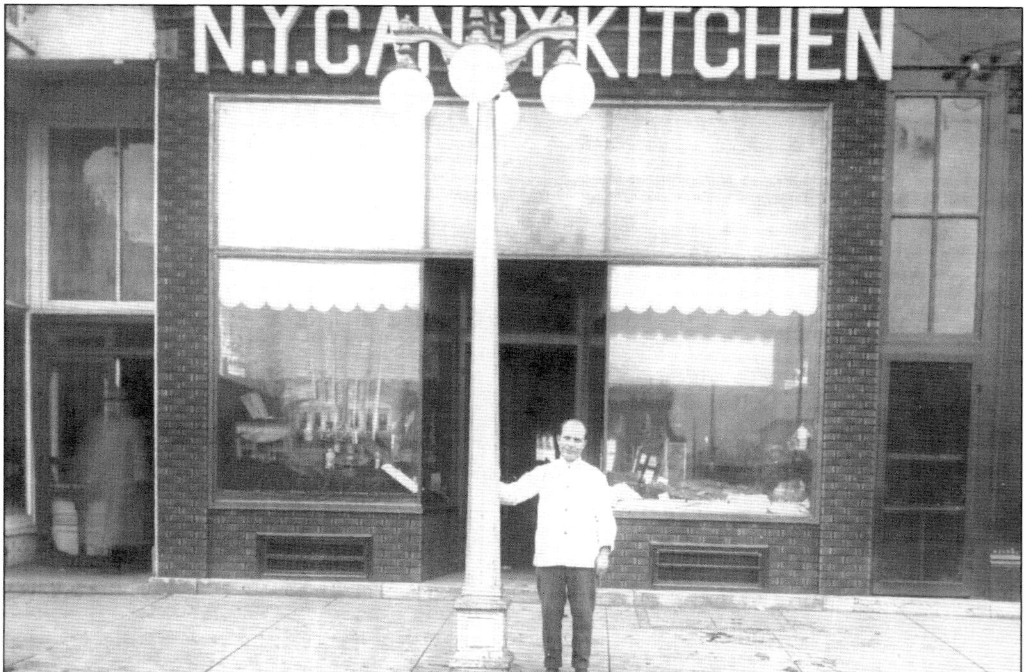

New York Candy Kitchen and Berghoff Café were owned by Pete and Louis Ninios. Candy and ice cream were manufactured in the basement from 1913 until a fire destroyed the building on September 9, 1949. The café was then moved to 1617 Main Street. The pictures of circus performers and other celebrities such as Hopalong Cassidy who visited the two businesses were donated to Fulton County Museum and can be seen there.

Rochester Bridge Company (RBC) was founded in 1893 and reorganized in 1897 by William Deniston. In 1902, the factory began producing structural steel for the construction of hotels, churches, temples, courthouses, and other buildings. During World War I, the company made steel for ships. It closed in 1932 because of the Great Depression. The buildings were sold to Cole Brothers Circus in 1934. An RBC bridge is preserved on the grounds of the Fulton County Historical Society.

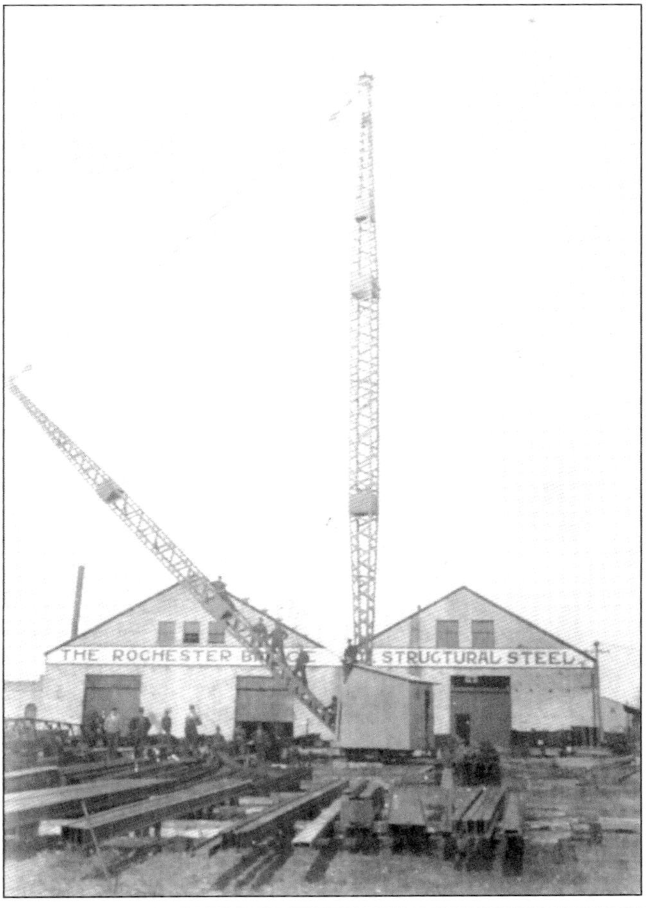

This is the famous Karn's Coffee Shop, where people gathered after dances at the Fairview and Colonial Hotels. It was owned by Oren Karn and son Harold Karn at 710 Main Street, with Karn's Hotel upstairs. Seen here from left to right are Joe Castle, Jay Clayton, Bill Delp, Oren Karn, and Lesle Wilson. Notice the circus posters in the windows.

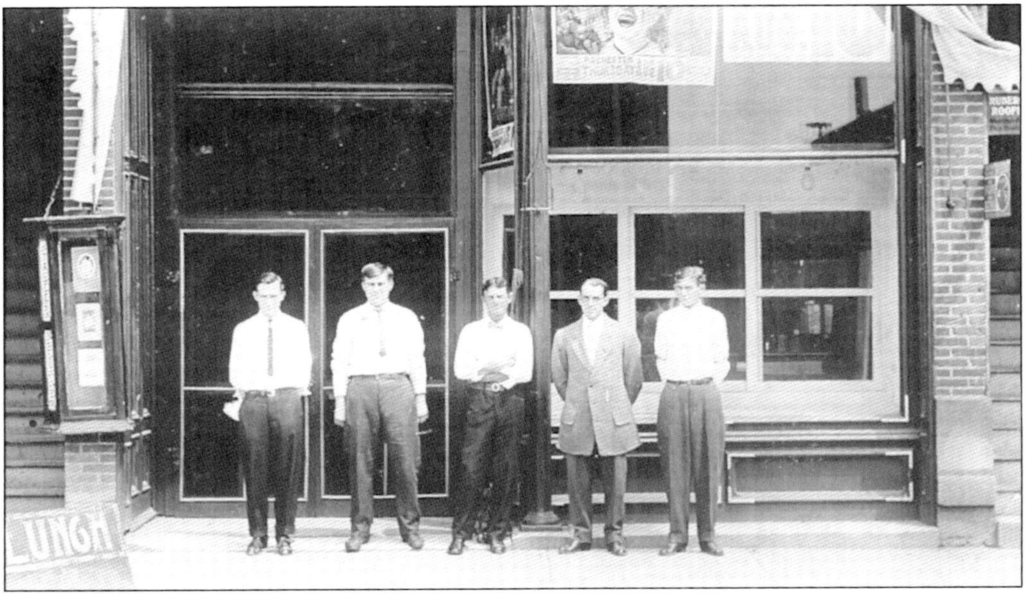

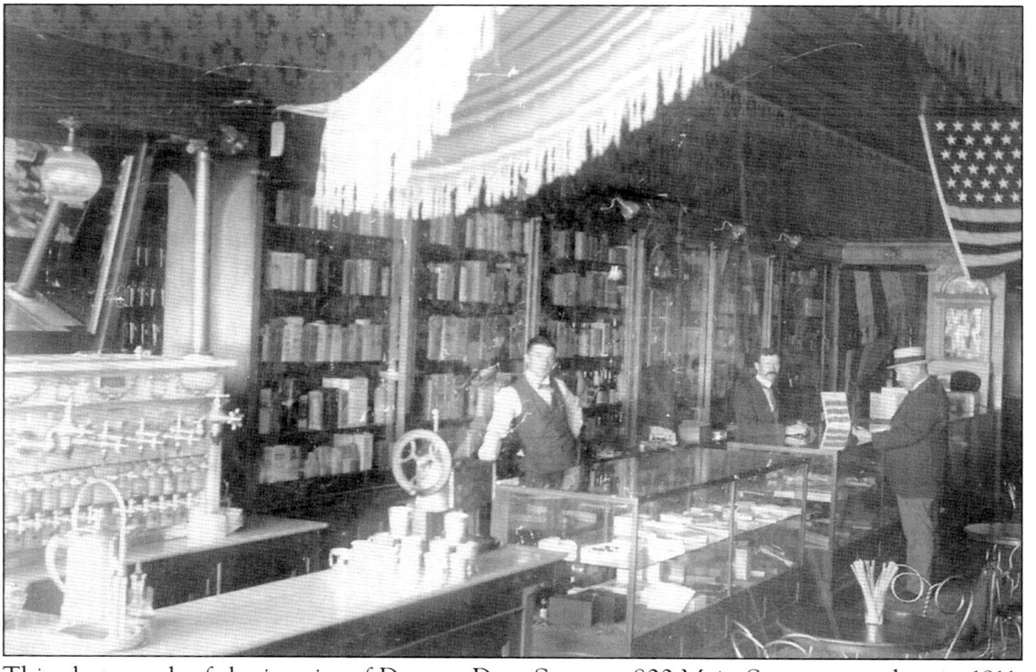

This photograph of the interior of Dawson Drug Store, at 800 Main Street, was taken in 1911. The proprietor was George Dawson. The drugstore soda fountain was a popular place for teenagers to hang out after school and get a cola or soda to drink. A hammock hangs from the ceiling, apparently for sale.

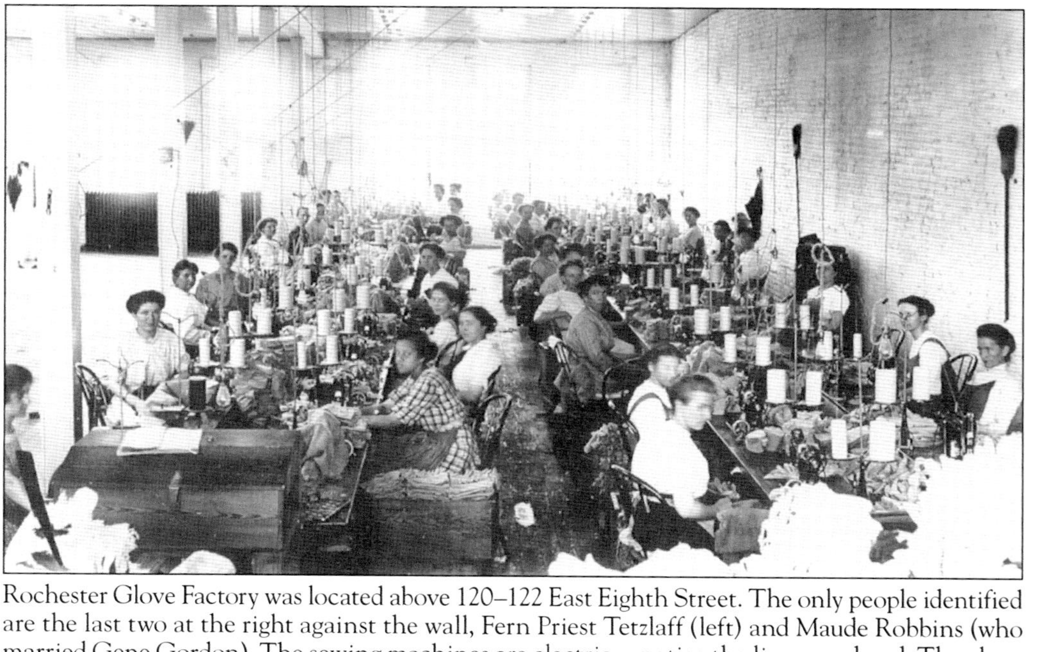

Rochester Glove Factory was located above 120–122 East Eighth Street. The only people identified are the last two at the right against the wall, Fern Priest Tetzlaff (left) and Maude Robbins (who married Gene Gordon). The sewing machines are electric—notice the lines overhead. The glove factory was constructed in May 1910 by Waring and Rafferty above the Manitou Theater. They hired 125 women at $7.25 per week.

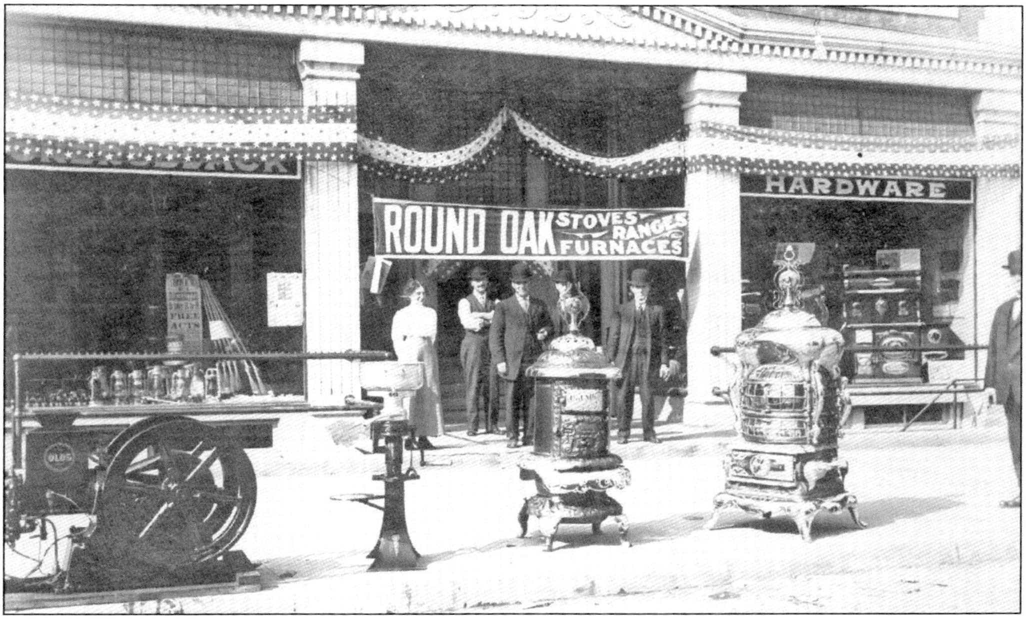

Stoner and Black Hardware, at 712–714 Main Street, preceded Bailey Hardware. George Black is third from left. George died in 1943, and his son Max partnered with Byron Bailey. In 1960, Black sold his interest to Byron, whose sons Robert and David worked there until 2006, when they sold it. A barbershop used to operate in the basement below; a bowling alley was on the third floor. (Courtesy of Tom Black.)

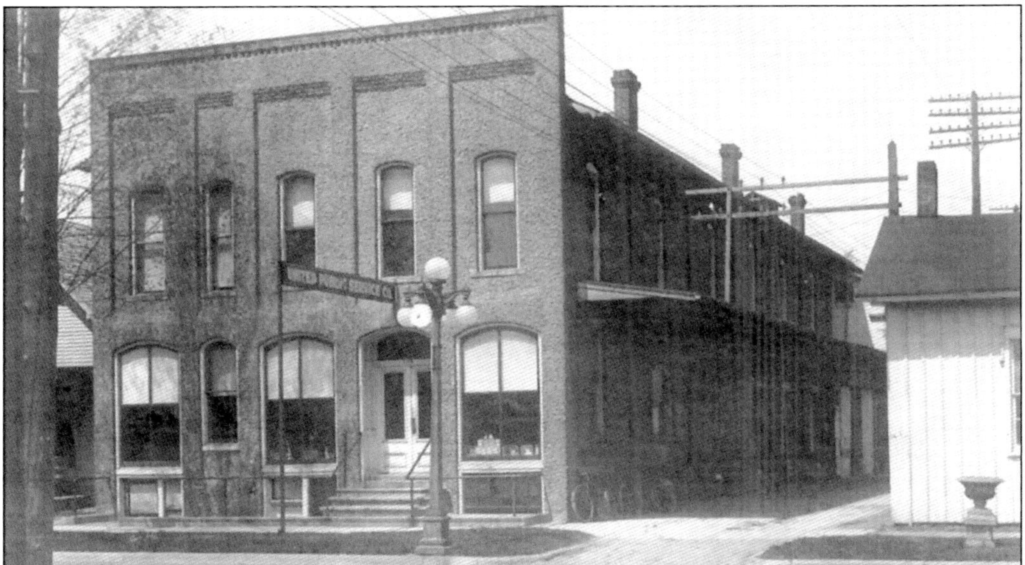

In 1917, United Public Service replaced the Rochester Electric Light Heat and Power Company, which brought the first electricity to Rochester in 1889. United also operated a plant to manufacture ice. The service was sold to Northern Indiana Power Company in 1922. In 1941, it became Public Service Indiana (PSI). The building was torn down in 1965, replaced by the PSI service center and headquarters, now known as Duke Energy.

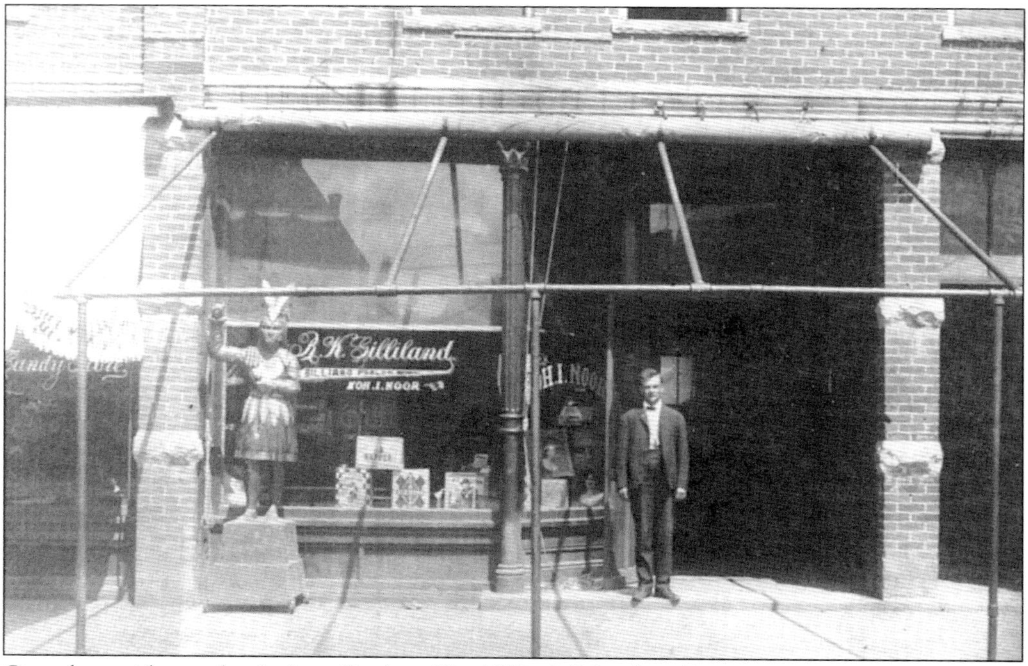

Complete with wooden Indian, Reuben "Reub" K. Gilliland's Billiard Parlor (at 709 Main Street from 1900 to 1929, afterwards at 502 Main) sold cigars named "Miss Rochester" and "La Planta." Reub operated a cigar factory on the south side of the courthouse square and made the "Town Clock" brand (which became one of the leading cigars in the state), as well as "Koh-I-Nor," "Gilliland's Little Rose," and "Gilliland's Hand Made." (Courtesy of *Rochester Sentinel.*)

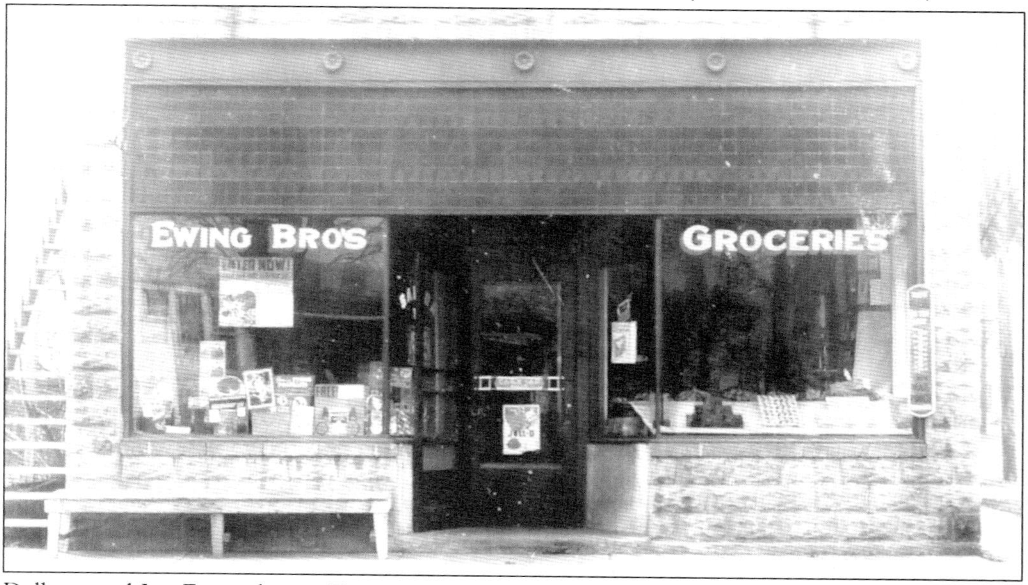

Delbert and Joe Ewing began Ewing Grocery in 1907 on Main Street, then moved in 1913 to the southeast corner of Ninth and Monroe Streets. They also had an IGA grocery store at 715 Main Street in 1927. The Ewings sold the store at 301 East Ninth Street in 1932 to Otto Cloud. (Courtesy of *Rochester Sentinel.*)

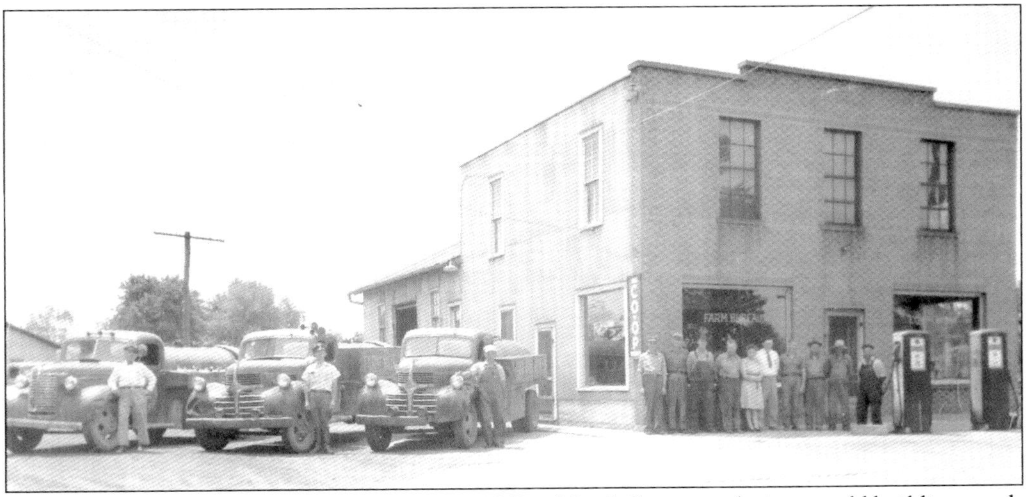

The Farm Bureau Co-op was built in 1940 at 423 East Ninth Street, replacing an old building south of this. Seen here are employees in 1945. From left to right, they are Bill Zink, Eldon Sherbondy, Bud Lewis, Bill Marshall, Vern Streyer, Josh Blacketor, Ernest Irvin, Mildred Irvin, James "Doc" Newcomb (manager from 1936 to 1950), John Denton, Emerson Reichard, Edward Pontious, and Claude Swears. A new elevator on North Main Street was built in 1949 and opened with a free community barn dance.

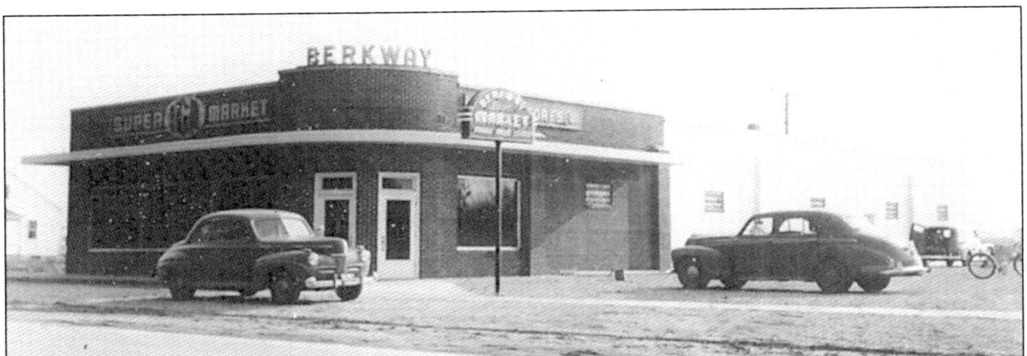

Berkway Super Market on East Ninth Street and Wabash Avenue opened in 1947, owned by Myron Berkheiser and Conde Holloway–hence the name Berkway. It was the first drive-up grocery, with ample off-street parking. It was also the first business building in the Manitou Heights subdivision. Berkheiser spent 46 years as a grocer, having worked for A&P, Kroger, and Morris Grocery on Main Street. Holloway later operated Conde's Farm Market on Race Street.

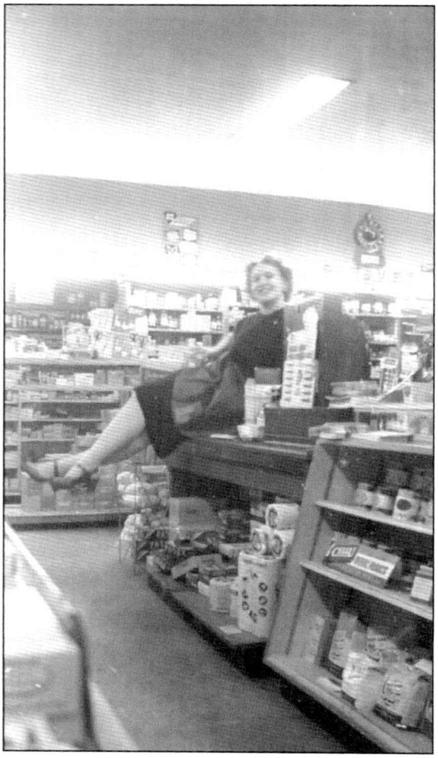

Heisler's Pharmacy (1950–1979) was located on the southwest corner of East Ninth Street and Wabash Avenue. At left, Jane Heisler, wife of co-owner Franklin Heisler, playfully poses on a counter in 1957. Franklin owned the drugstore with his father, Wayne Heisler. In 1980, Franklin closed his drugstore and went to work as pharmacist at Super X next to Kroger's in Rochester Plaza. (Courtesy of Jane and Wayne's daughter, Phyllis Heisler.)

Theodore Johnson and his son Claude started Johnson's Meat Market in 1929, having purchased Vine Curtis's market at 316 East Ninth Street. Theo died in 1934. Fire damaged the store in 1945, but Claude restored and enlarged it, adding 200 to 400 locker units. At that time, home freezers were considered too expensive for most people to own, so families would commonly rent a locker in which to store their frozen meats and vegetables. (Courtesy of *Rochester Sentinel.*)

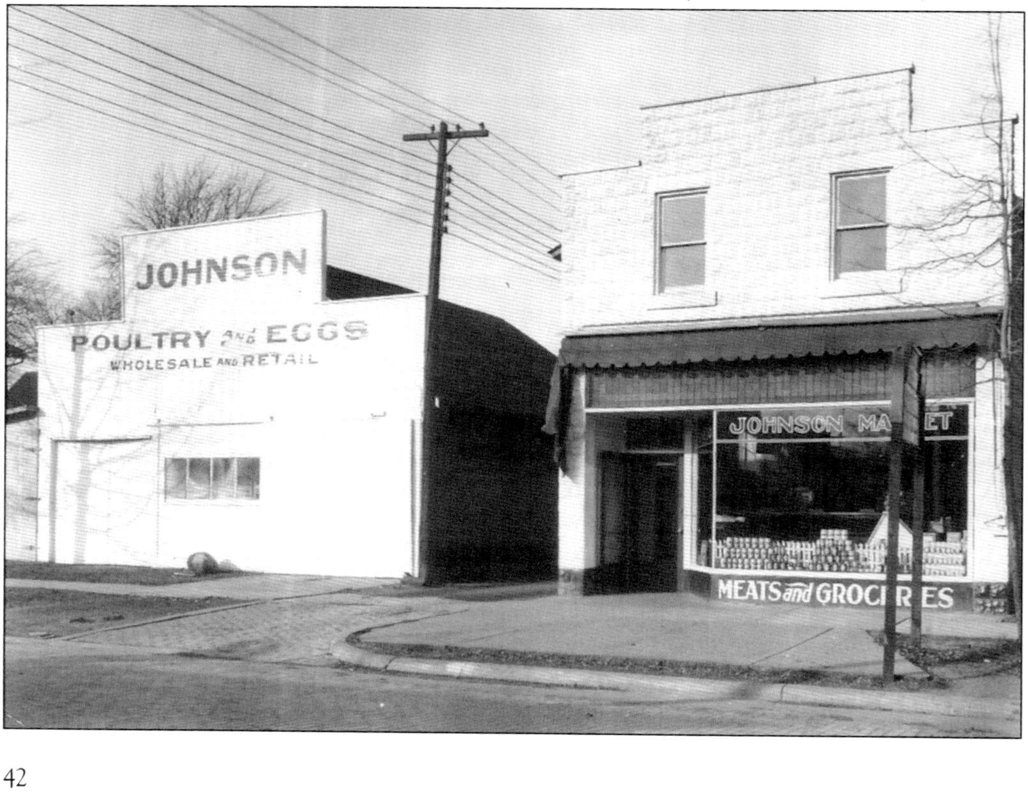

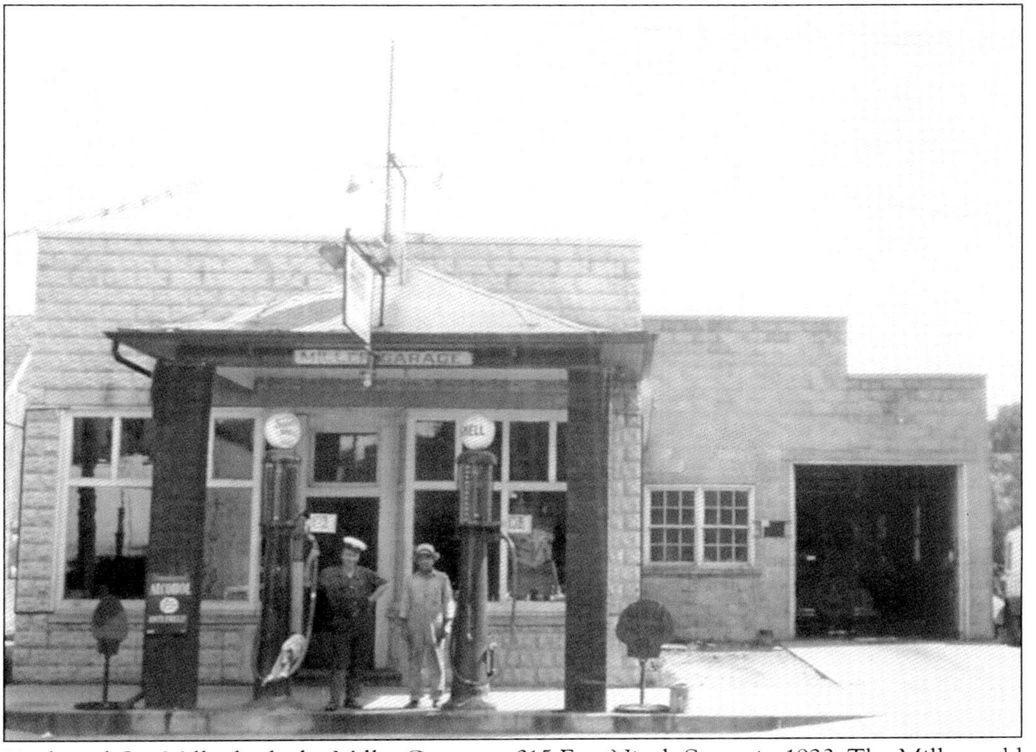

Hugh and Ott Miller built the Miller Garage at 315 East Ninth Street in 1923. The Millers sold Paige and Jewett automobiles there in 1925. They sold Plymouths in 1934 and added Studebakers in 1936. Millers leased the garage in 1945 to Voris Hoffman, who made it a Ford Ferguson dealership. Millers also ran the Western Oil filling station that opened at 520 Main Street in 1927. In 1945, it moved to 625 Main Street.

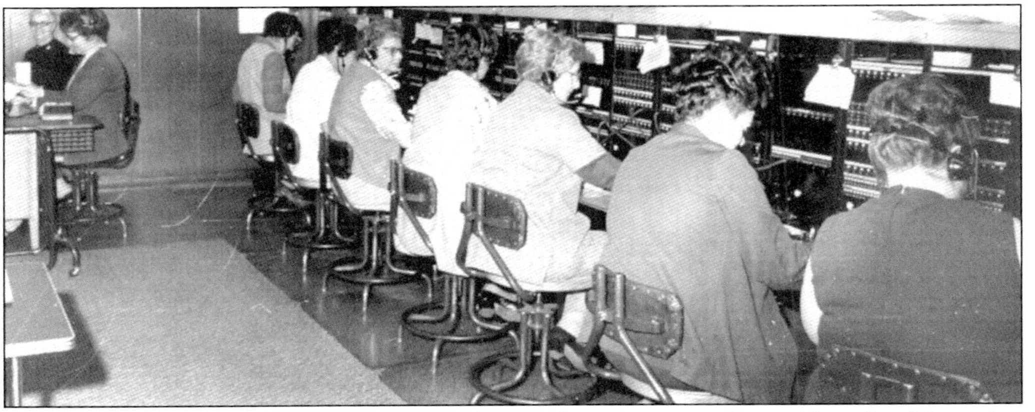

Rochester Telephone Company operators work at the long distance toll switchboard on November 16, 1974. At the left are Lura Kirkendall and Nina Ogden at the information desk. From left to right, the other operators are Helen Reese, Kathryn Shireman, Willetta Miller, Erlene Irwin, Gladys Hall, Gloria Heinold, and Martha Cloud. The job of local telephone operator was eliminated by the dial system in 1957; long-distance dialing came in late 1974. (Courtesy of Rochester Telephone Company.

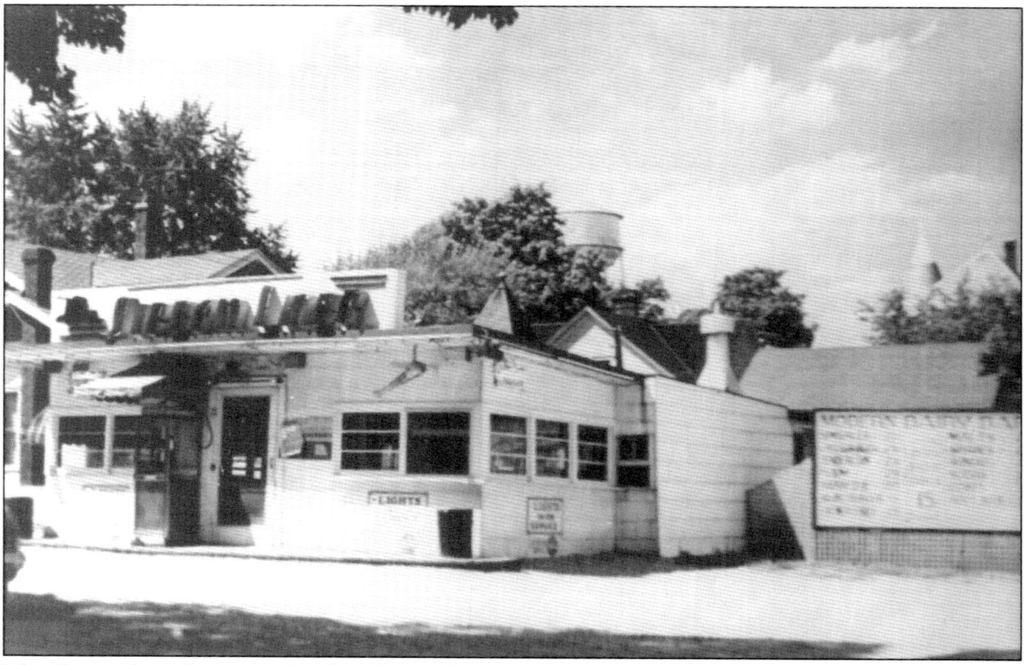

The Streamliner began as Modern Dairy Bar in 1939 at 202 East Ninth Street. It was moved to the junction of U.S. 31, 14, and 25 at the south edge of town in 1949. When owner Larry Calhoun opened a new restaurant at Ninth and Madison Streets in 1988, he named the new one Streamliner Central and the old one Streamliner Junction. Streamliner Junction was torn down in 2004.

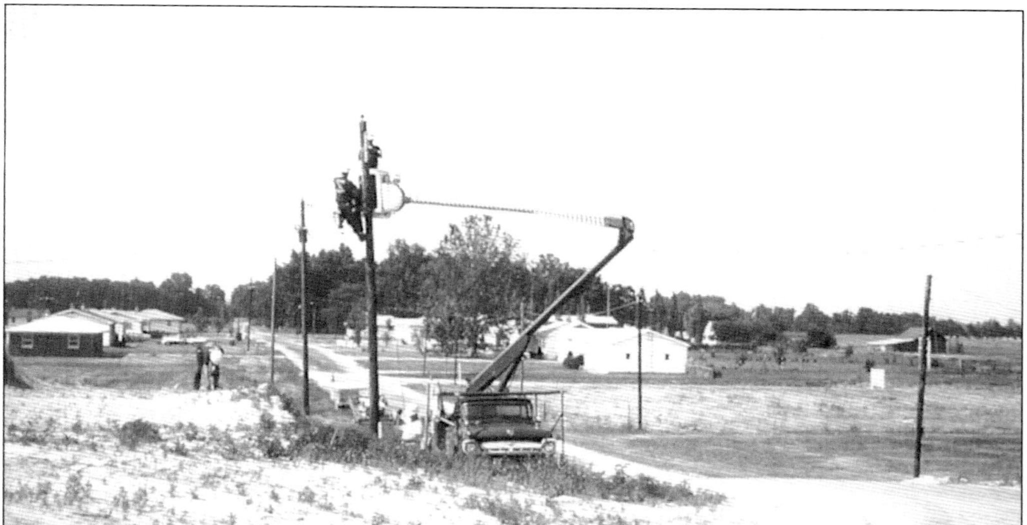

Rural Electric Membership Corporation (REMC) put electric in for Hillcrest Baptist Church at 1010 West Ninth Street July 1963. This is in the Reese Addition on the west side of Rochester from Ninth Street on Reese Road (now 50 East). Hillcrest Baptist Church is now on the left. The houses seen here, from left to right, belonged to Kenneth Hood, Arnold Snipes (first to build in the addition), Bernice Mow, and Harold Reese (on Sixth Street). Later, Eighth Street was built at right front.

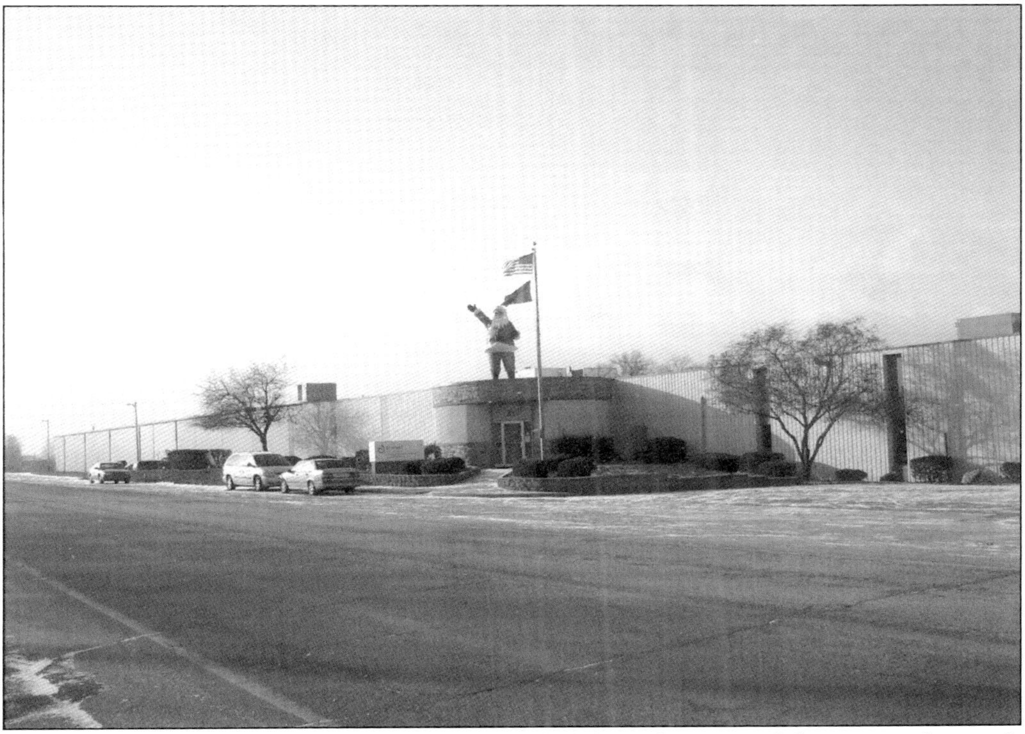

Since 1968, Santa Claus has waved from the roof of the Indiana Metal factory 4 miles north of Rochester on Old 31. Val Pemberton, the plant manager, bought the Santa for $1,000. It is made of fiberglass and looks like new, being laid to sleep in a shed atop the roof when not standing for Christmas season. The factory's name was changed to Torx Camcar and now is Acument Global Technologies.

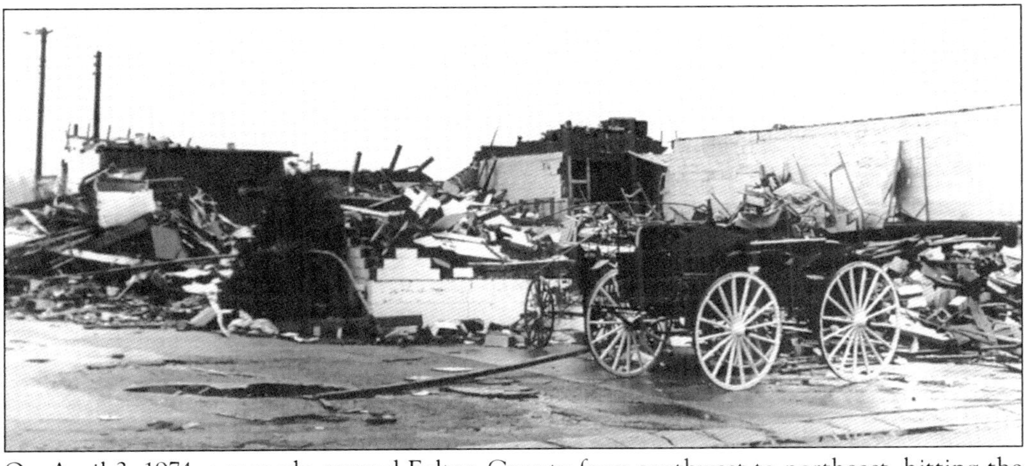

On April 3, 1974, a tornado crossed Fulton County from southwest to northeast, hitting the northwest corner of Rochester, destroying many buildings and killing four people in the area. One of the buildings destroyed was Buttermilk Bob's, pictured here. Also destroyed were the Ghrist Motel, Clevenger round barn, and Talma School. Riddle School and many houses near it were damaged. High school students picked up debris from farm fields so that the year's planting could proceed.

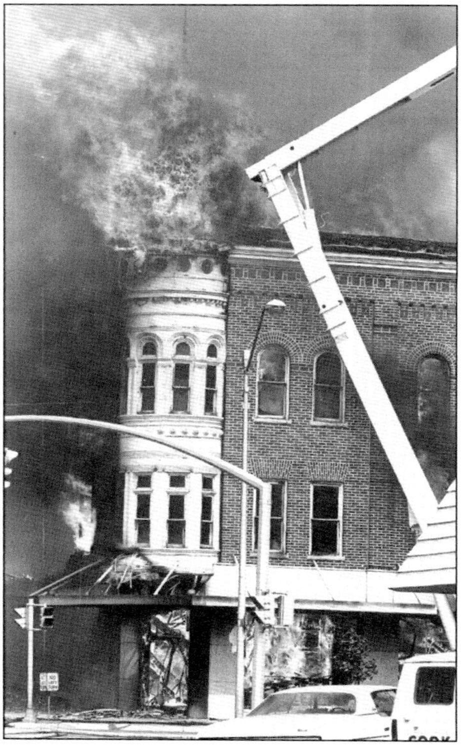

Wile's Department Store (the former Arlington Hotel) burned on July 19, 1975. The hotel was built in 1890 at 701 Main Street. Fred Senger purchased Wile's Department Store in 1947 and moved the store to the hotel building in 1964. At left, flames are engulfing the collapsing building, and the corner tower is disappearing in flame. Many of Rochester's old historic buildings were destroyed by fires through the years. (Courtesy of *Rochester Sentinel.*)

Rochester Post Office was built in 1925 at Madison and Eighth Streets. Albert Bitters, local postmaster, placed the big iron key to the old jail in the cornerstone. Seven rural routes delivered mail to people living in the country. Mail carriers walked to deliver mail in town. The new post office was built in 2001. The sheriff's department moved offices into the old post office in 2009.

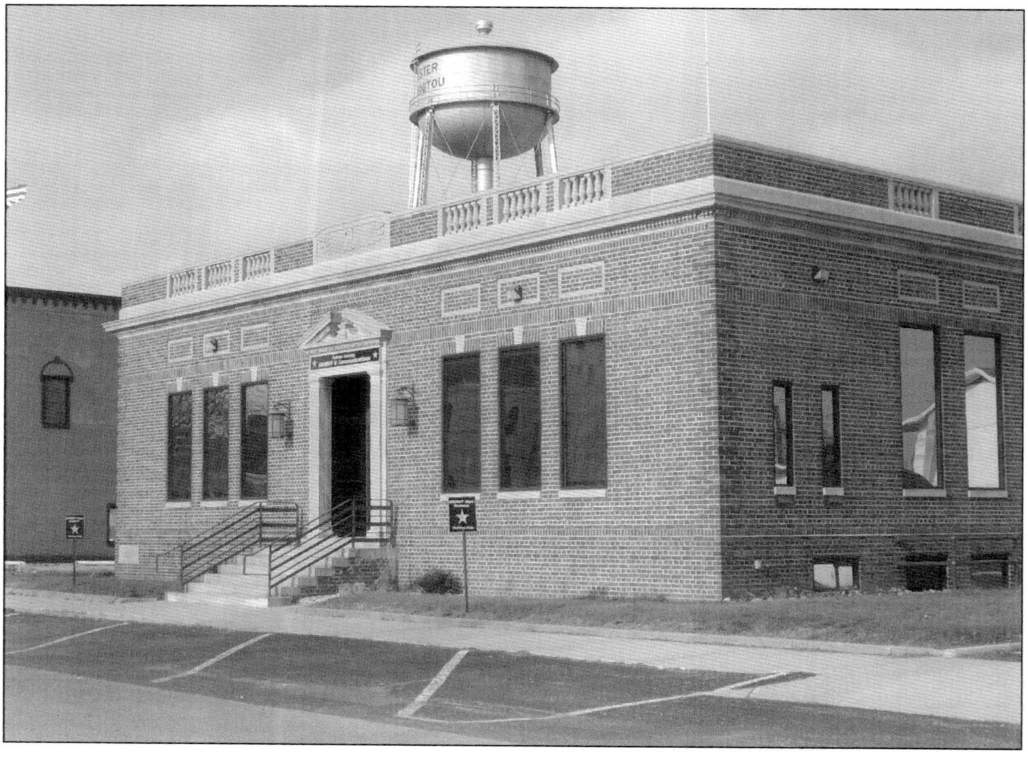

Four

Lake Manitou and Tippecanoe River

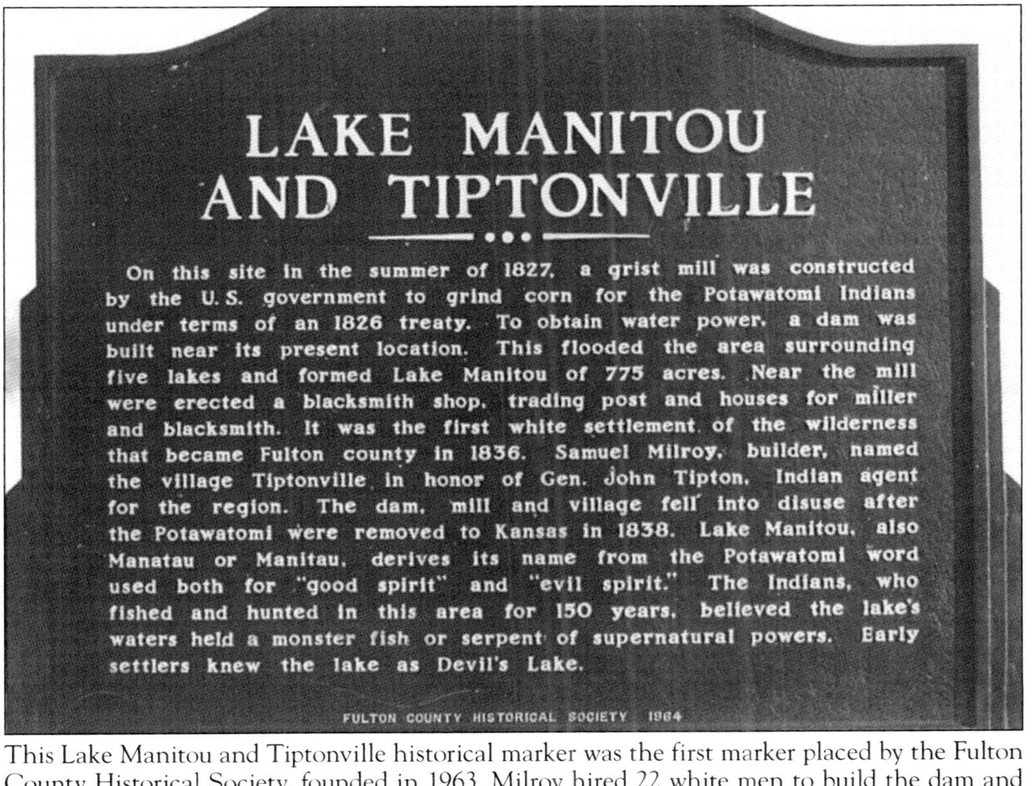

This Lake Manitou and Tiptonville historical marker was the first marker placed by the Fulton County Historical Society, founded in 1963. Milroy hired 22 white men to build the dam and mill. Blacksmith John Lindsey brought his wife, Elizabeth, and six small children. She died in 1832, the first white woman to die here. A George Winter sketch of the Manitou Monster was published in the Logansport newspaper in 1834.

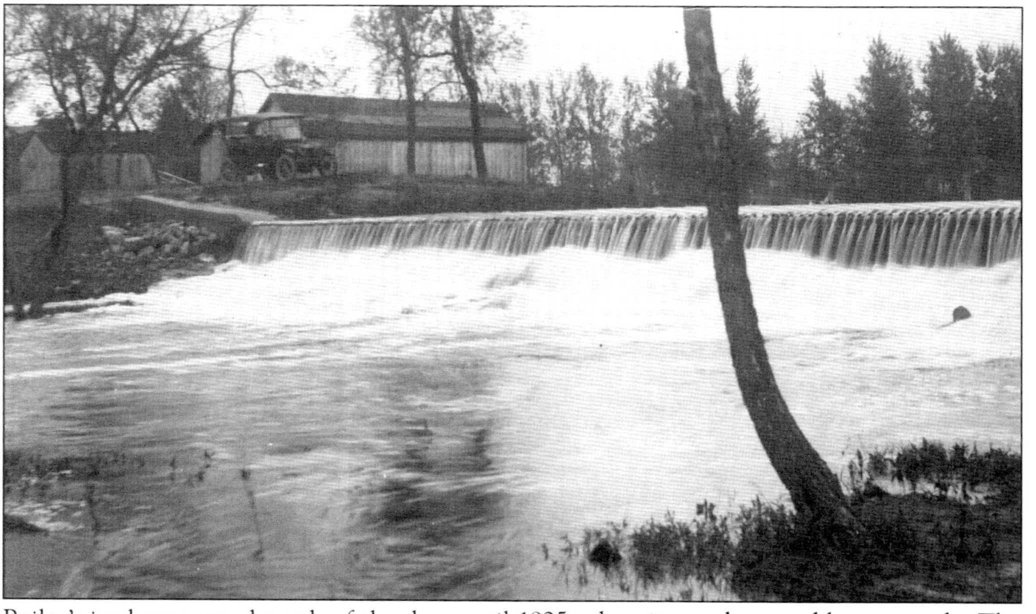

Bailey's ice house stood north of the dam until 1925, when it was destroyed by a tornado. The dam was built as a result of the 1826 treaty with the Potawatomi Indians, which was signed at Wabash at Paradise Springs. It provided a mill and a blacksmith for the Potawatomi. John Lindsey and wife Elizabeth had a son, Nathan Lindsey, born October 4, 1831—the first white baby born in what became Fulton County in 1835.

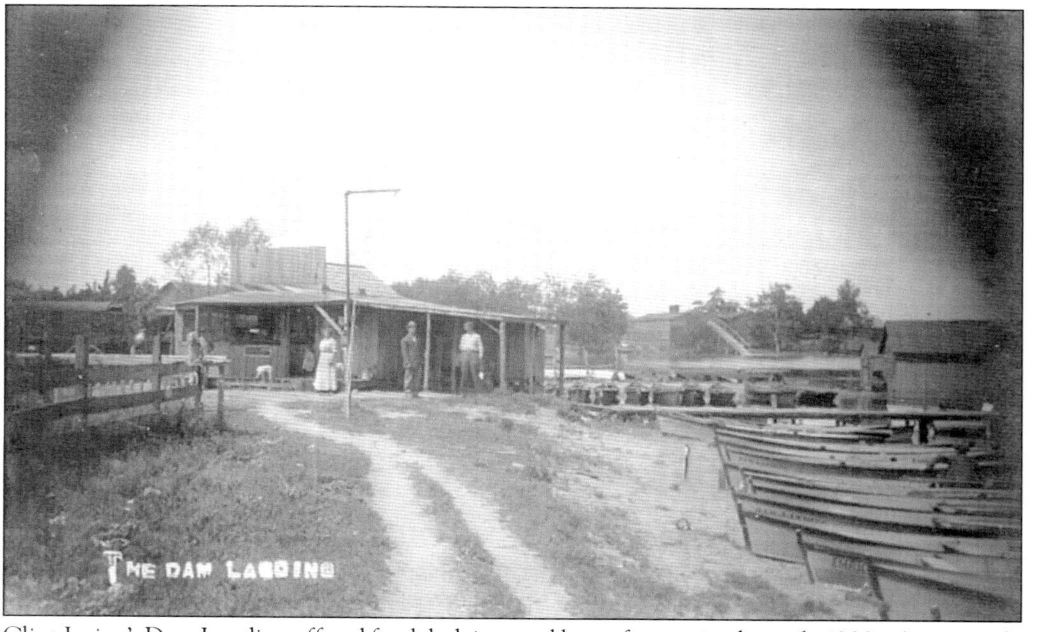

Clint Irvine's Dam Landing offered food, lodging, and boats for rent in the early 1900s. A peninsula ran out into the lake, and Irvine had 52 boats parked around it that he rented out. The land also had a bunkhouse for men who came to fish. Boats rented for 10¢ for the first hour and 5¢ for each additional hour. (Courtesy of Tom Black.)

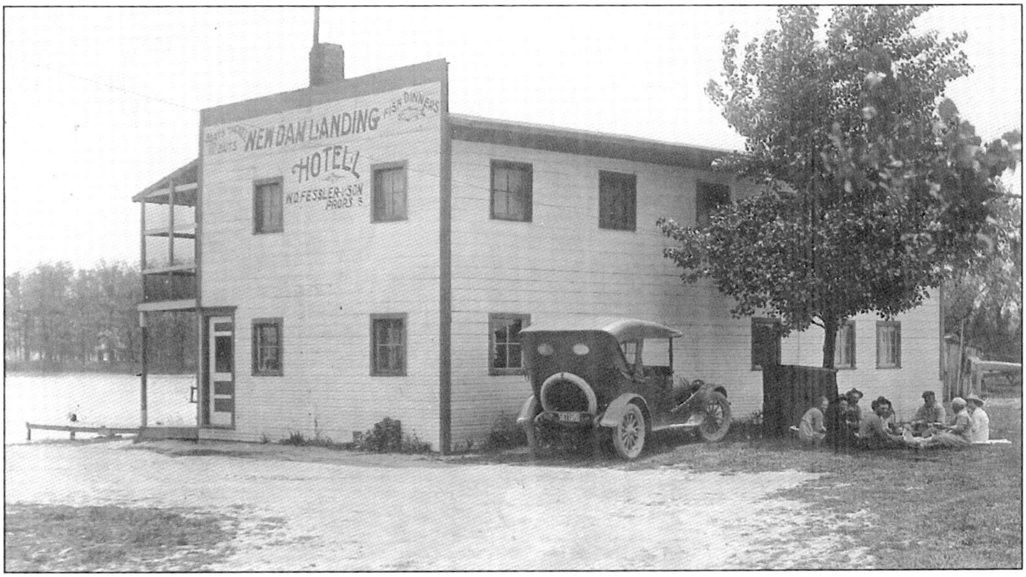

"New Dam Landing Hotell–Boats Tackel Baits and Fish Dinners–W. O. Fessler and Son" read the sign on this two-story wood frame building around 1920. Located south of the dam and mill race, it continues today as Pat's Landing restaurant. The mill race was dug in 1840 or possibly as late as 1858 to provide water power to Rochester factories.

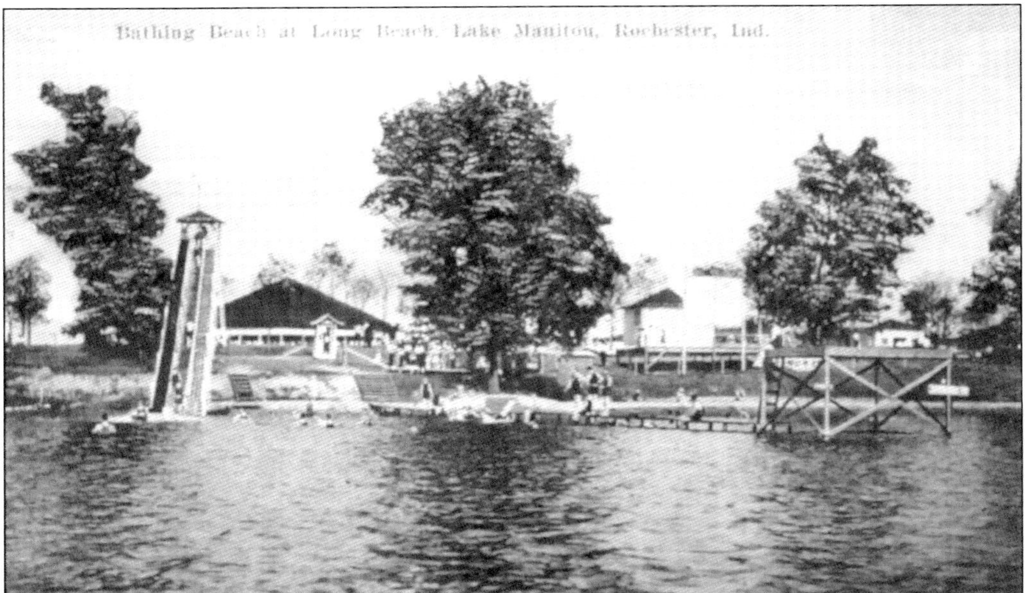

Long Beach Amusement Park and Manitou Hotel were on the north shore near Bessmore Park. It was incorporated in 1921 by Charles and Martha Shank of Indianapolis. It was purchased by A. J. Barrett in 1924. A 1925 tornado damaged it, so a new pier, bathhouse, and dance pavilion were built. It became White City, added a toboggan slide, and held dance marathons in the hotel in the early 1930s.

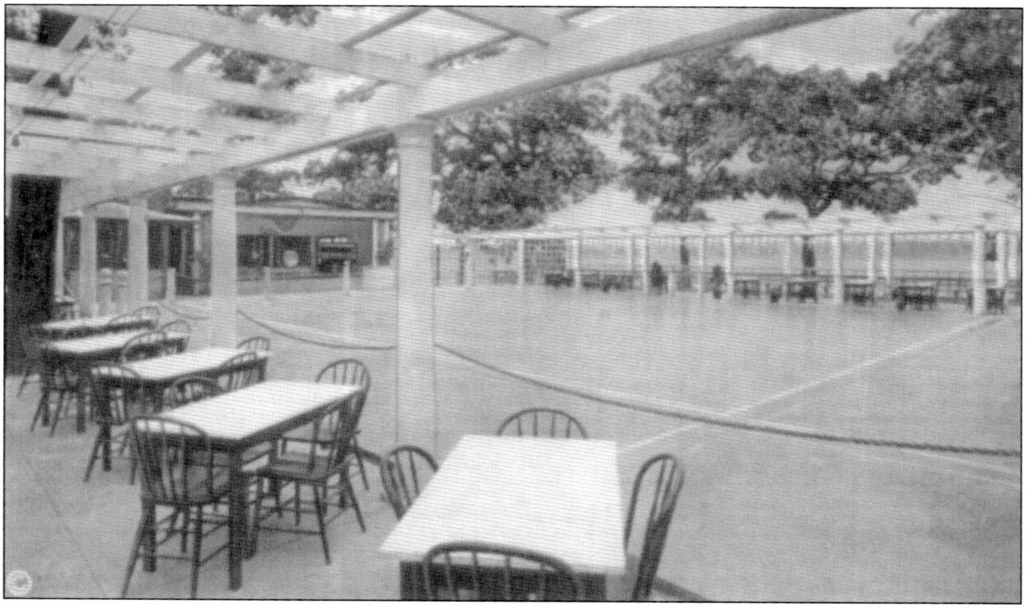

Fairview Hotel offered swimming, diving, dining, dancing, and music by big bands of the 1920s and 1930s. The dance floor was crowded with dancers and listeners to the marvelous music and singing. Both old and young loved the same music in those days! The trains brought big crowds of 2,500 to 3,000. Harry Paige was the proprietor from 1914 until the hotel was destroyed by fire on January 25, 1939. (Courtesy of Tom Black.)

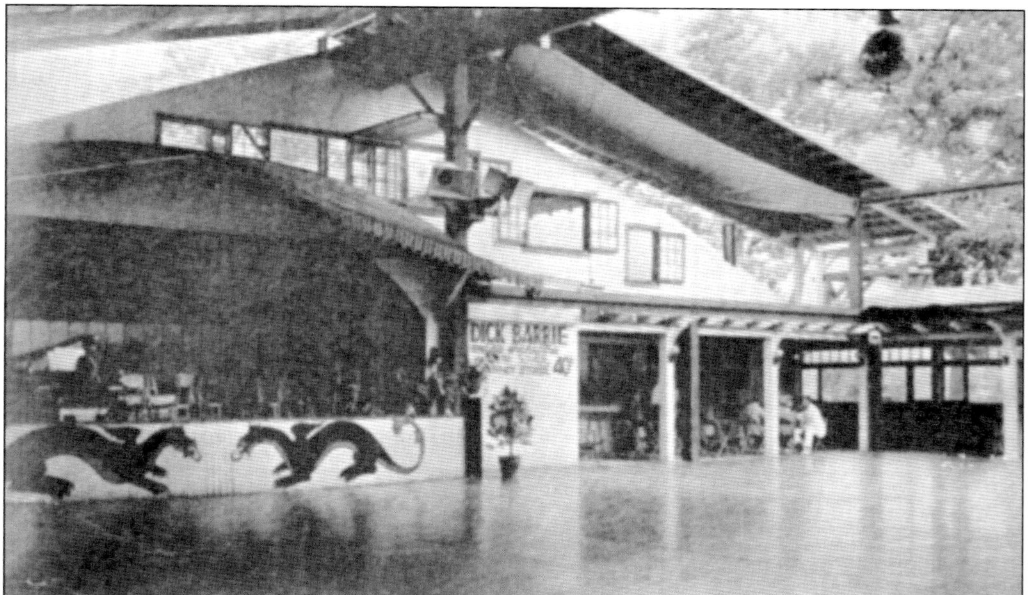

Colonial Hotel on Lake Manitou was owned by A. C. Bradley until it burned on October 25, 1938. Big bands played and crowds came by train and automobile to dance on the open floor on starry nights. Bradley sold it after the fire to Harry Paige, who rebuilt it and continued to book big names, such as Glen Miller, Duke Ellington, Cab Calloway, and Louis Armstrong. RHS held junior-senior proms there.

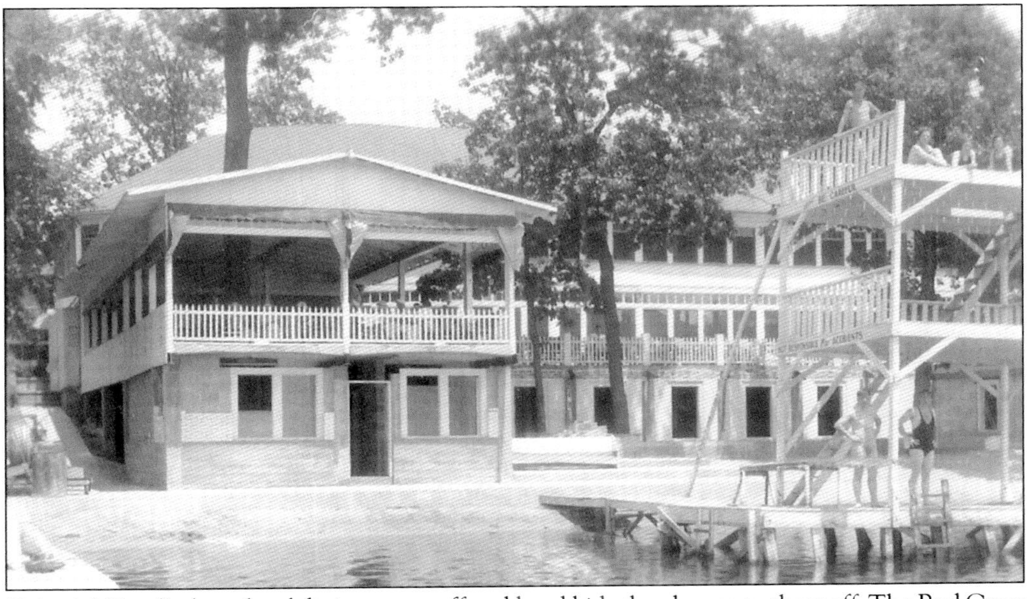

Colonial Hotel's three-level diving tower offered local kids the chance to show off. The Red Cross gave swimming lessons there. Paige sold the Colonial to Dave Shafer in 1947. Swing music was declining, and rock and roll soon replaced it in popularity. It continued as a restaurant but was torn down in 1977, replaced by Colonial Condos in 1982.

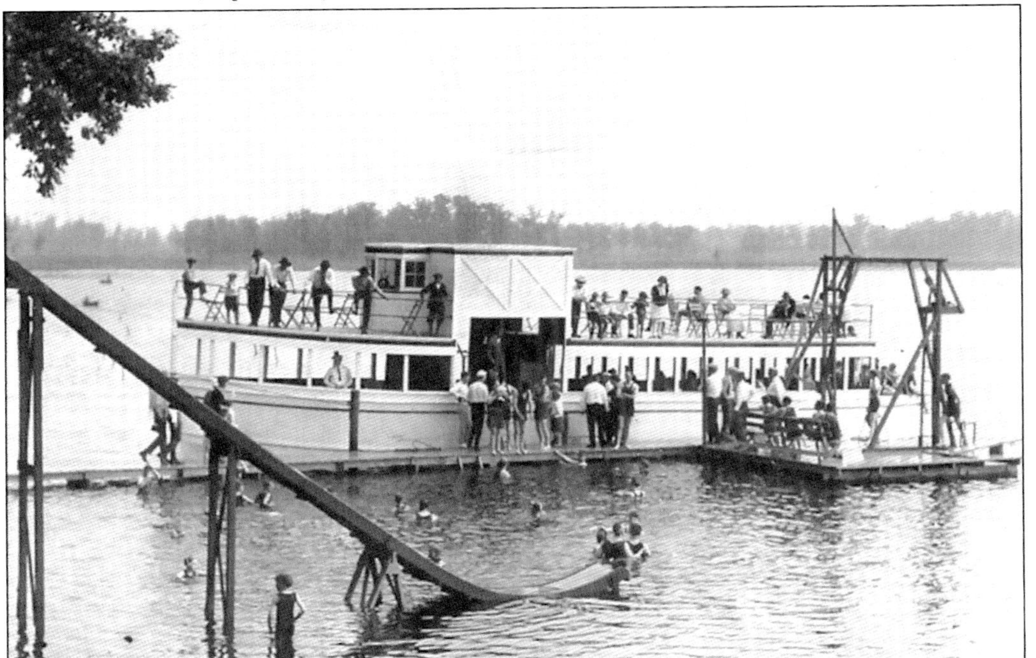

The *Pastime*, a double-decker excursion boat, is shown landing at Colonial Hotel. It was owned by George Pollock and later by Emerson Enyart. For 25¢, passengers could take a leisurely cruise around the lake. Another excursion boat was the *Redwing*, a single decker that was later moved to Lake Maxinkuckee. (Courtesy of *Rochester Sentinel*.)

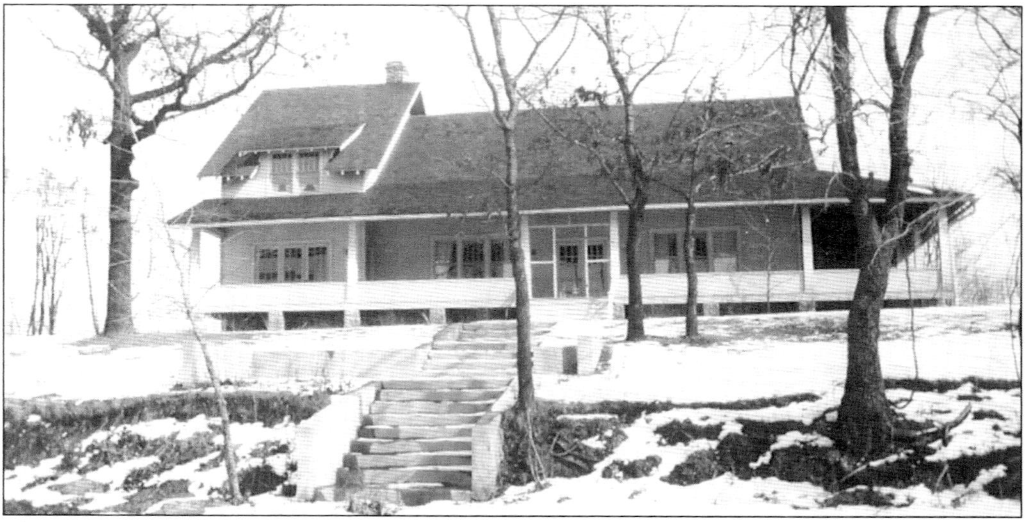

The Elks Country Club was a snowy place in the winter of 1927. The lake was covered with ice, perfect for ice fishing. In spring, summer, and fall, the golf course is a busy place, but in winter, the clubhouse remains a popular restaurant. This is on the east side of Lake Manitou, at 2506 Country Club Drive.

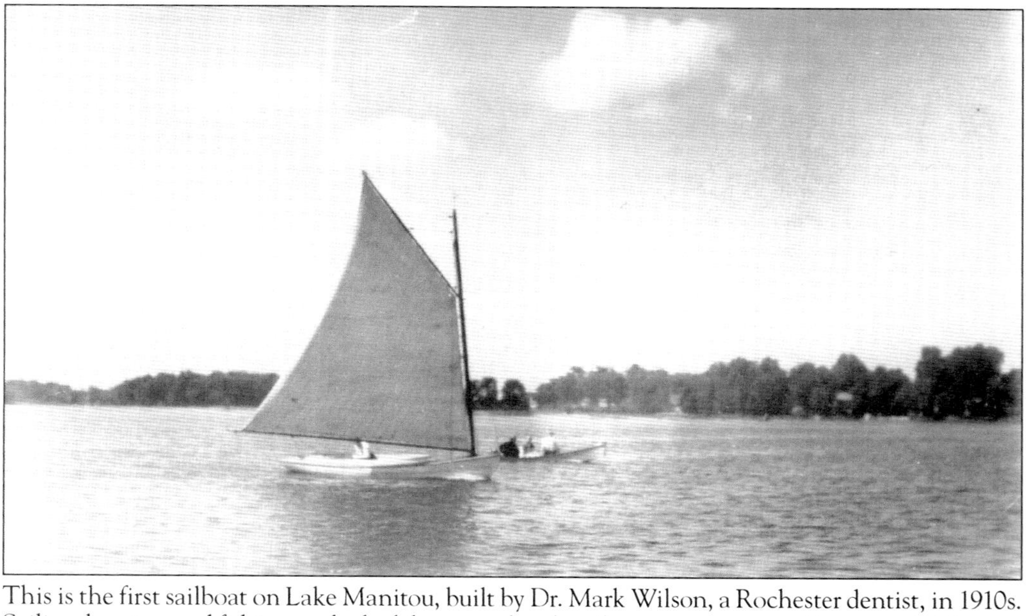

This is the first sailboat on Lake Manitou, built by Dr. Mark Wilson, a Rochester dentist, in 1910s. Sailing, boating, and fishing made the lake a popular place for summer tourists. Gangsters Al Capone and John Dillinger are rumored to have visited the lake. Today the Lake Manitou Association sponsors a parade of decorated boats to open the season. (Courtesy of *Rochester Sentinel*.)

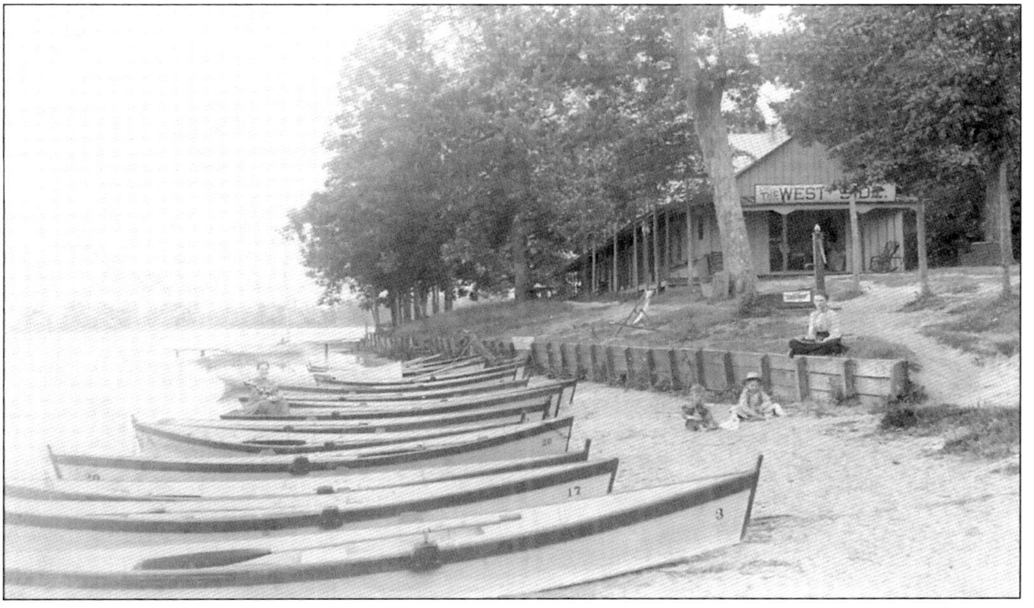

West Side Hotel in early 1880s had boats for rent. Formerly Jewel's Landing, additional rooms were built facing the lake, porches of which appear under the trees. The hotel soon added a large dining room. A tall water pump is seen behind the seated woman at right, who watches over two children. Moose Lodge purchased the West Side Hotel on October 20, 1948. (Courtesy of *Rochester Sentinel.*)

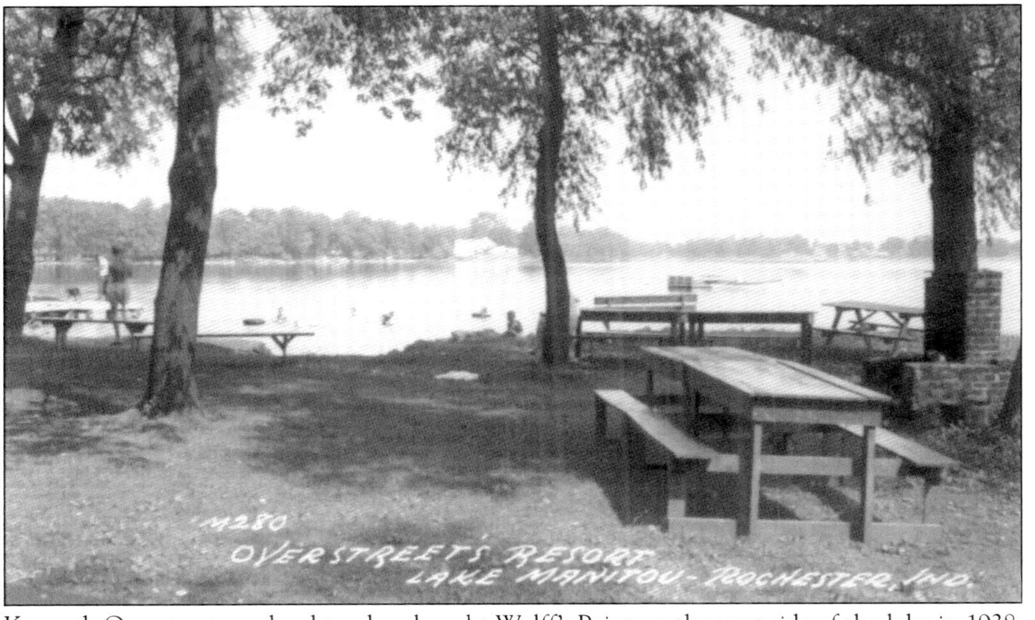

Kenneth Overstreet, a school teacher, bought Wolff's Point on the west side of the lake in 1938. He made Overstreet's Resort, adding a 32-foot pier. It was a popular place for free parking, free swimming, free picnicking, fishing, and renting boats and cottages. Snacks like ice cream and pop were sold at the concession stand. Local farm kids even brought their ponies to swim. (Courtesy of Tom Black.)

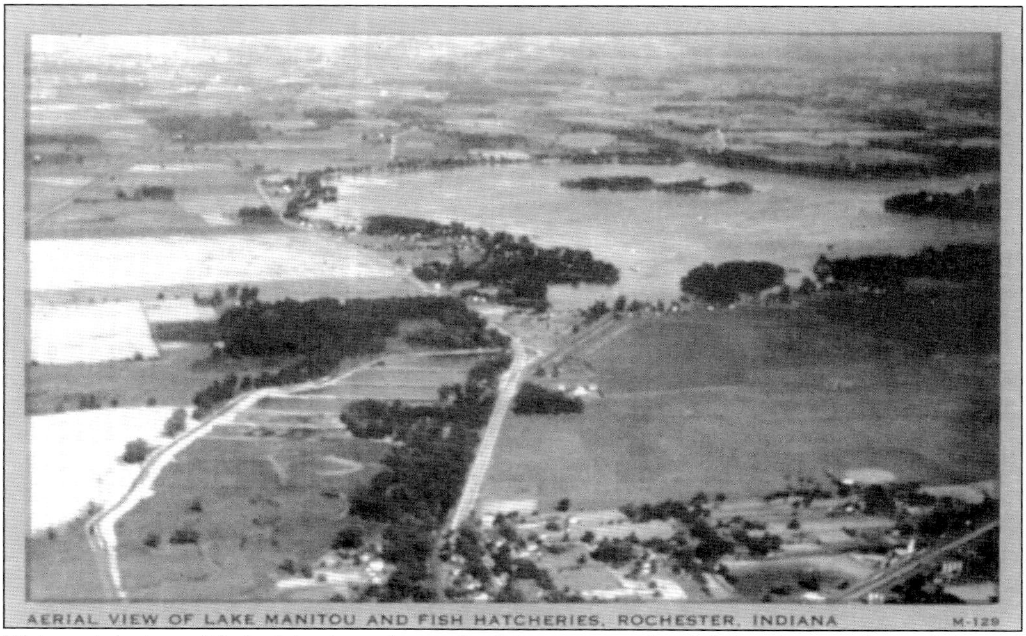

This aerial view of Lake Manitou shows the lake at top right, fish hatchery at lower left, and Fansler Addition at lower right. Rochester's first air field was there in 1920s. Rochester High School's first football field was donated by Art Fansler in 1951 and named Fansler Field in his honor. (Courtesy of Tom Black.)

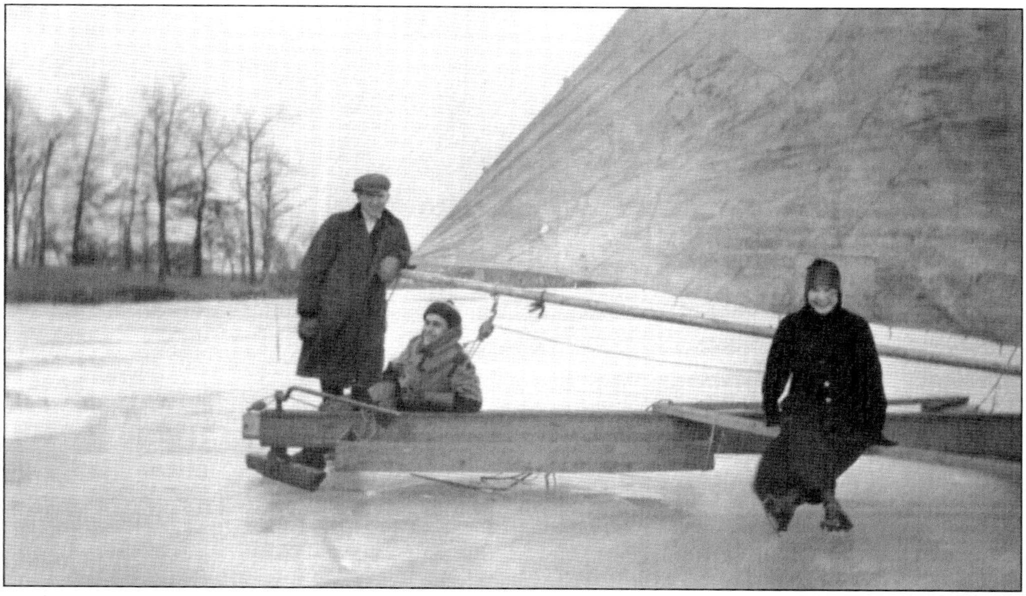

Ice boats provided a thrilling ride across the lake before snowmobiles. Riders said ice boats went at speeds faster than the wind because of the ability to tack. Today the lake is a popular place for ice fishing and skating. When the ice expands and makes booming noises, old-timers said it was the Manitou Monster trying to get his head above the ice. (Courtesy of *Rochester Sentinel.*)

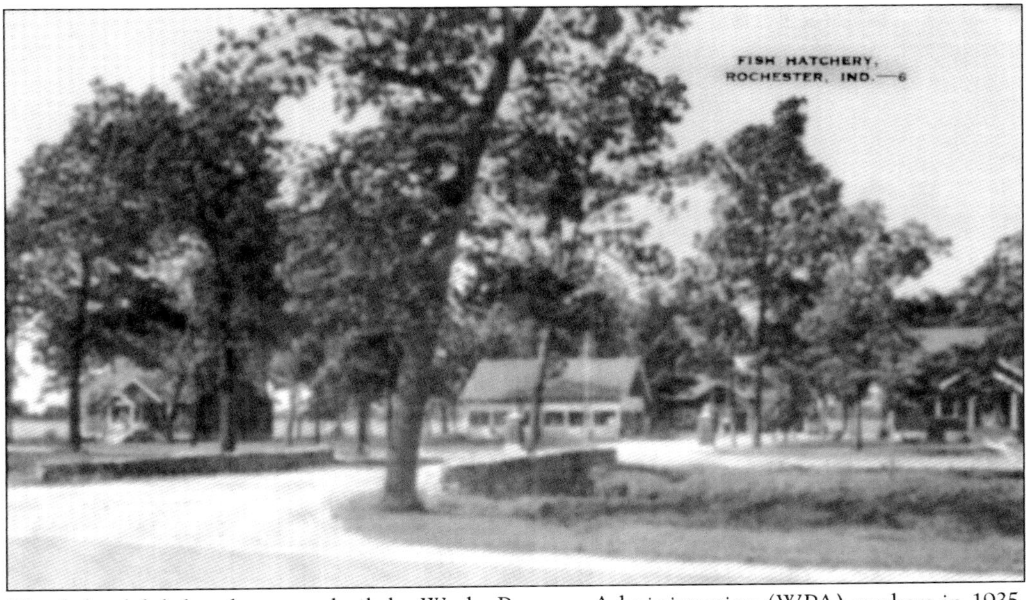

The federal fish hatchery was built by Works Progress Administration (WPA) workers in 1935. The stone bridge over the Mill Race still stands today. A metal fish was installed in each of the brick posts by the driveway, but these disappeared years ago. When the fish hatchery closed in 1965, it was sold to the City of Rochester for a park, swimming pool, and golf course. (Courtesy of Tom Black.)

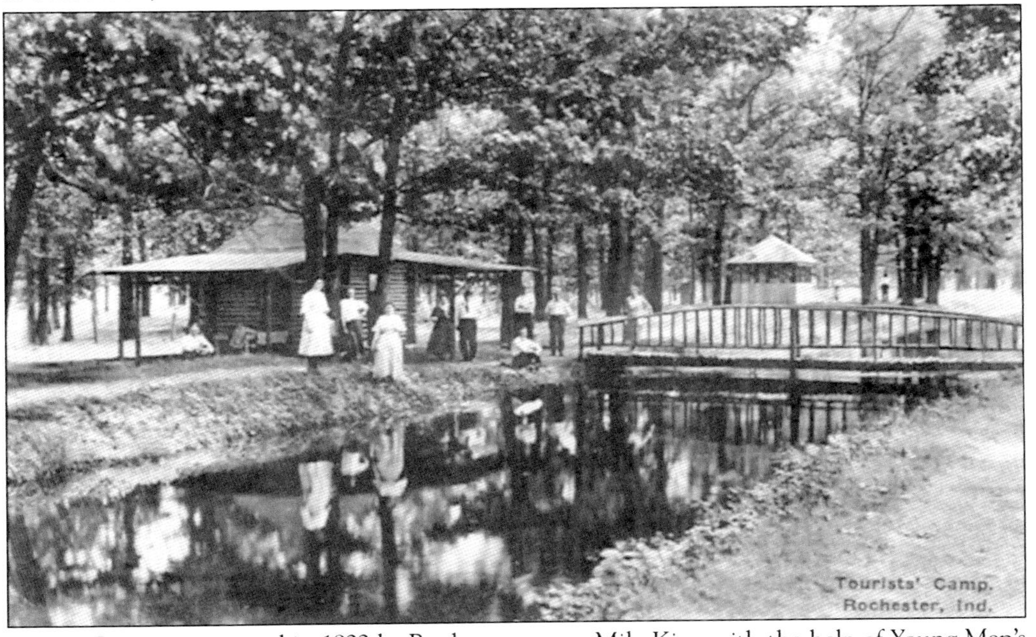

Tourist Camp was created in 1922 by Rochester mayor Milo King with the help of Young Men's Business Association (president Hugh Barnhart), which cut trees in the tamarack marsh at Akron and built log cabins for travelers. The cabins were moved to City Park when the fish hatchery was built. The last cabin to survive was moved to Fulton County Historical Society grounds in 1985. (Courtesy of Dave Burkett.)

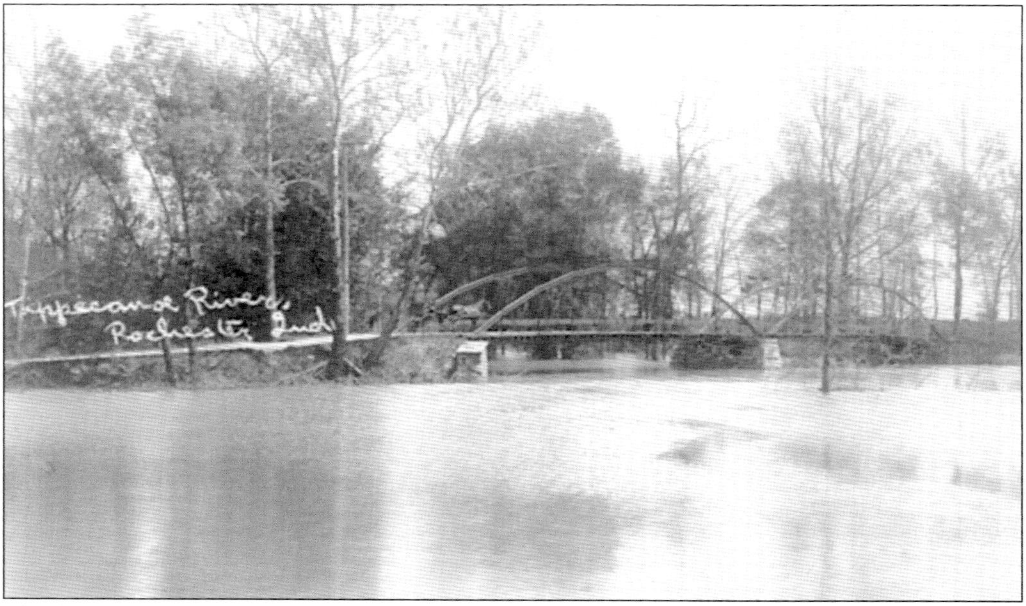

This bridge, built in 1875 across Tippecanoe River and Michigan Road (Old U.S. 31), was a curved truss design. It was replaced by a square truss bridge in 1916. The current concrete bridge was built in 1982, thus alleviating the problem of the old bridge having become a one-lane bridge and a bottleneck for travelers going from South Bend to Indianapolis. (Courtesy of Dave Burkett.)

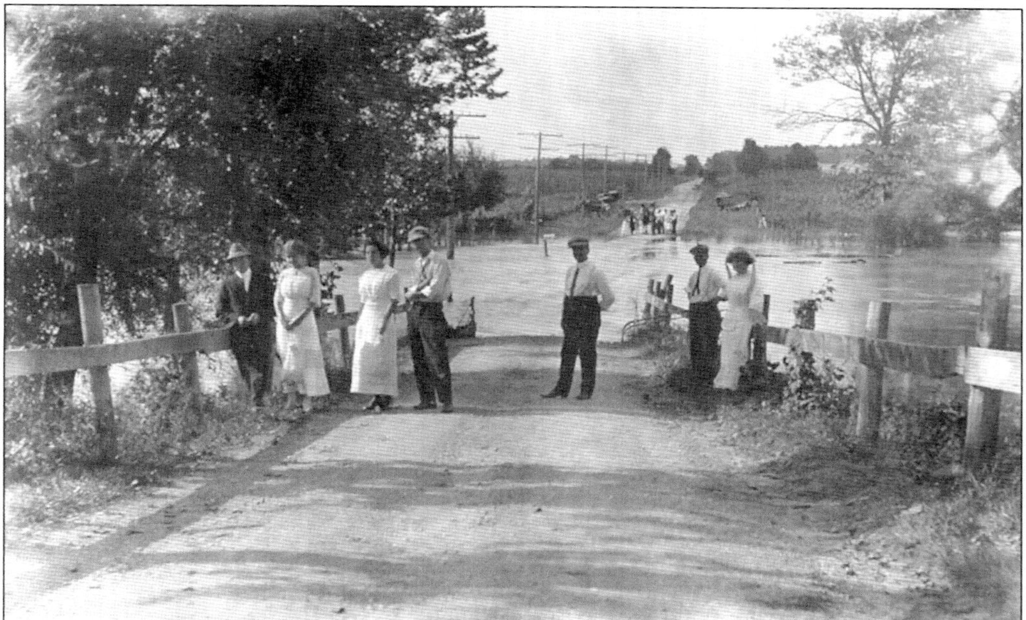

The Tippecanoe River flood in August 19, 1912, killed Thomas Rush (age 72) when his buggy spilled and he was trapped under water. His daughter, Laura Rush, and three-year-old grandson were in the buggy but were rescued by William Rea, Charles Snepp, and Joe Baker. The flooded area about 100 feet wide was on Old 31 just north of the river bridge. The camera is facing south toward Rochester.

Five

MILITARY AND POLICE

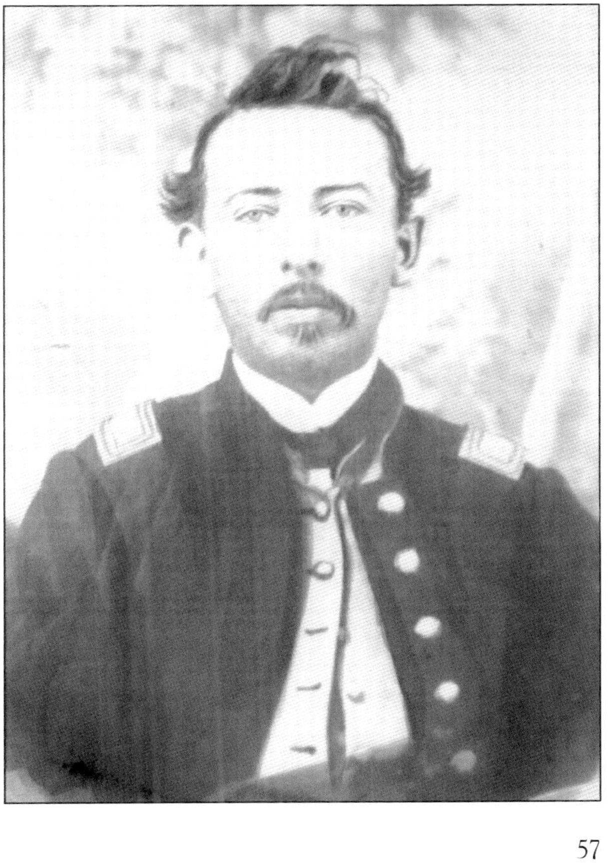

John McClung, a Mount Zion farmer, was killed at Sabine Crossing, Louisiana, on April 8, 1864, the first Fulton County man killed in the Civil War. He was a first lieutenant in Company K, 46th Indiana Regiment. The Rochester Grand Army of the Republic (GAR) post was named for him. It was established in 1882 and continued to be active until 1934. The GAR record book is in the Rochester library.

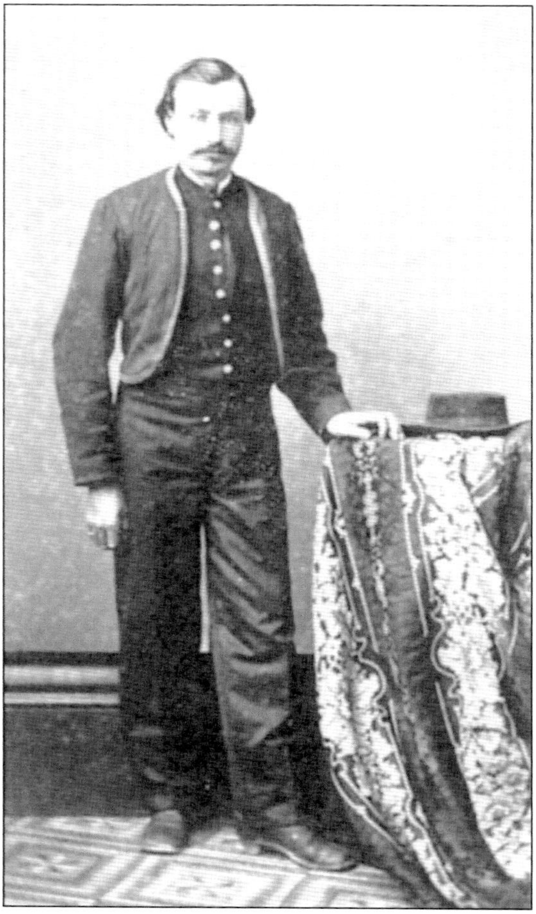

George Moore was a Civil War corporal in Company K, 46th Regiment, from December 1861 to September 1865. Moore was captured at Sabine Crossing, Louisiana, and spent several months in a Confederate prison in Tyler, Texas, where he caught rheumatism. He and his wife, Catherine Bowen, had eight children. She died in 1920. In 1922, at age 85, George, suffering from shaking palsy, hung himself in his son's barn near Athens.

The A. H. Skinner Spanish-American War veterans gathered for the last time in 1958. Seen below from left to right are Austin McIntire, Ben Noftsger, Jack Irwin, Fred Logan, Oliver Krom, and Ben Freeman (in wheelchair). An encampment was held in Rochester in 1937 that was attended by over 600 people, including the Women's Auxiliary. Capt. Otis Minter was mayor of Rochester from 1939 to 1945. When Minter died in 1966, Fred Logan was the only local member still living.

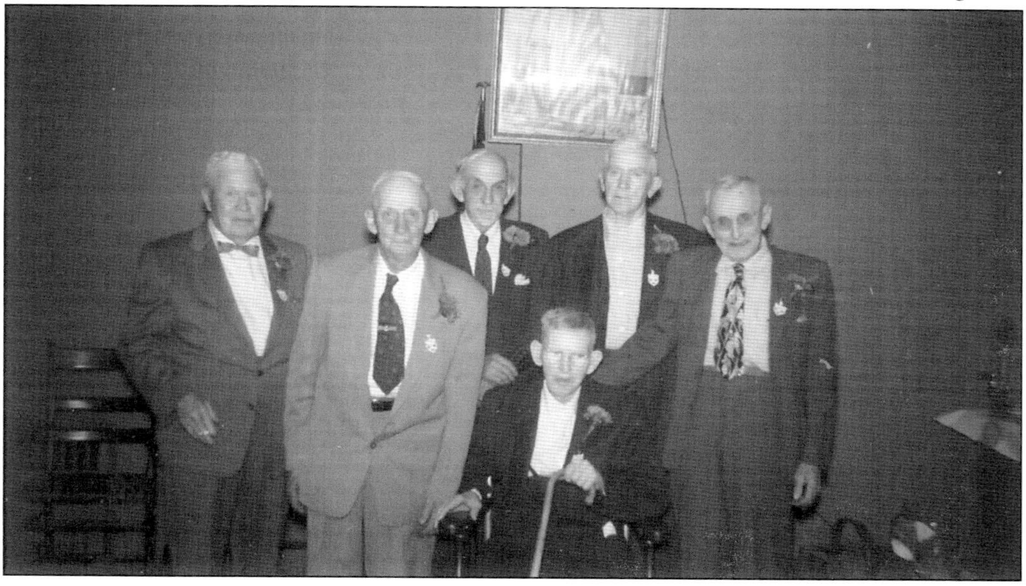

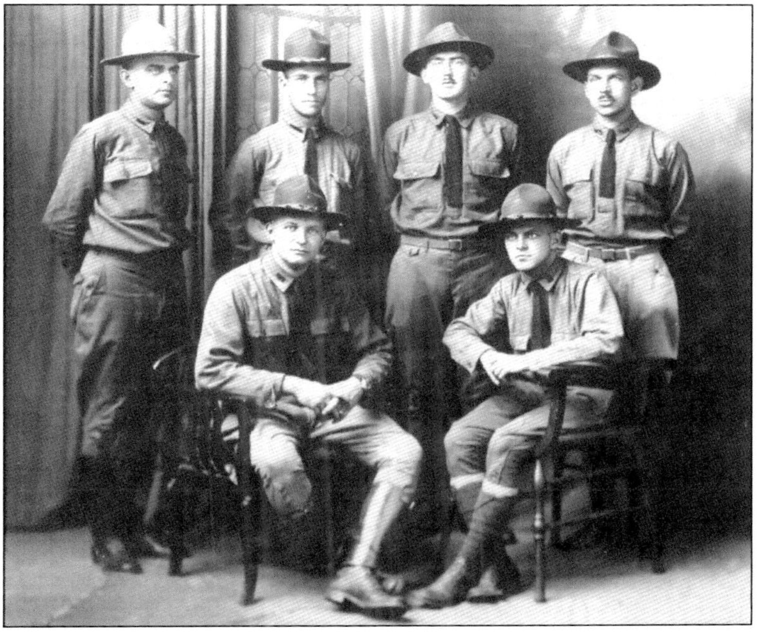

Rochester men who volunteered and attended the First Officers Training Camp at Fort Benjamin Harrison from May to August 1917 were getting ready for service in World War I. From left to right, they are (seated) George Brower and Percy Smith; (standing) Lee Wile, Charles Rees, Lyman Brackett, and Hugh A. Barnhart. (Courtesy of *Rochester Sentinel.*)

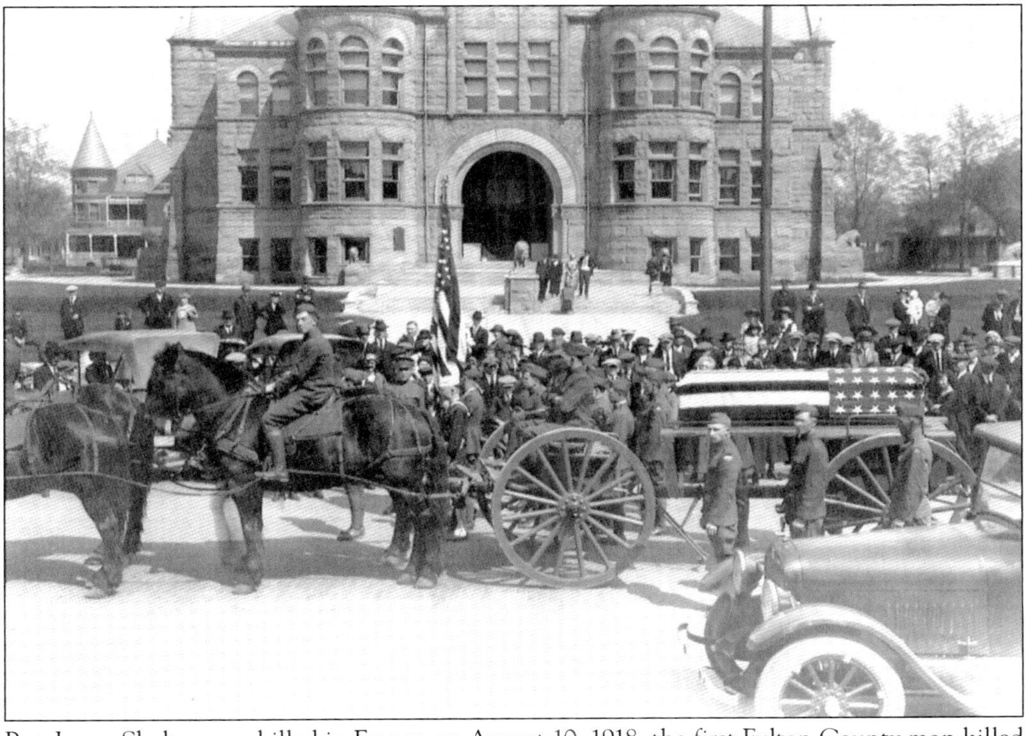

Pvt. Leroy Shelton was killed in France on August 10, 1918, the first Fulton County man killed on the front line in World War I. His body was returned for burial in 1922. By that time, the Leroy Shelton American Legion Post had been established. Post members conducted a military funeral on May 1, 1922. The funeral was at the Methodist church, and the burial was at the Mount Zion cemetery.

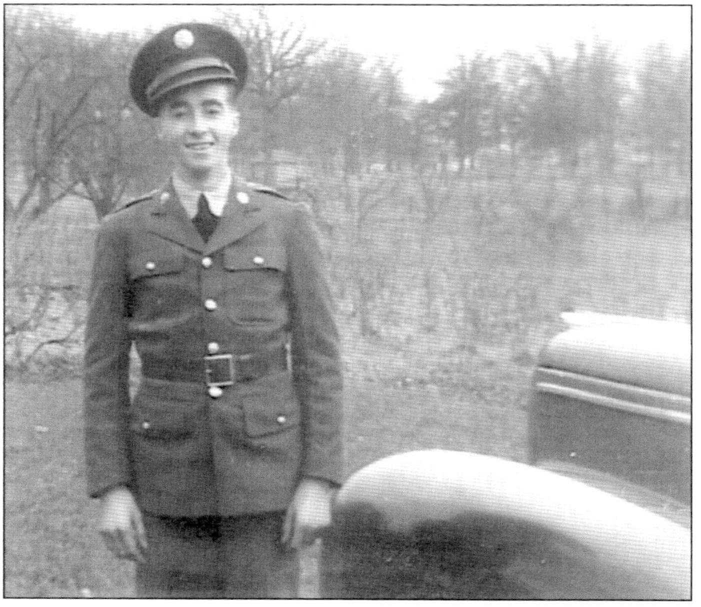

Fred Brown, pictured in 1942, was a sergeant in the 6th Division, 1st Infantry Regiment, G Company 1942 to 1945. In the Philippines, he was in continuous combat for 112 days in 1945. Brown earned the World War II Victory medal, American Theater ribbon, Asiatic–Pacific Theater ribbon with Bronze Stars, Philippine Liberation medal with bronze star, and other awards honoring him for good conduct and as a rifle sharpshooter, combat infantryman, and rifleman. (Courtesy of Fred Brown.)

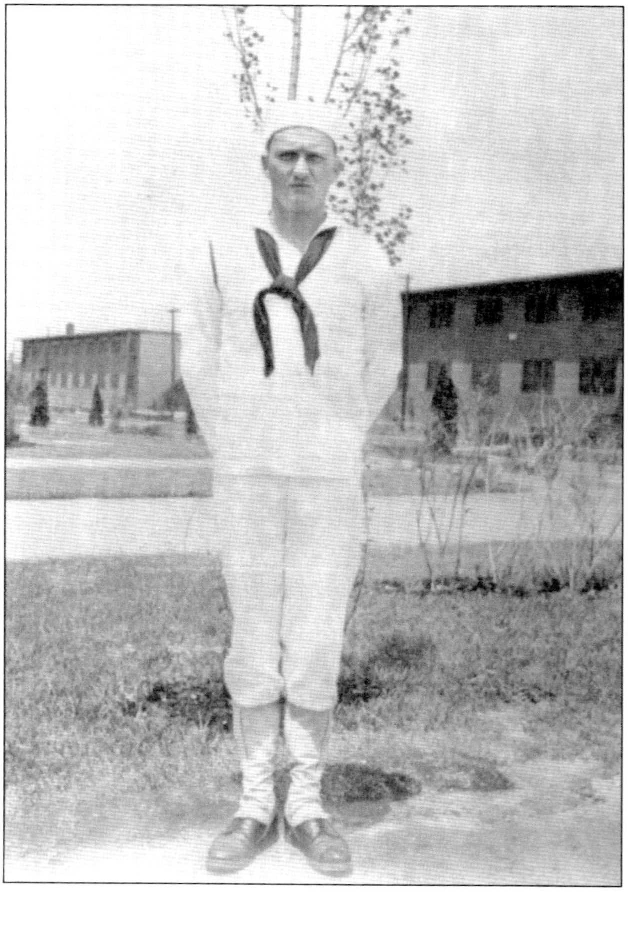

Raymond Craig was in the navy from May 1944 to December 1945. He was on an LST ship engaged in battles in the Panama Canal and Leyte (where he was wounded), Mindanao Island, and Manila Bay in the Philippines. He was discharged as a seaman first class. He received a Purple Heart, Pacific Theater ribbon, Philippine Liberation ribbon, three Bronze Stars, and a Victory medal. (Courtesy of his daughters, Sue McFarland and Judy Shepherd.)

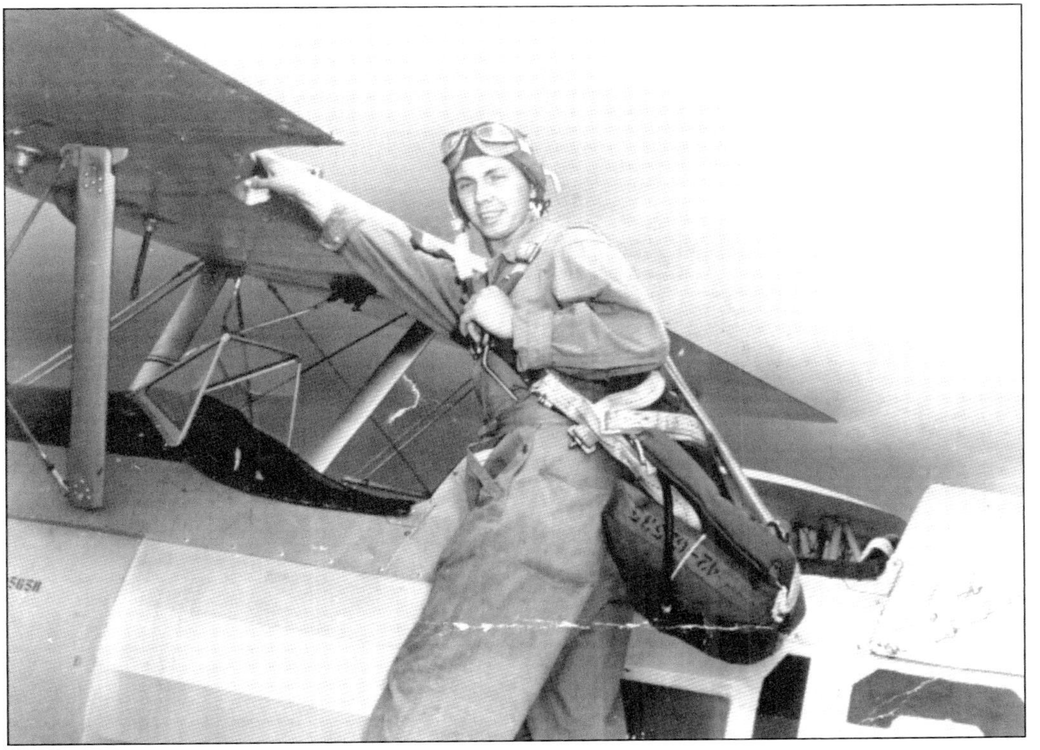

Harrison Crabill was a flying cadet in 1945 at Lakeland, Florida, in this BT-17. In 1943, Crabill entered the U.S. Army Air Forces, and he was discharged in 1945. The U.S. Army Air Forces became the U.S. Air Force in 1947. He had his first airplane ride with Helen House in 1937 at Rochester airport. Crabill became a flight instructor for Mentone Flying Club and at Rochester airport, where he taught many local people to fly.

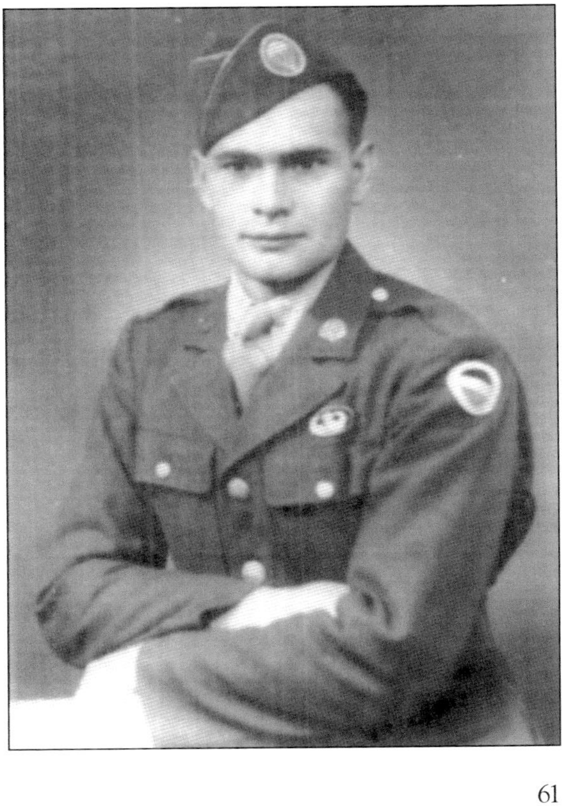

Clarence Thomas was killed on D-Day, June 6, 1944. He was a member of the 507th Parachute Infantry, 82nd "All American" Airborne Division. His rank was technician fifth grade. Gen. M. B. Ridgway's letter to Clarence's father, William A. Thomas, was published in the *News Sentinel* on October 3, 1944. Clarence is buried in Plot B, Row 3, Grave 17, Normandy American Cemetery, St. Laurent-sur-Mer, France. (Courtesy of Melinda Clinger.)

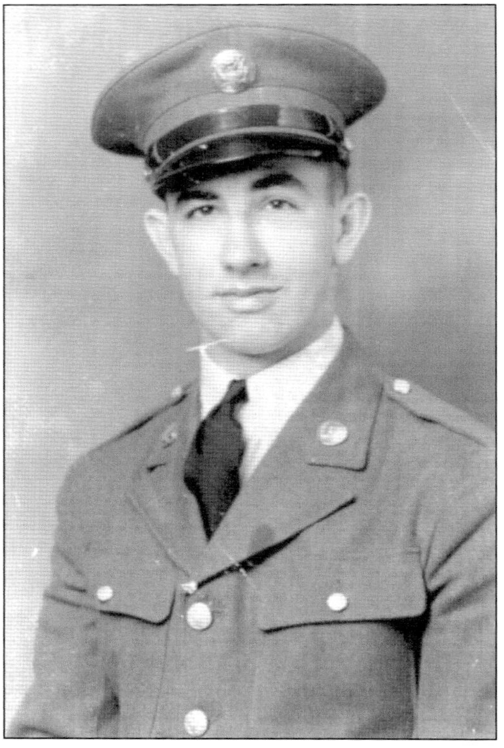

Kenneth Zartman enlisted in the army in May 1940. He wouldn't turn 18 until that August, so he had to lie about his age to enlist. He was at Pearl Harbor when it was bombed on December 7, 1941. He was in the 2nd Ranger Battalion, 27th Infantry, Forward Observer 15th Field Artillery. He served in the central Pacific islands from 1942 to 1944 and was discharged in July 1945. (Courtesy of Ruth Mills Zartman.)

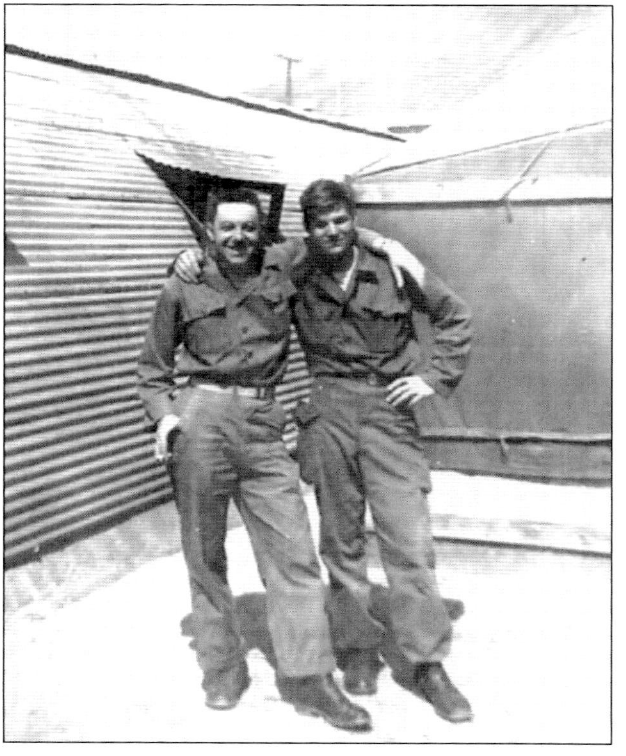

Ted Davis (left) and Willis "Bill" Willard, two Rochester soldiers, met in the Korean War one day in 1953. Notice the mountains in the background. Davis was a corporal and chief clerk of chemicals for Pusan Base in 1952 and 1953. Willard was also a corporal and a gunner on a half-track quad 50 (artillery). He later drove a truck at Pusan. Willard was also stationed at Inchon and Suwan. He was in the army from 1952 to 1954. (Courtesy of Ted Davis.)

Ernest Hiatt enlisted on April 10, 1952, at age 17. Sheriff Laurence Norris had to sign to show that he had no arrests before he could join the U.S. Navy Reserves. He graduated from Great Lakes Naval Base on October 3, came home, and married Carolyn Wood on October 5. He served 16 years but never went overseas. The last six years were spent as a recruiter in South Bend. He was honorably discharged in 1969. (Courtesy of Ernest Hiatt.)

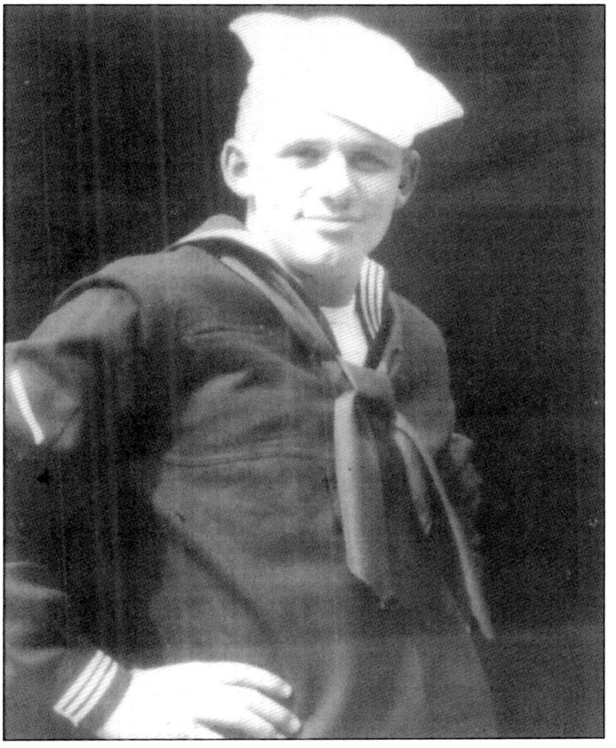

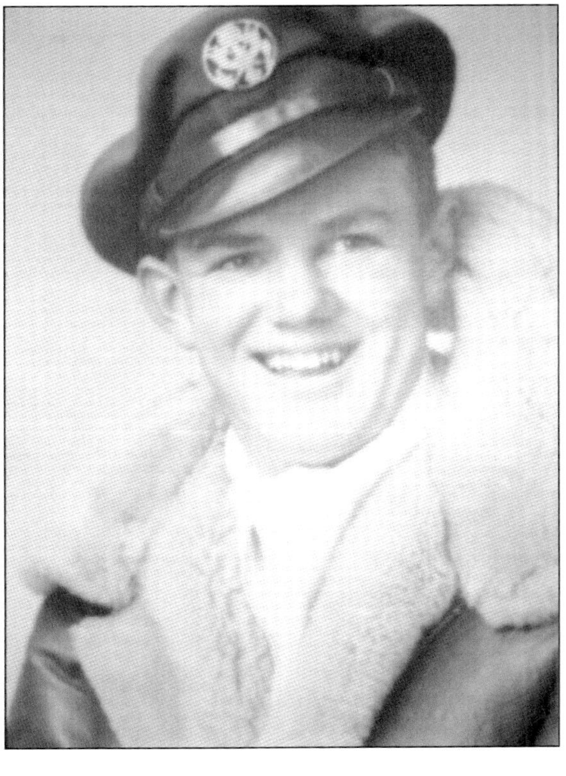

Cpl. Robert Helt, son of Ralph and Mildred Helt, was one of four U.S. Air Force men who were killed on June 5, 1951, in the explosion of a Flying Boxcar near Jackson, Tennessee. A 1949 graduate of Rochester High School, Helt had been active in Burton Church and 4-H. His body was brought home on the Erie Railroad and buried in the IOOF cemetery. (Courtesy of Dave Helt.)

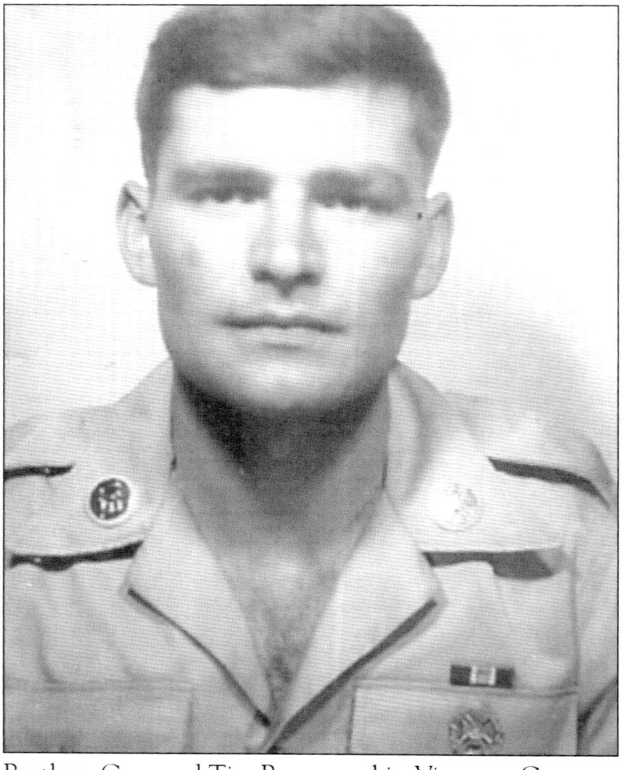

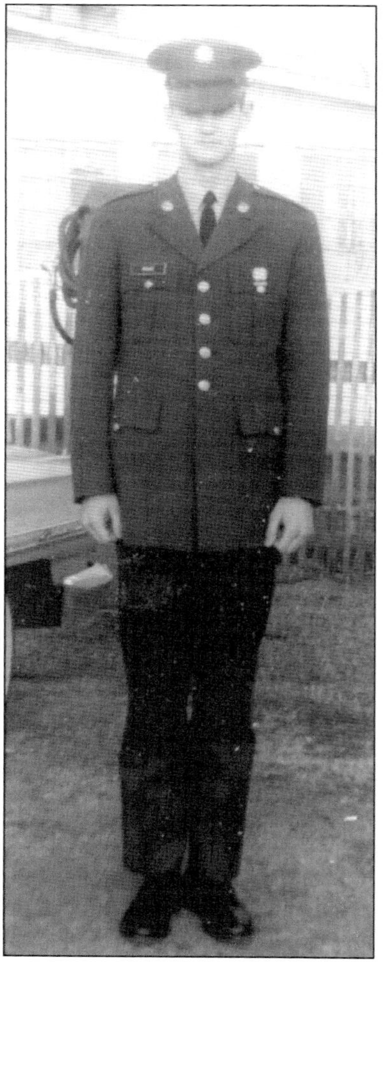

Brothers Gary and Tim Roe served in Vietnam. Gary (above), an E-5, served in the 1st and 5th Cavalry Air Mobile Division from May 1967 to May 1968, directing an 81-mm mortar. Sp4c. Timothy Roe (right) quit Rochester High School on his 18th birthday, one month short of graduation. A tank driver, his first big battle was August 12, 1969. He wrote home "One day in the field and we got hit bad. . . . Our whole troop got wiped out—21 men wounded and we don't know how many killed." The 11th Armored Cavalry was hit by 8,000 enemy troops and lost 8 of 17 tanks in 36 hours of combat. "God was definitely looking out for me," Tim wrote. "Everyone around me was dropping like flies." He was later badly injured and died on February 26, 1970. (Courtesy of Gary Roe and Nick Roe.)

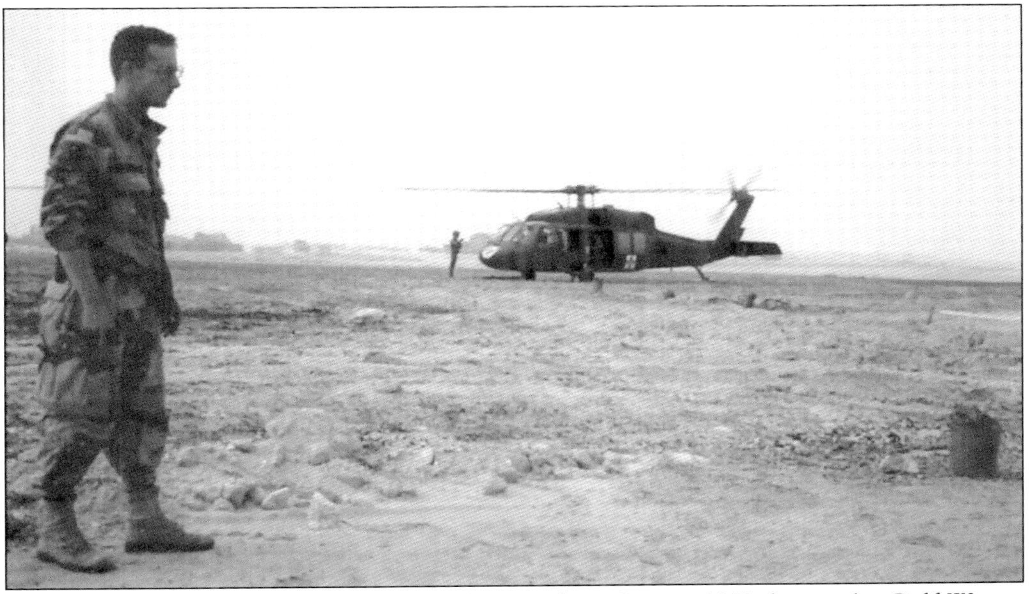

Sgt. Tom Butler watches a helicopter land in southern Iraq in 1991 during the Gulf War or Desert Storm. His job was a medic and overseeing operations of a medical unit, known as FAST or Forward Army Surgical Team. FAST was between the MASH units and the combat troops at the front. He helped with enemy prisoners of war, assisting in heart surgery, amputations, and other medical procedures. (Courtesy of Tom Butler.)

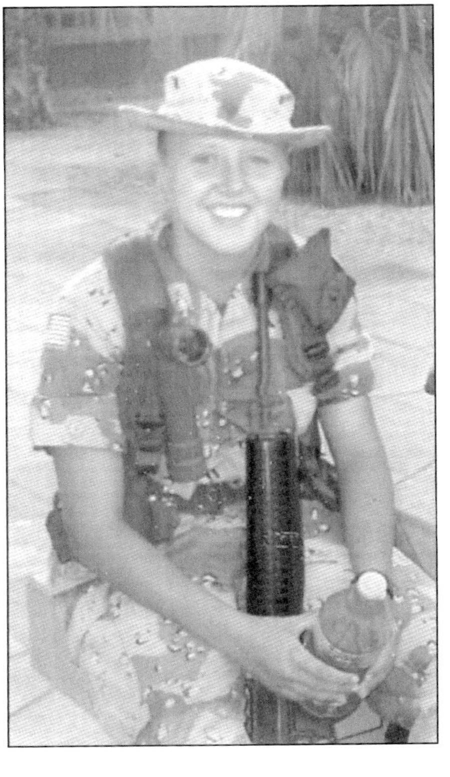

Samantha Kidd married Tom Butler in September 1990 in a military wedding ceremony presided over by 595th personnel. Less than a month later, the 595th deployed to Saudi Arabia. Samantha's rank was specialist fourth class in medical logistics from 1988 to 1992. She stated in the company yearbook: "I didn't want my husband to see me dirty . . . or when he was in charge of latrine burning." (Courtesy of Samantha Butler.)

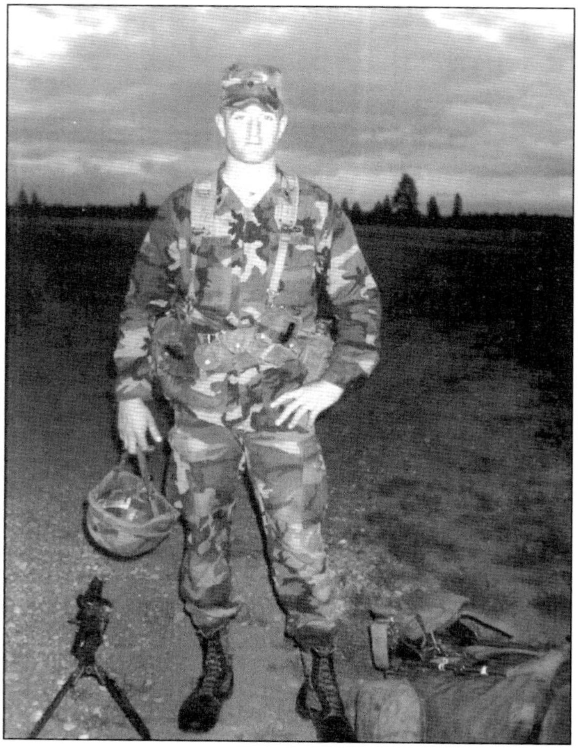

Sgt. Jeff McLochlin died on July 5, 2006, of wounds received in small arms fire on the Afghanistan–Pakistan border. His funeral was attended by 700 family and friends and 200 Patriot Guard motorcyclists. A former police officer in Rochester and Plymouth, he was in the Indiana National Guard, led a parachute drop in Panama, served in Bosnia, and deployed twice to the War on Terror in Iraq and Afghanistan. (Courtesy of McLochlins.)

Jason Snyder took time out from teaching at Rochester Middle School (RMS) to serve in Iraq in 2003 and 2004. He was a first lieutenant with the 293rd Infantry Battalion. His second deployment to Iraq was in 2008 as a captain in 76th Infantry Brigade Combat Team with a specialty in chemical weapons. Snyder returned to teaching at RMS for the second semester, beginning in January 2009. (Courtesy of Jason Snyder.)

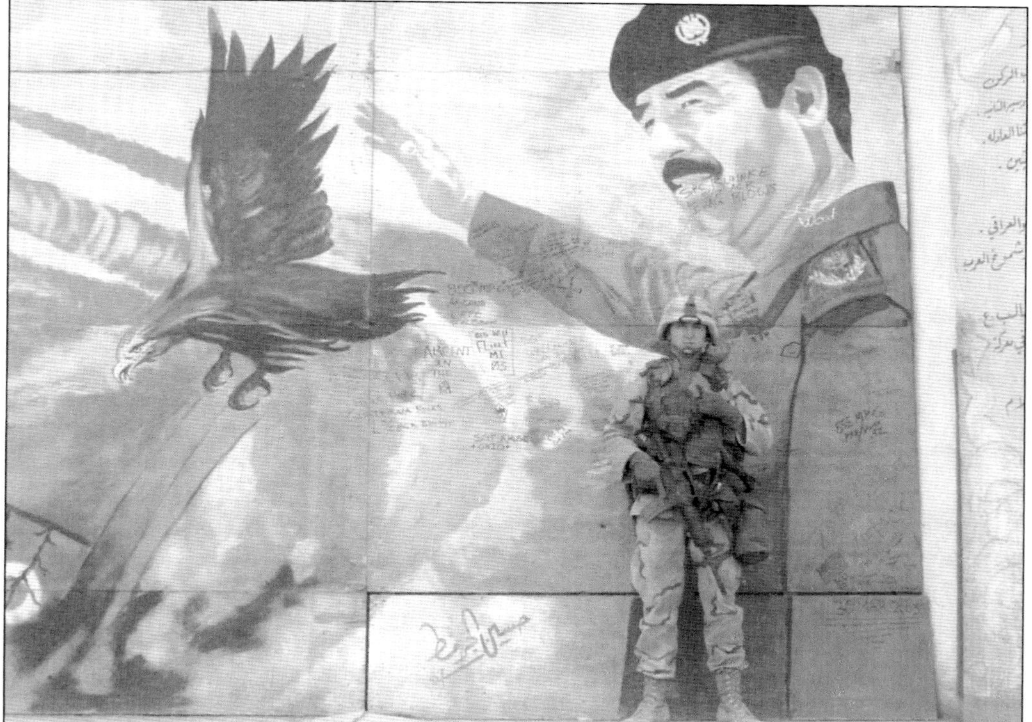

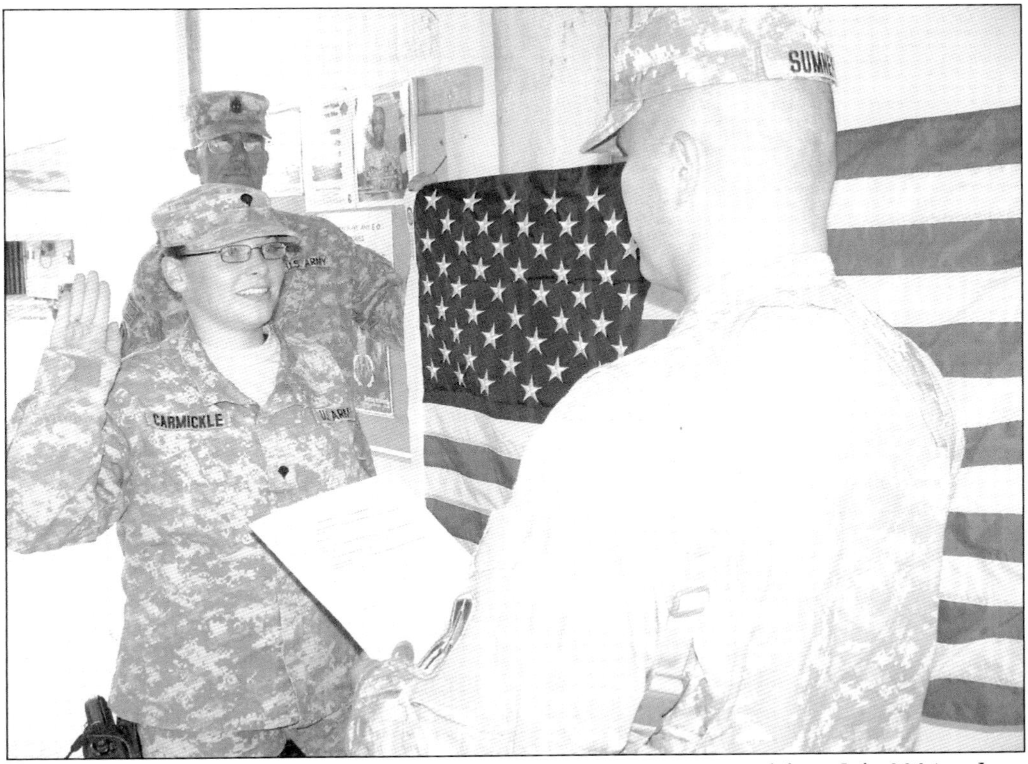

Samantha Carmickle (center) reenlisted in Iraq in 2008. Sammi served from July 2004 to June 2005 in Afghanistan and from March 2008 to November 2008 in Iraq. She will be in until 2014. She is a petroleum supply specialist (a "fuel jockey") for Delta Company, 113th Forward Support Company for the 152nd Cavalry. Samantha graduated from Rochester High School in 2000 and joined the Indiana National Guard in 2002. (Courtesy of her sister, Cynthia Thomas.)

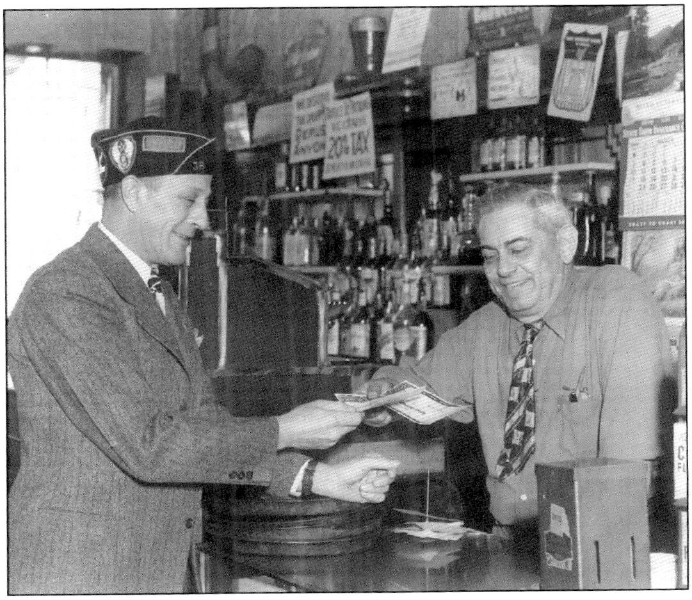

Leroy Shelton American Legion Post began on June 4, 1919, with Hugh Barnhart as first president. The Woman's Auxiliary began in 1922. The legion hall was at Madison and Thirteenth Streets from 1928 to 1945. Louis Ninios is shown presenting checks to Post Commander Ray Roy to pay off debt from purchasing the Val Zimmerman building at 611 Main Street in 1945. A new Legion building on Indiana 25 was constructed in 2007, but in 2010, they moved back to 611 Main Street. (Courtesy of the American Legion.)

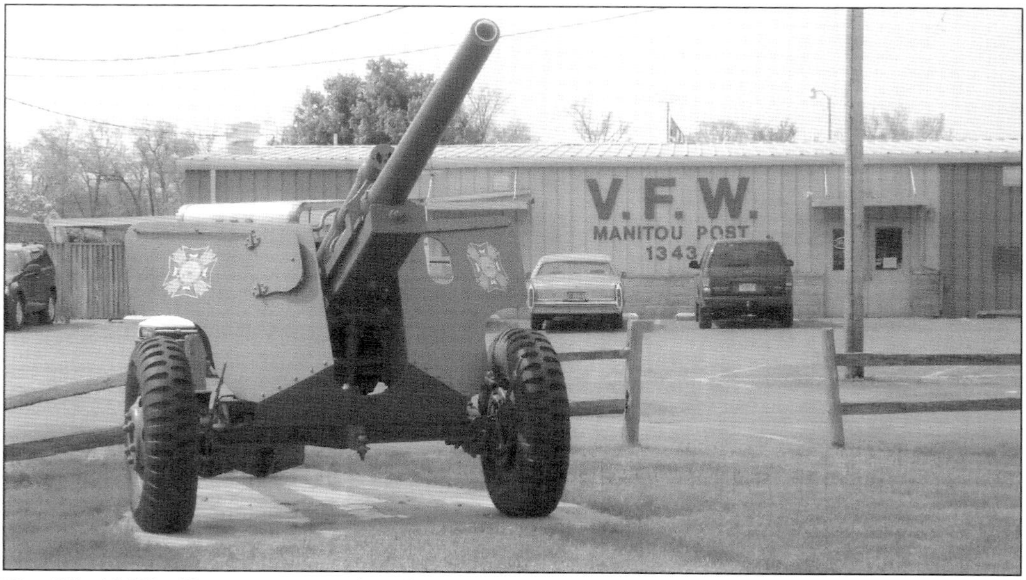

Two World War II cannons stand at the Veterans of Foreign Wars at Lake Manitou. They were donated by the government at the end of World War II to replace the Civil War cannons the county had donated to the scrap drive in September 1942. Sheriff Willard Clark got the cannons moved to the VFW about 1960 because children played on them and presented a liability.

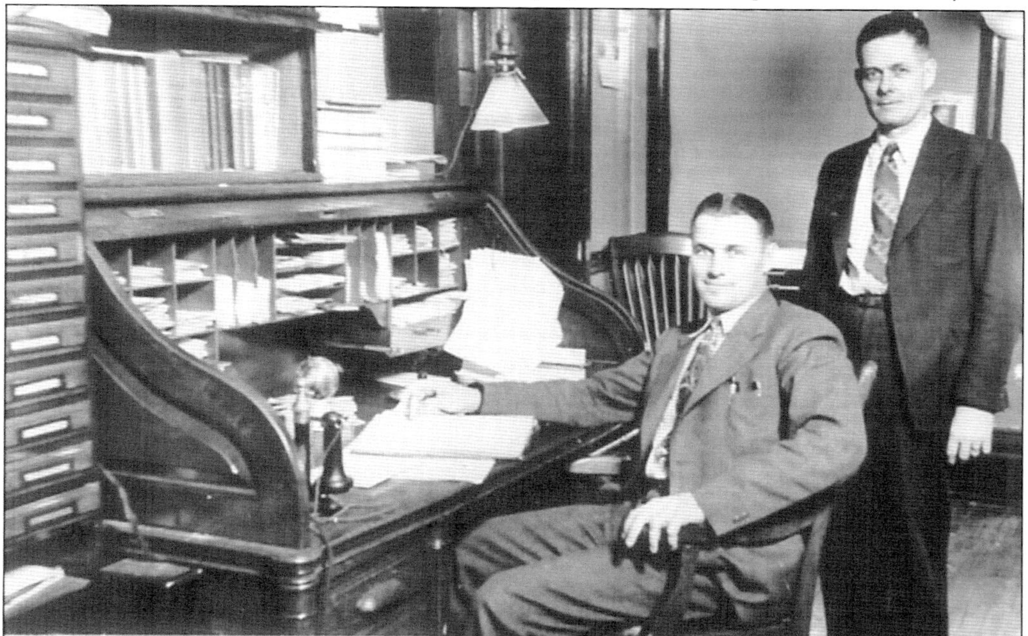

Russell Voorhees (seated), sheriff from 1938 to 1942, is shown here with deputy Frank Summers in the Fulton County jail office. While Voorhees was sheriff, druggist Charles Dyche was found dead in a woods on the east side of Lake Manitou on June 18, 1941. It was ruled a suicide, but gossip considered it a murder. The place was called Dead Man's Woods for many years and was a scary spot for teenagers to park.

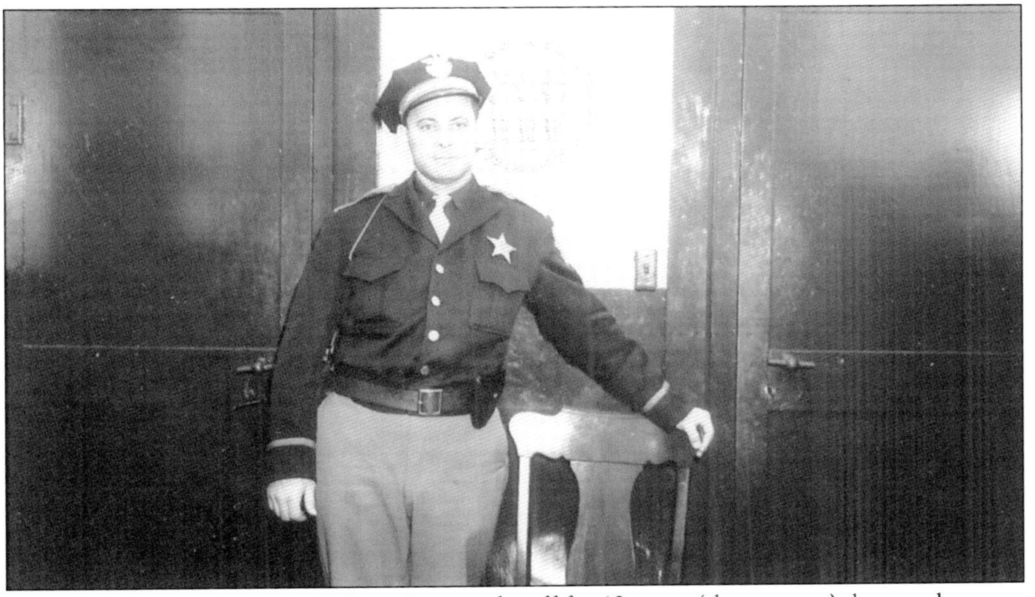

Laurence "Buck" Norris was Fulton County sheriff for 12 years (three terms), longer than any other sheriff. His wife and three children lived in the sheriff's living quarters in the old jail. Norris designed his own brown and tan uniform, which was adopted by all Indiana counties for their sheriffs. Behind him is the Safety Legion plaque, created by Herman Daake for the Erie Railroad. (Courtesy of the Norris daughters.)

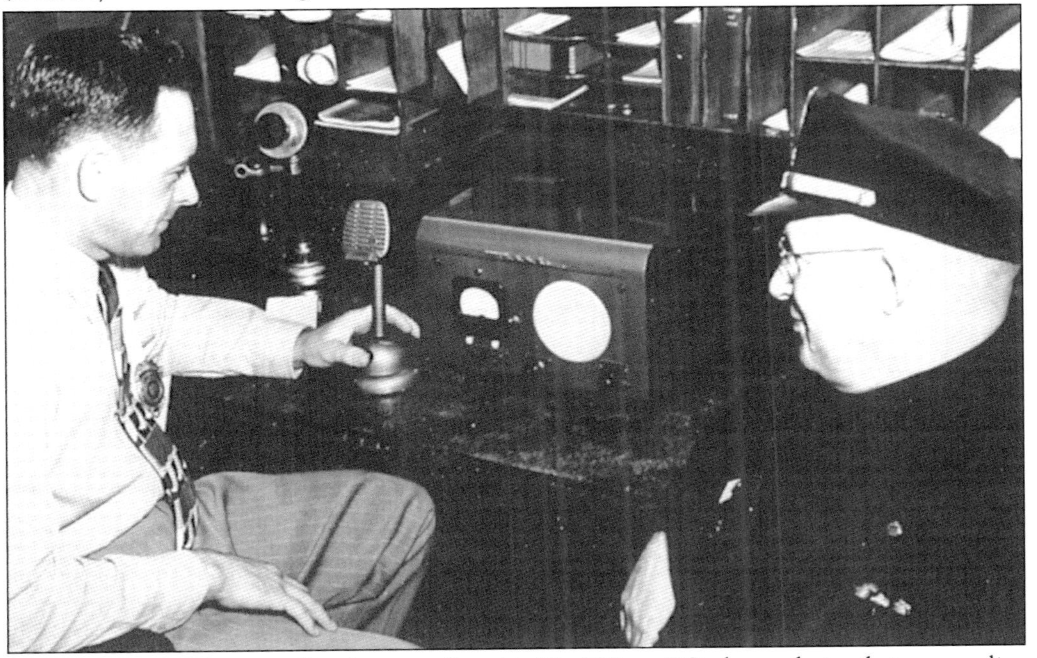

Sheriff Laurence Norris and Rochester police chief Earl "Rusty" Graham admire their new police radio. Graham did not want to get it, and called it a "squawk box." Norris, a World War II veteran, was sheriff from 1946 to 1958. No sheriff records were kept of calls or runs until Norris set up a file system for prisoners. He also kept radio records. The city police station was in city hall.

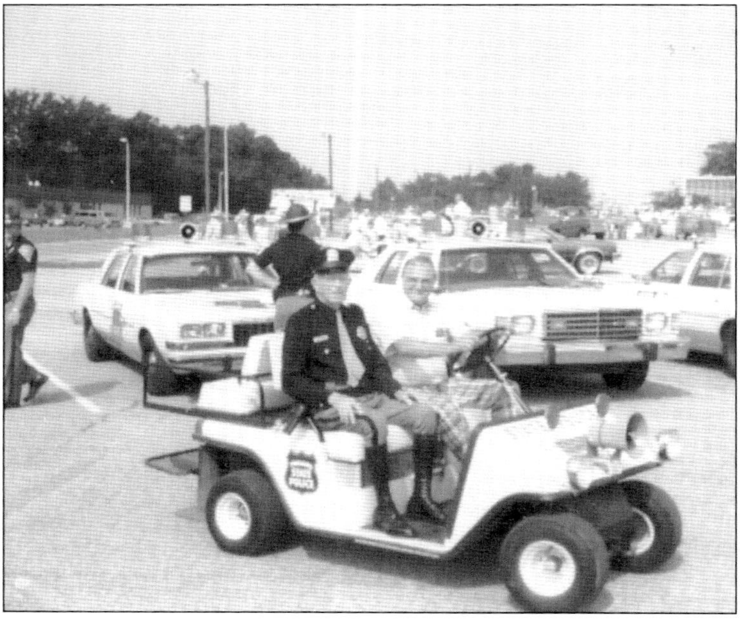

Estel Bemenderfer, the oldest-living member of the Indiana State Troopers, wore his original uniform and was driven by Jim Heyde in an Indiana State Police golf cart in the 1979 Round Barn Festival parade. At left, the parade is forming at Rochester High School parking lot. Bemenderfer was in the Indiana State Patrol (now Indiana State Police) from 1933 to 1947. He was Rochester police chief from 1956 to 1961. (Courtesy of James Heyde.)

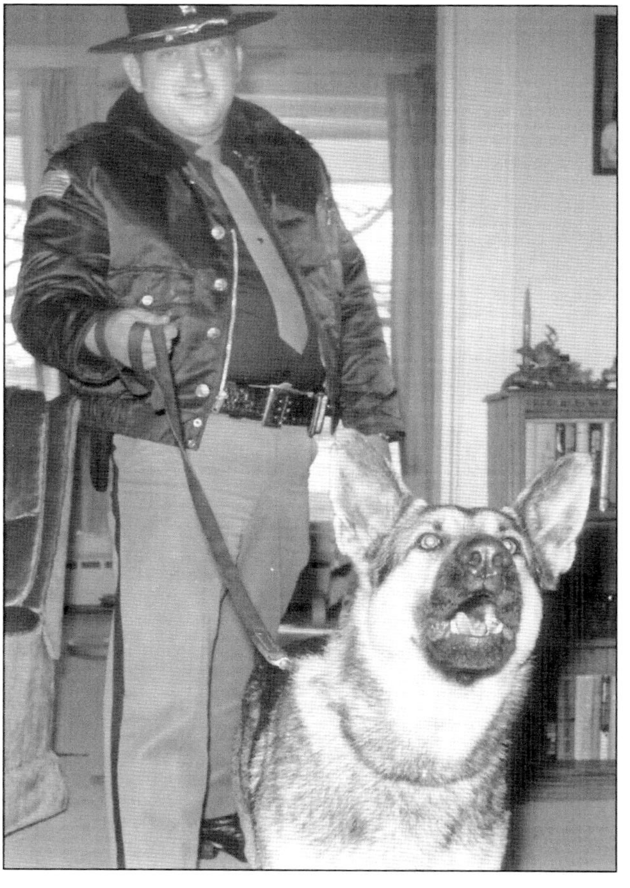

Sheriff Robert Newgent holds tight to his police dog Rocky in 1976, part of a statewide K-9 program. He and deputy Earl Vance took training at the Edelheim Kennel at Bunker Hill. Willard Clark, sheriff from 1959 to 1966, had the first local police dog, a German shepherd, in 1964, which he purchased for $50 from Mrs. Gray at Argos. Clark took the dog for a walk around the courthouse every evening.

Six

Schools and Sports

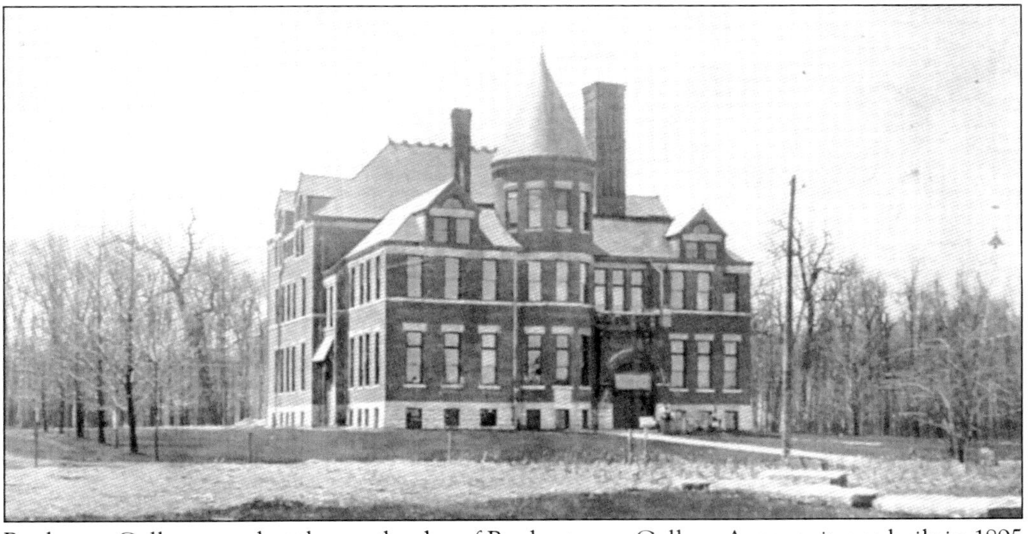

Rochester College stood at the south edge of Rochester on College Avenue; it was built in 1895 and closed in 1912. Demolished in 1923, its bricks were used to build the Times Theater. The Rochester College Alumni Association continued to meet annually until 1974. The cornerstone of the college now stands on the courthouse lawn at Main and Ninth Streets, with a historical marker that gives a history of the college.

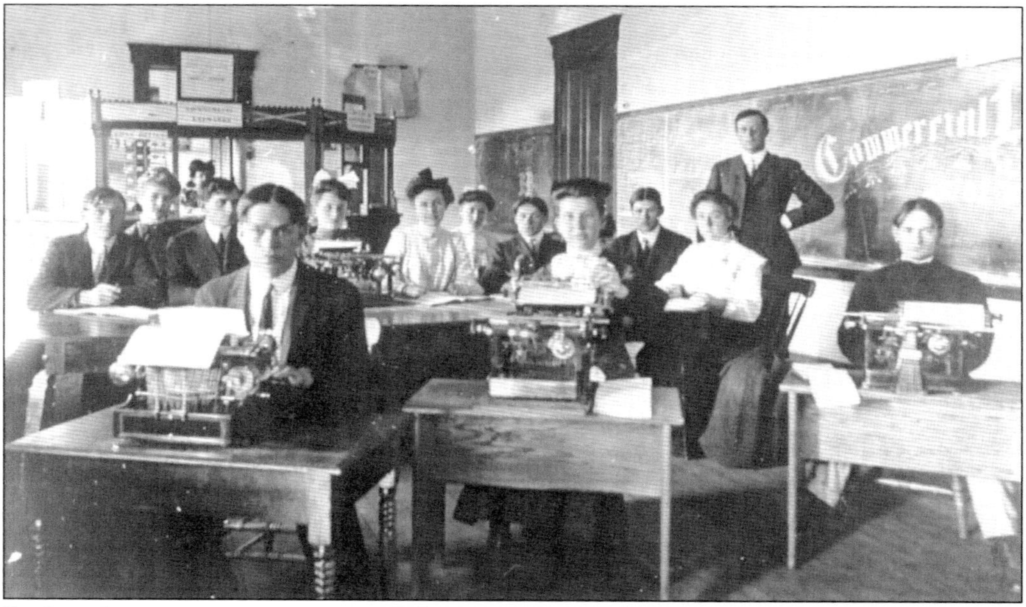

Students learn to type in commercial class in 1904 at Rochester College, which was founded by Dr. Winfield S. Shafer as a normal school, meaning it trained teachers. Art, music, business, and other curricula were also offered. Rochester Township high school students' tuition was paid by the township trustee. When Rochester Joint High School was built in 1912, the college lost all its high school students, and it closed.

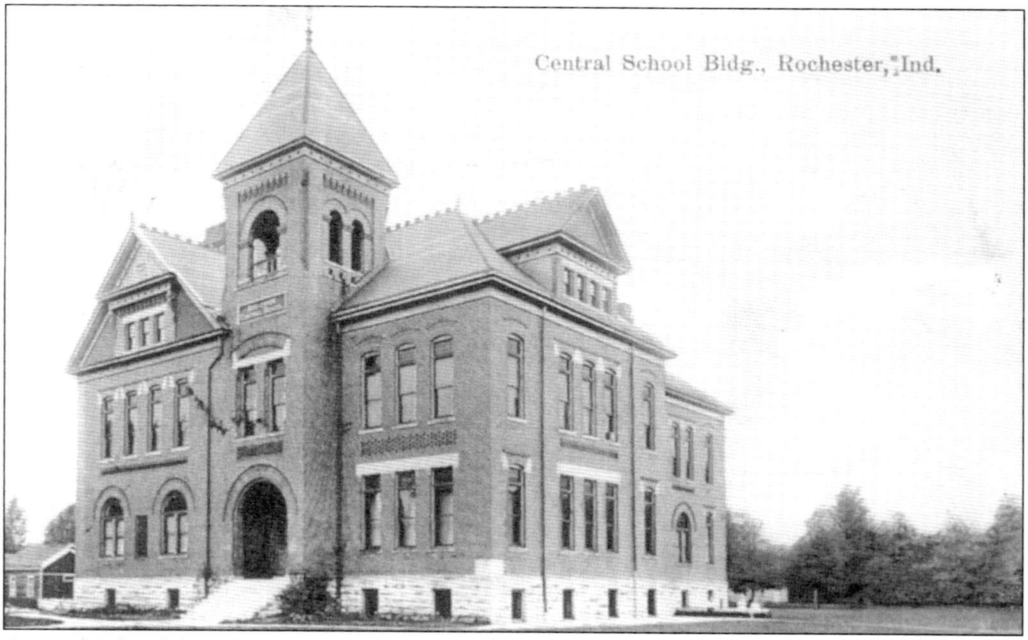

Central School, later named Lincoln School, was built in 1887 on the southwest corner of Sixth and Pontiac Streets. The high school and junior high were located on the upper floor. After the 1912 high school was built, Lincoln housed only the junior high. It was abandoned in 1957, when the new Riddle School was opened. The old Lincoln School was demolished in 1966.

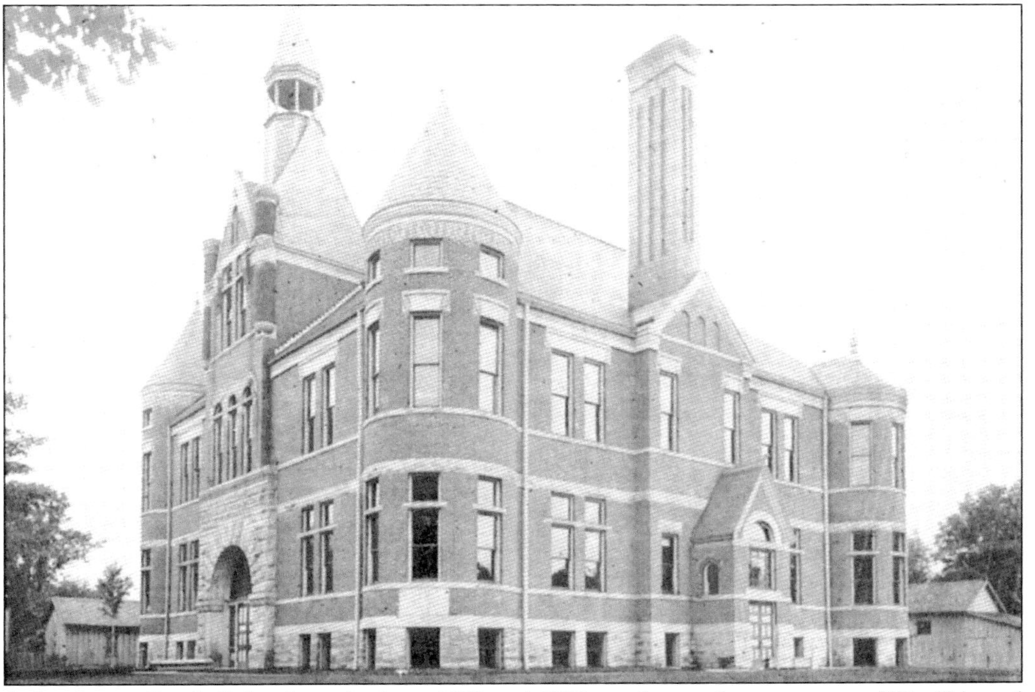

Columbia or South School was built in 1897 and 1898 on the southwest corner of Twelfth and Monroe Streets, where the Jaycee Park is now. Pupils could be promoted to the next grade at the end of the first semester, as well as in the spring. Boys played basketball in the third-floor attic. Everybody walked to school and walked home for lunch. In 1897, Lincoln and Columbia Schools battled in the first basketball game ever played in Rochester.

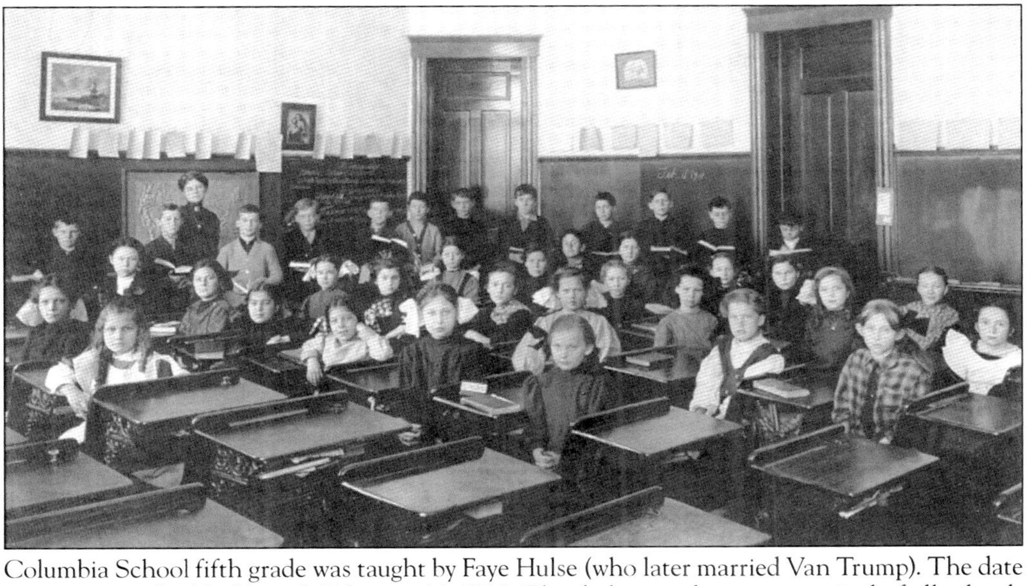

Columbia School fifth grade was taught by Faye Hulse (who later married Van Trump). The date is written on the blackboard: February 18, 1910. The desks seen here were typical of all schools until the 1960s or later. Each desk was attached to the seat in front of it, and the seat folded up. The desk had a round hole for a bottle of ink and an open shelf below for students' books.

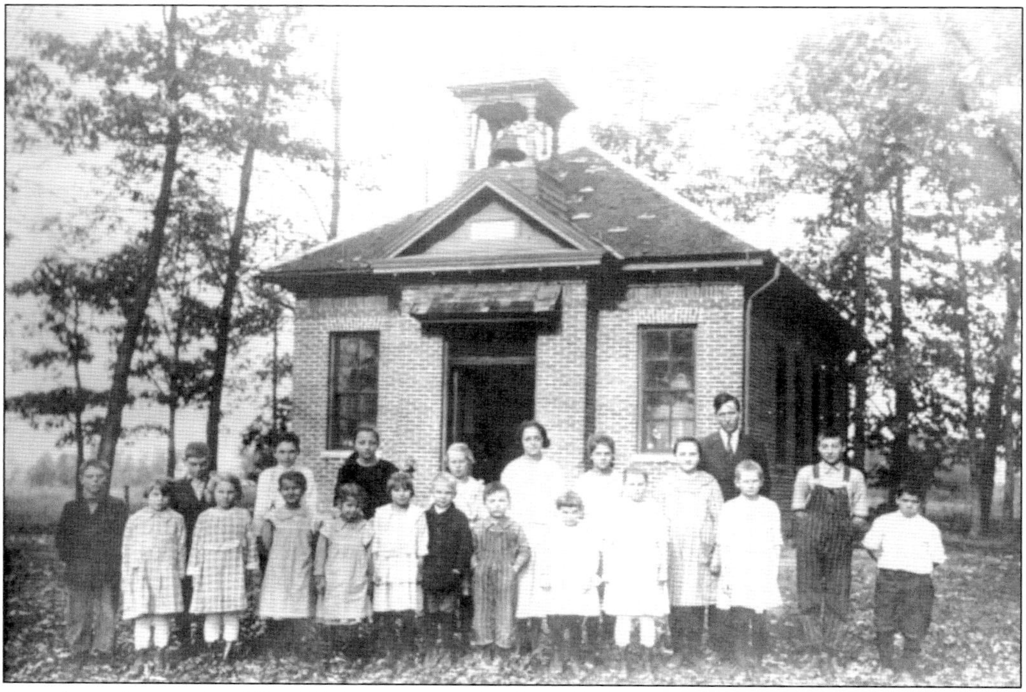

Seen here during the 1920–1921 class year, the Sprinkleburg one-room school was located near the country club's golf course. From left to right are (first row) Herbert Myers, Frances Sibert, Clarabelle Myers, Mary Edna Ducker, Florence Ducker, Bernice Bick, Vernice Brunson, Richard Rogers, Geraldine Nelson, Catherine Myers, Jessie Rogers, Alfreda Henning, Lee Becker, and Porter Sibert; (second row) Walter Becker, Luroy Bick, Lois Shobe, Elma Myers, Mable Shobe, Lula Bick, and teacher Estil Ginn.

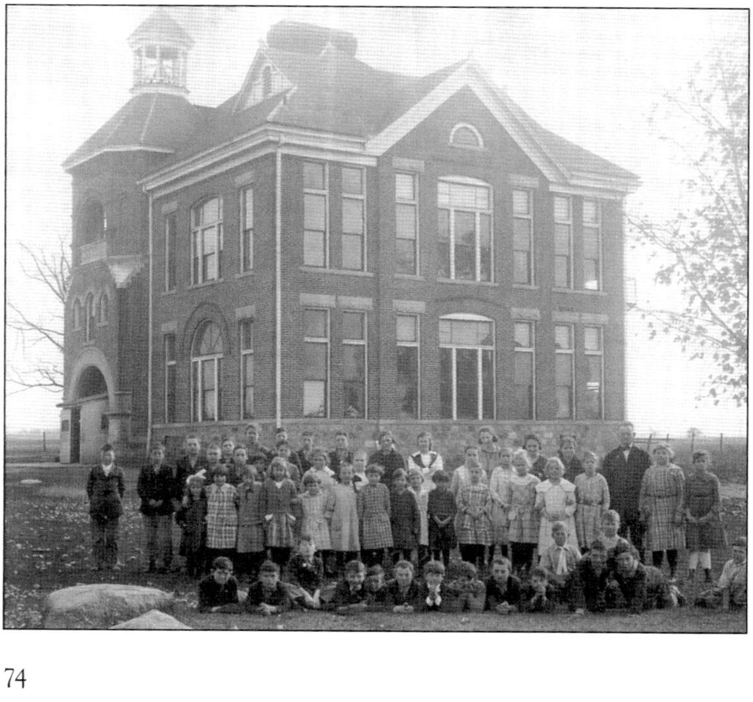

McKinley School, pictured 1920–1921, stood on the south side of Fort Wayne Road between 450 East and 500 East. It was the first consolidated rural school in Fulton County and is mistakenly said by some to be the first consolidated school in the state. It was built in 1901 and closed in 1931, when students were transferred to Rochester city and township schools. The teachers were Vernon Miller, Lavoy Oliver, and Bernice Eash.

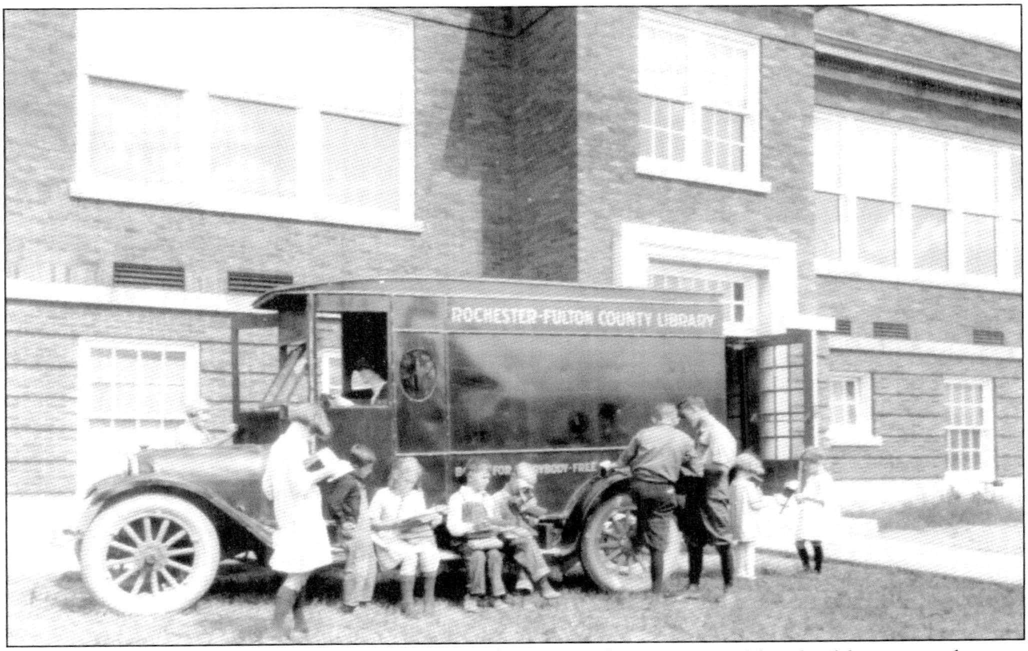

Woodrow School, built in 1917 on Old 31 and 300 South, was visited by the library truck once a month so students could borrow books. Pictured here in 1923 is Fulton County's first library truck. Some people said that Fulton County had the first library truck in Indiana, but that is not true. After the end of the school year, the library truck also took books to area farmhouses so kids could continue to read all summer.

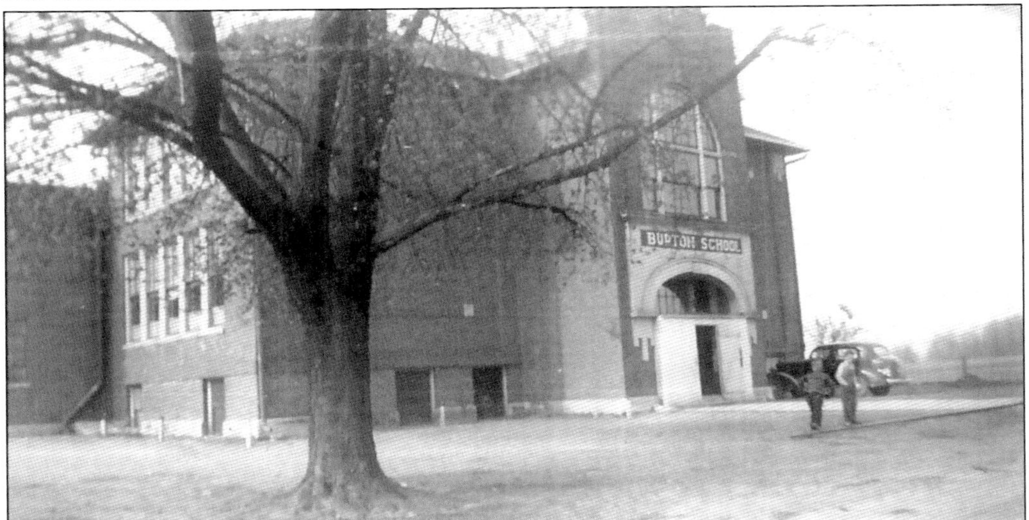

Burton School was built 1912 on the south side of 200 North, halfway between 300 West and 400 West. Many people of German extraction founded Germany Station, Germany Bridge, and Germany Telephone. The town of Germany became Pershing and then Loyal, Indiana. Burton School was originally named Germany School, but its name was changed in World War I because the United States was at war with Germany. The gymnasium is on the left. The school was closed in 1959. (Courtesy of Glen Cleland.)

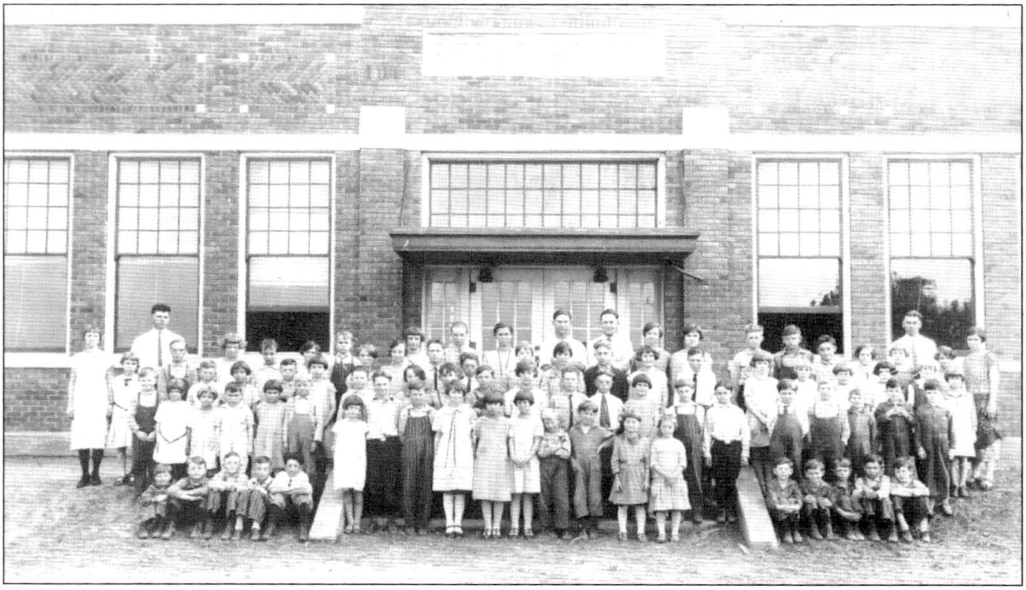

Reiter School was located at the intersection of 125 West and 200 South, southwest of Rochester. Teachers in 1925 were Clifford Baggerly (left), grades seven and eight; Fred Van Duyne (right), grades five and six; Vera Carey, grades 3 and 4; and Esther Enquist, grades one and two. Reiter School, named for township trustee Marion Reiter, opened in 1925 and closed in 1960, when students were transferred to Columbia and Riddle schools in Rochester.

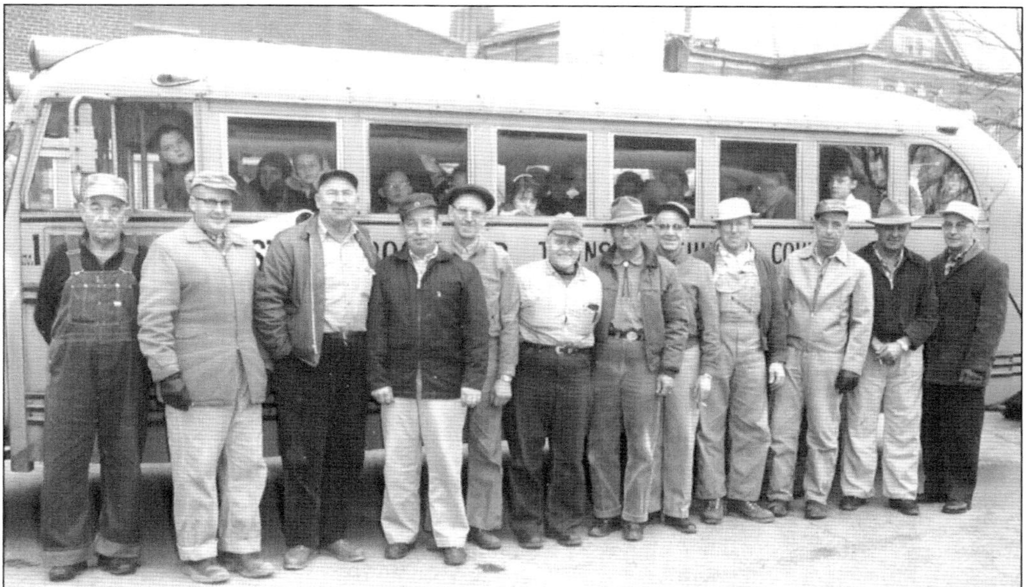

Rochester Township school bus drivers, 1958, pose in front of a bus parked south of Whitmer Gymnasium and Lincoln School, seen in the background. They hauled students to Woodrow, Reiter, and Burton Schools and then to Rochester High School. From left to right are Harry Rush, Jim Tobey, Vic Skidmore, Bill Werner, Bill Wagoner, Charlie Ogle, Kenneth Hall, Lester Heckathorn, Ted Merley, Howard Taylor, Ira Baker, and Byron Martinson. All were farmers.

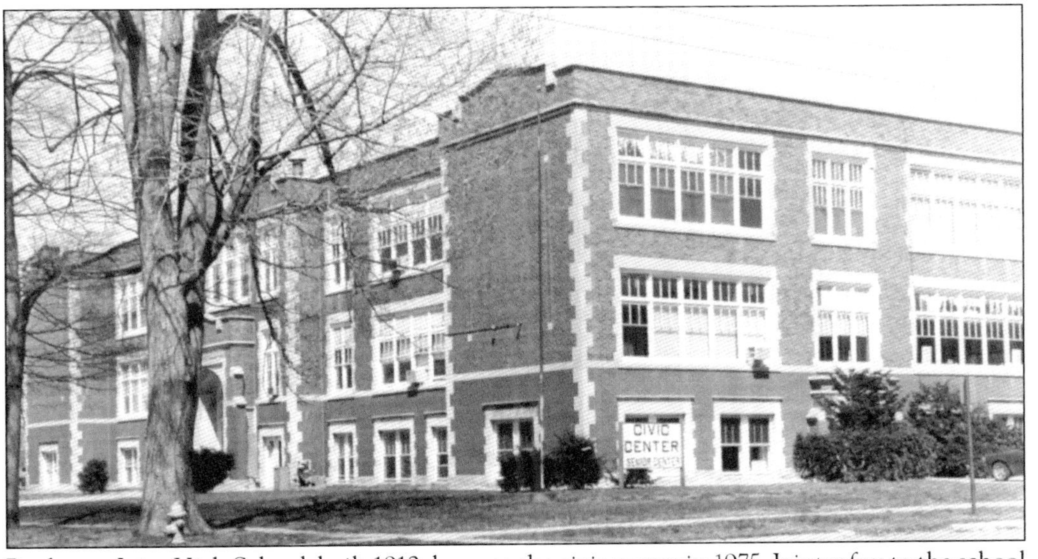

Rochester Joint High School, built 1912, became the civic center in 1975. Joint refers to the school being paid for jointly by Rochester city and township. Before 1912, the township students had to either pay tuition or attend Rochester College, where the township trustee would pay their tuition. It became Rochester Middle School in 1957, when a new high school was built, and closed in 1977, when a new middle school was completed. It became the civic center, and rooms were rented for a museum and various public service offices. It was torn down in 1993.

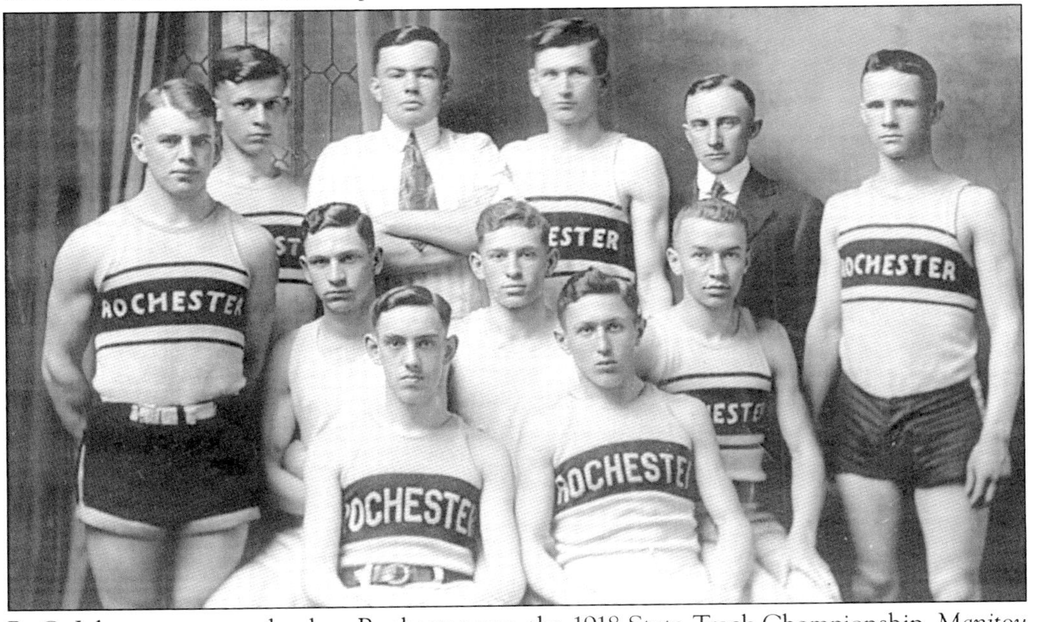

R. C. Johnson was coach when Rochester won the 1918 State Track Championship. *Manitou Ripples* published this photograph but not the names. They were, in no particular order, captain Charles Ivey, Orville Whitmer, Walter Perry, Walter Smith, Harry Karn, George Wylie, Harley Schmitt, Dee Miller, Ray "Candy" Miller, ? Newcomb, and Winston Robbins. Candy Miller was inducted into the Indiana State Basketball Hall of Fame. Ivey was inducted into the Indiana Track Hall of Fame.

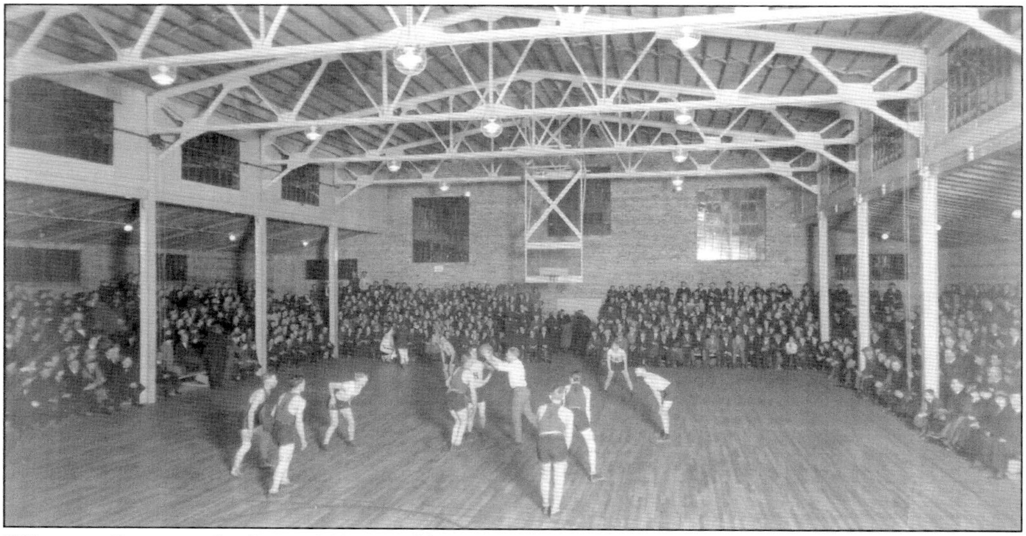

Whitmer Gym was built in 1920. In addition to sporting events, the gym was also the scene for fish fries and other public and political gatherings. One end had a stage with curtains for plays and graduation ceremonies. The new Rochester Community High School and gym were built in 1965. Whitmer Gym was used for a YMCA but was torn down in November 1988, and an arboretum was created there.

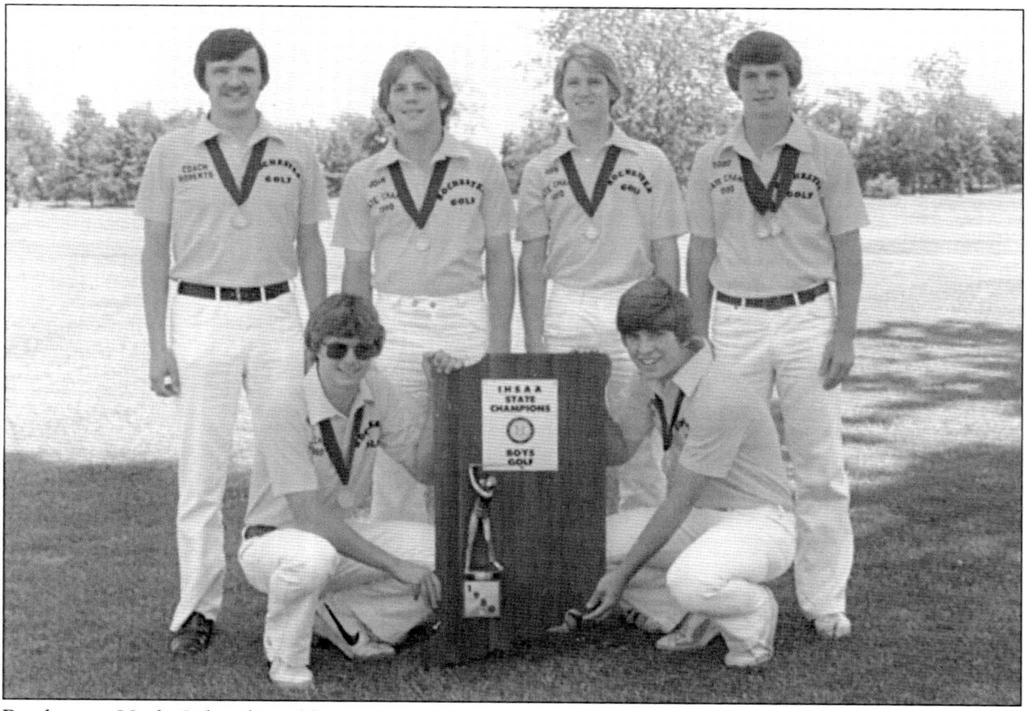

Rochester High School's golf team won the Indiana State Championship in 1980. From left to right are (kneeling in front) Mike Shafer and Terry Smith; (standing) coach John Roberts, John "Jack" Sawyer, Rob Sawyer, Todd Smith. The Smiths and Sawyers are cousins and have continued to play and support golf. (Courtesy of RHS.)

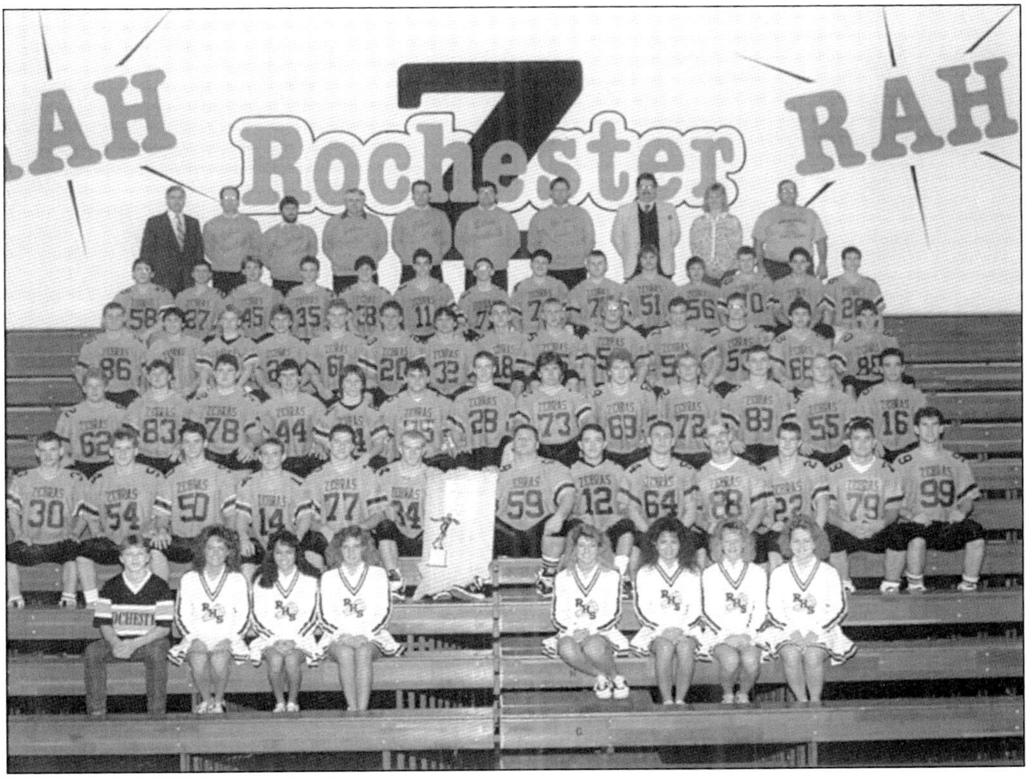

The RHS football team won the Class AA State Championship in 1987. In the front row are Zebby the Zebra mascot (out of costume) and the cheerleaders. Space does not allow naming all the players. Standing in the back from left to right are Principal Dennis Eller, Coaches Brash, McKee, Kelly, Coplen, and Whirledge; Head Coach Miller, Assistant Principal Huffman, Cheerleader Sponsor Eller, and Maintenance/ Groundskeeper Copeland. (Courtesy of RHS.)

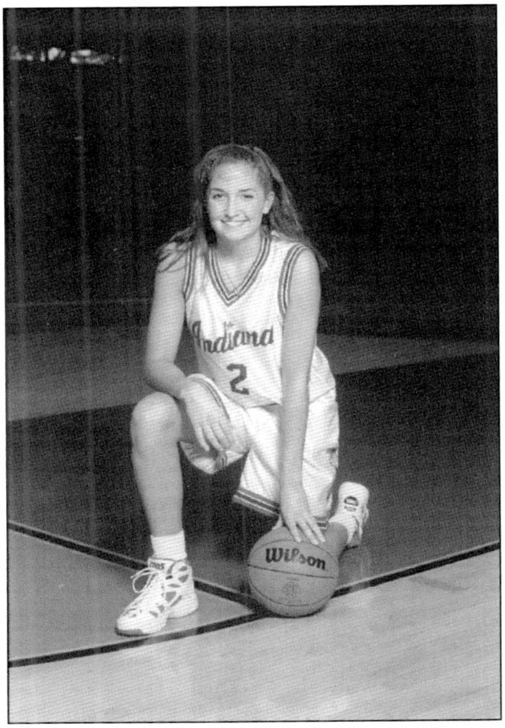

Sheila McMillen won state and national honors in 1995. She was an Indiana All-Star, Nike and Reebok All-Star, *Parade* All-American, AAU All-American and National Champ, first-team All-State, 1,000-point scorer, and South Bend Tribune Area Player of the Year. At Notre Dame, she was the first player to participate in four straight NCAA tournaments, received the O'Connor Award in 1999, and was a Big East All-Star. She was inducted into the RHS Hall of Fame in 2005. (Courtesy of RHS.)

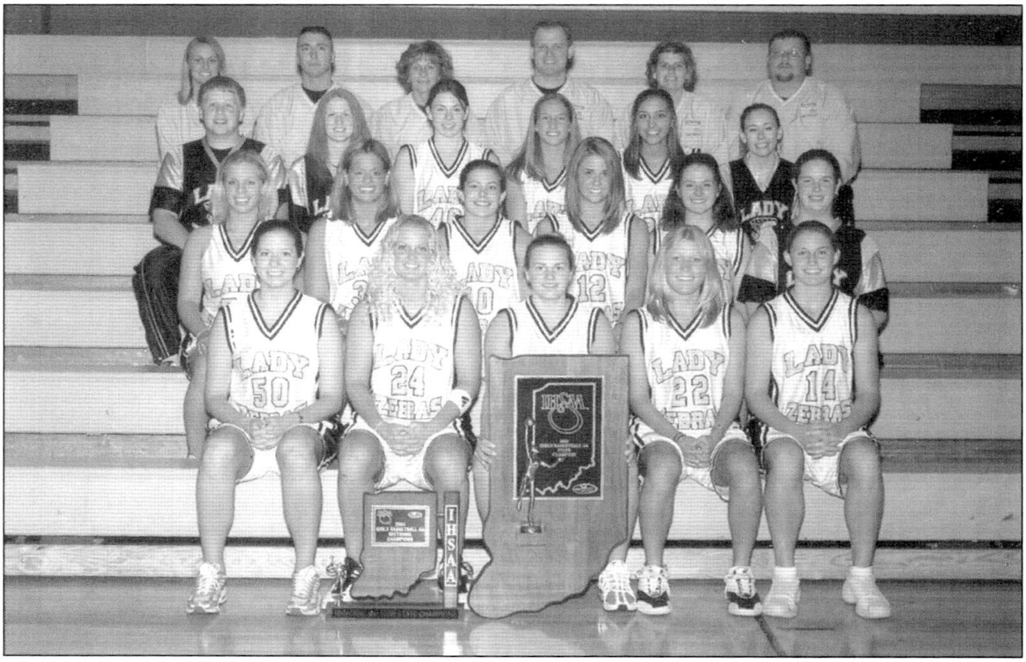

The RHS girls basketball team won the Indiana State Championship in 2004. From left to right are (first row) B. Riddle, J. Formal, C. Felke, L. Dishman, and A. Roe; (second row) K. Howard, J. Easterday, R. Carr, M. Thomas, R. Heyde, and manager L. Bright; (third row) managers S. Williams and L. Helstern, C. Greives, L. Cox, B. Sewell, and manager A. Hunt; (third row) coaches Andrea Milliser, Jason Snyder, Katie Felke, head coach Tony Stesiak, Stacy Stesiak, and coach Randy Wynn. (Courtesy of RHS.)

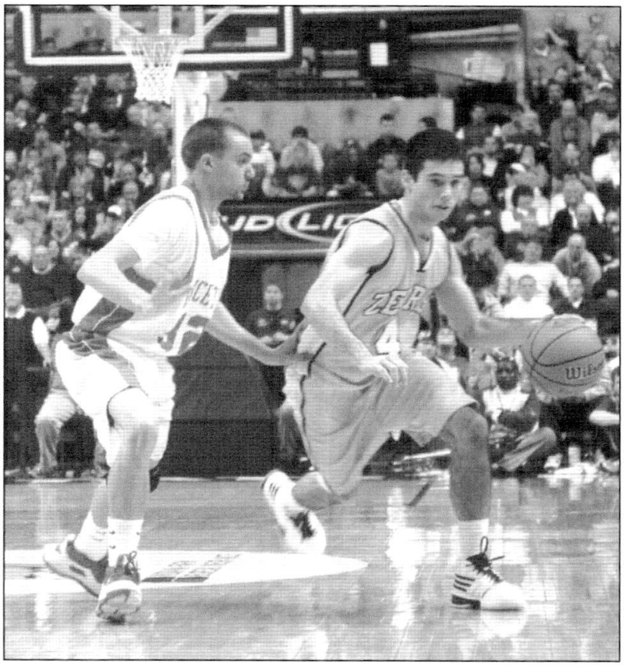

Bruce Grimm Jr. (right) is the all-time leading scorer in RHS history with 1,477 points. He was thrice chosen All Conference and first team All-State. At left he is playing in the ISHAA Class 3A boys' basketball championship at the Conseco Fieldhouse, Indianapolis, in March 2009, against Princeton. His team lost in double overtime, 81-79. Grimm scored 40 points, which set a state finals scoring record and earned him Tournament MVP. (Courtesy of Mike Kenny, *Rochester Sentinel* photographer.)

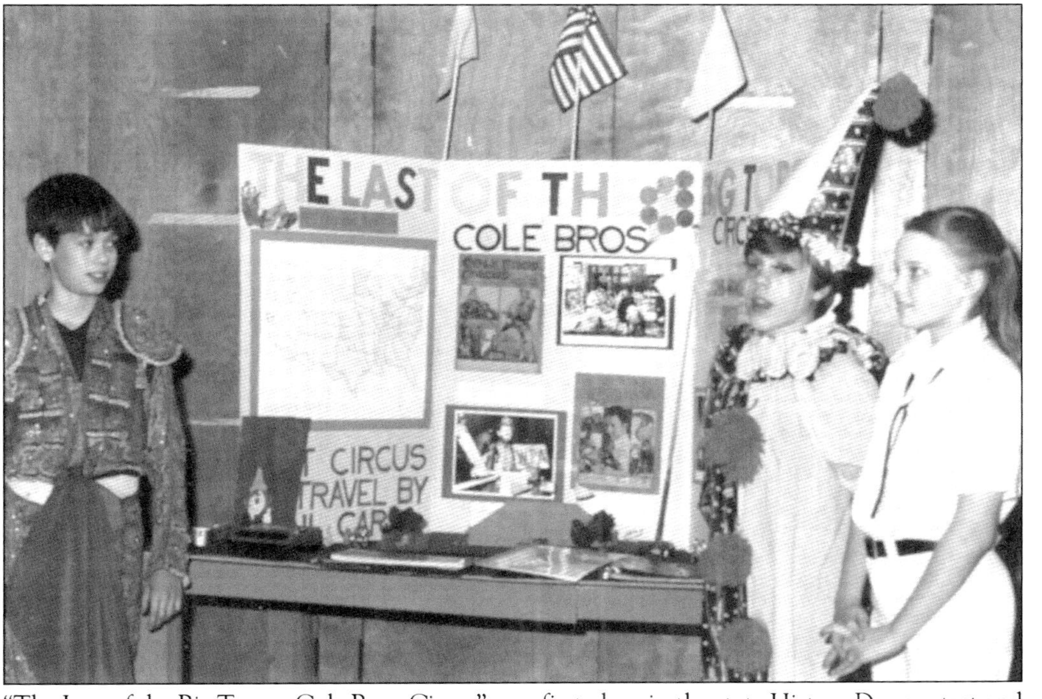

"The Last of the Big Tops—Cole Bros. Circus" won first place in the state History Day contest and placed fourth nationally in Washington, D.C., in 1983. Linda Hewitt was the students' teacher. Here Rich Howell wears a bullfighter suit that belonged to Bobo Zoppe. Elaine Peterson is dressed as a clown, and Coleen Williams is dressed as lion tamer Clyde Beatty. These three created the exhibit, which is now in the Fulton County Museum.

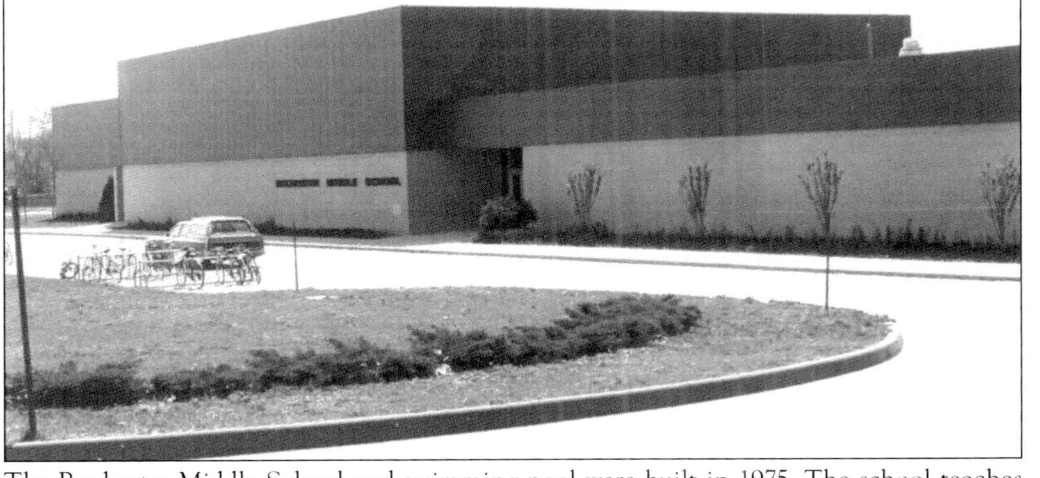

The Rochester Middle School and swimming pool were built in 1975. The school teaches grades six, seven, and eight, replacing the junior high, which taught grades seven and eight. It was designed according to the Open Concept, without walls to separate it into rooms, but in 1987, walls were added. The school buses park here, and pupils change buses to go to Riddle and Columbia Elementary Schools.

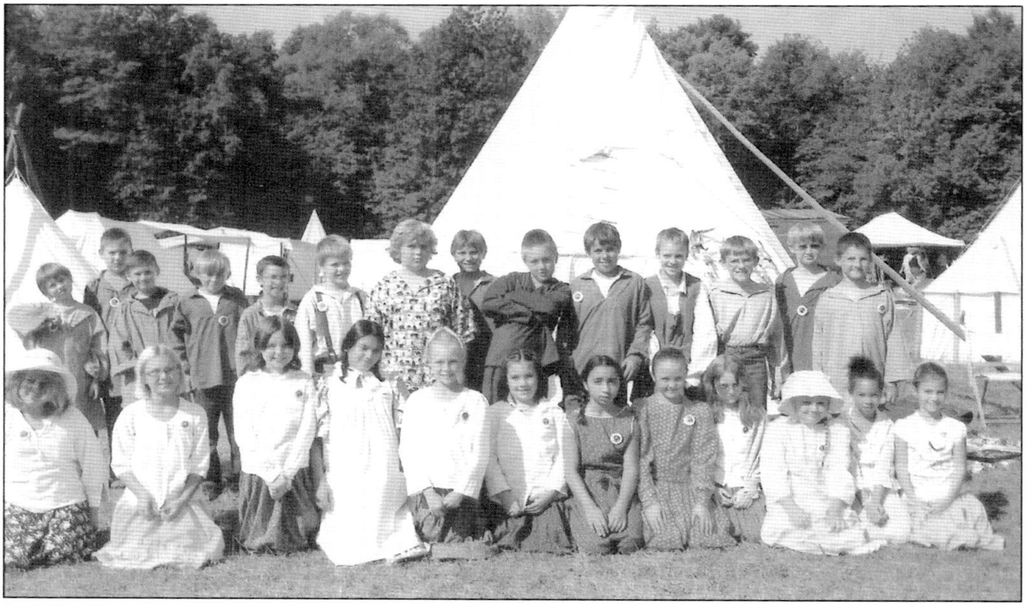

Riddle Elementary School fourth graders performed pioneer dances at the Trail of Courage Living History Festival in 2008, dressed in pioneer outfits. Jean Clements taught them from 1992 to 1999 as Miss Tabitha's School of Dance and Decorum, accompanied by musicians Liza and Mark Woolever. Since 2000, the dances have been taught by physical education teacher Charlee Schwenk and music teacher Lisa McMillan. (Courtesy of Charlee Schwenk.)

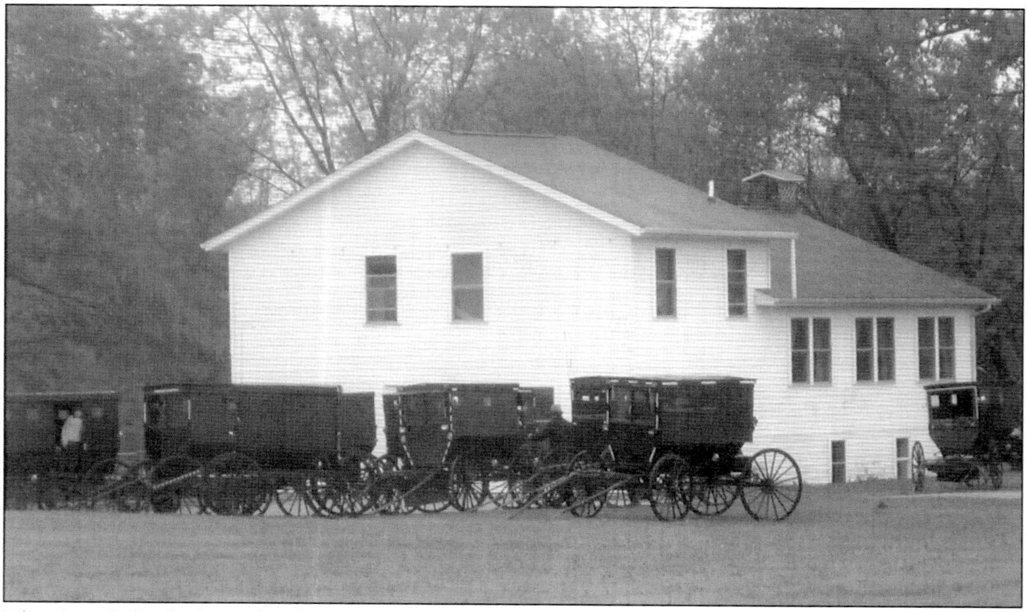

The Amish built this school a quarter of a mile east of Mount Zion in 1999 on County Road 250 South. They had bake sales every Saturday in 1998 in the McCrosky little red round barn at the Fulton County Museum to earn money to build the school. The school has 32 students in grades one through eight and two teachers: Robert Schrock and Laura Detweiler. In the image above, buggies are lined up for the last day of school in 2009.

Seven

Historic Architecture, Churches, and Houses

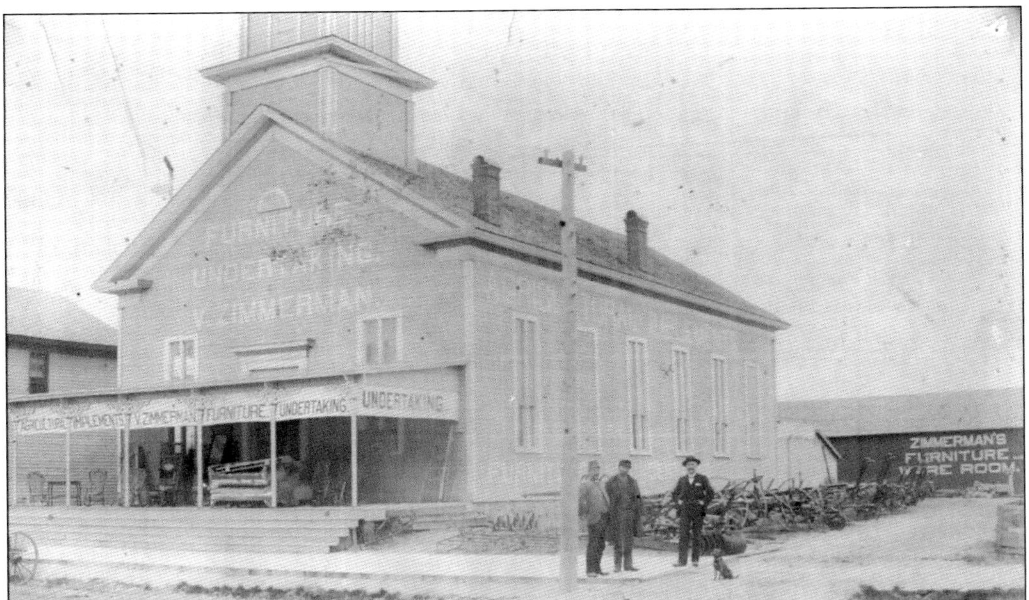

This building at 611 Main Street, one of the oldest in Rochester, was the Rochester First Baptist Church from 1867 to 1879. Val Zimmerman used it for a funeral and furniture store from 1879 to 1944. State senator Valentine Zimmerman is at the right above. When he died in 1900, his sons Val II and Leo continued the business. The old church was sold to the American Legion in 1945, when the Zimmerman Funeral Home moved to 1101 Jefferson Street.

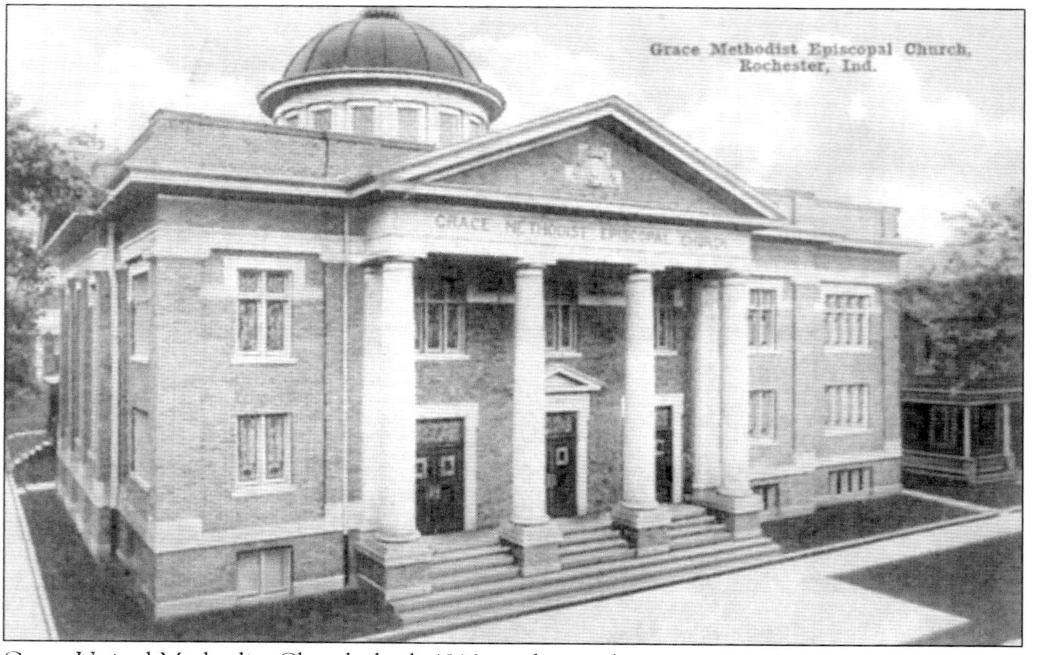

Grace United Methodist Church, built 1916 on the southwest corner of Seventh and Jefferson Streets, is the largest church in Rochester. The dome was removed in 1969. This neoclassical building replaced a brick church built in 1880 in the same location. The Methodist church was the first congregation established in Fulton County; the Rochester Circuit of the Methodist Episcopal Church was established in 1839. (Courtesy of Dave Burkett.)

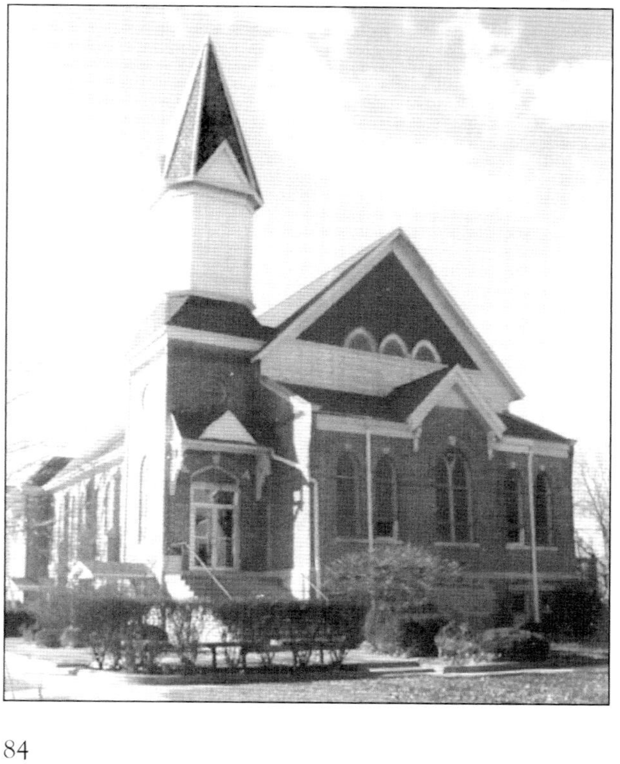

The First Presbyterian Church, at 530 Jefferson Street, was built between 1888 and 1891 in Gothic Revival style. The congregation first met in 1839 with Rev. Robert Rankin. One of the first churches in Rochester, it was formally organized in 1840 under Rev. Edward Wright. The congregation built the first church in 1844 and 1845 on the same corner of Jefferson and Sixth Streets. (Courtesy of First Presbyterian Church.)

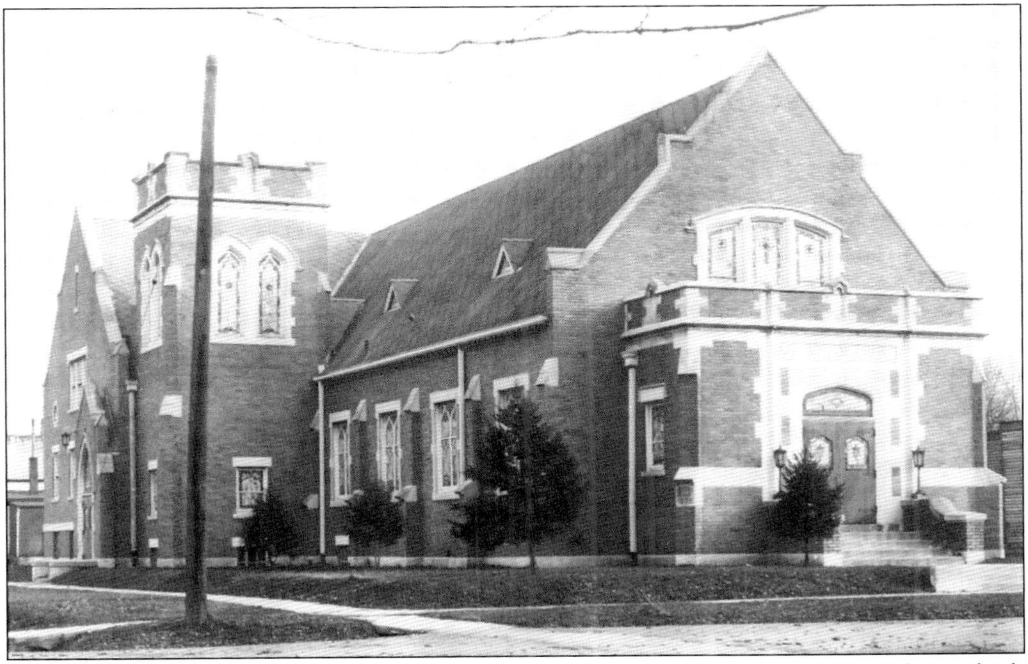

Church of Christ, now known as the First Christian Church (1101 Madison Street), was built in 1925 in the Tudor Revival style. The congregation started in 1879 and built its first church building in 1880. Akron sold its own Christian church building in 1939, donated money from the sale to the Rochester church, and united with them. (Courtesy of *Rochester Sentinel.*)

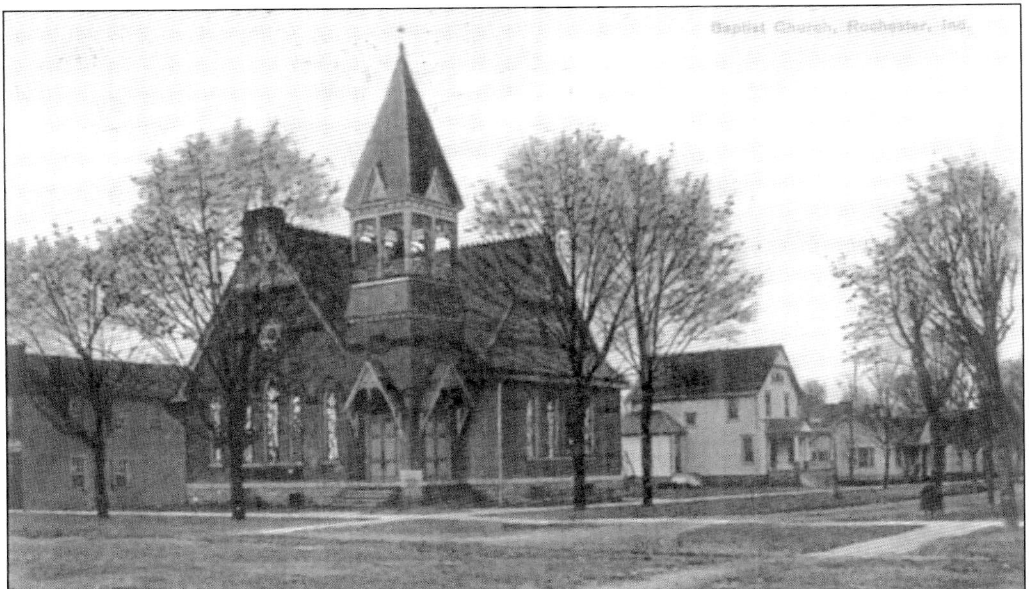

The Baptist congregation was established in Rochester in 1853 and built a wooden church at 611 Main Street in 1867. The next First Baptist Church was built in 1889 at Main and Tenth Streets (pictured above), and the educational addition was built in 1914. Both were replaced in 1960 by the present church complex. (Courtesy of Dave Burkett.)

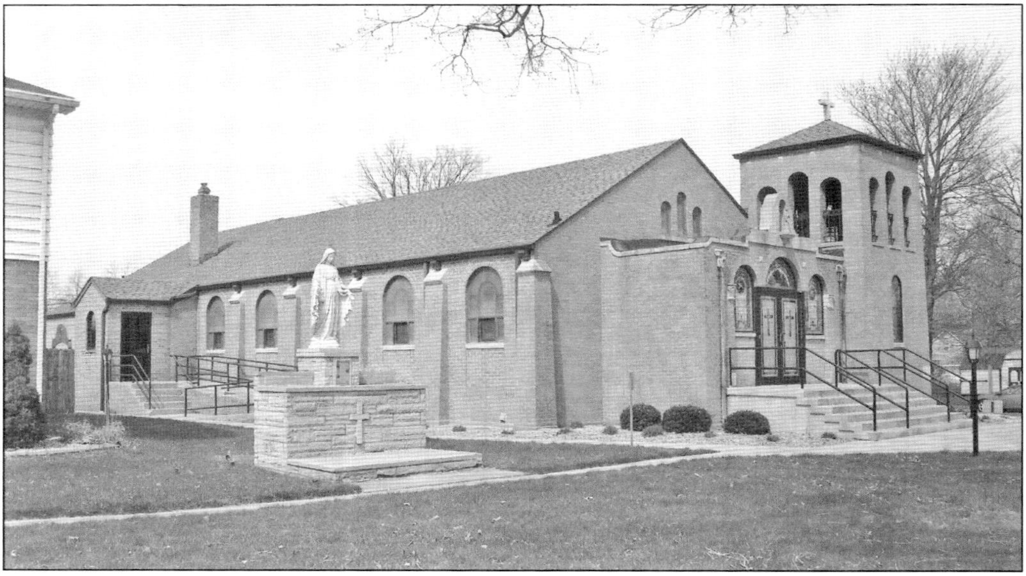

St. Joseph Catholic Church was built in 1930. Rev. John Schall, the pastor of Monterey, purchased land and built the Mediterranean Eclectic–style church at 1300 Main Street. The congregation was formed about 1900, and the first church was located on West Eighth Street. The shrine of the Virgin Mary was donated by Fr. George Lanning's mother in 1963. The rectory and parish hall were built between 1967 and 1971 under Fr. Harold Weller.

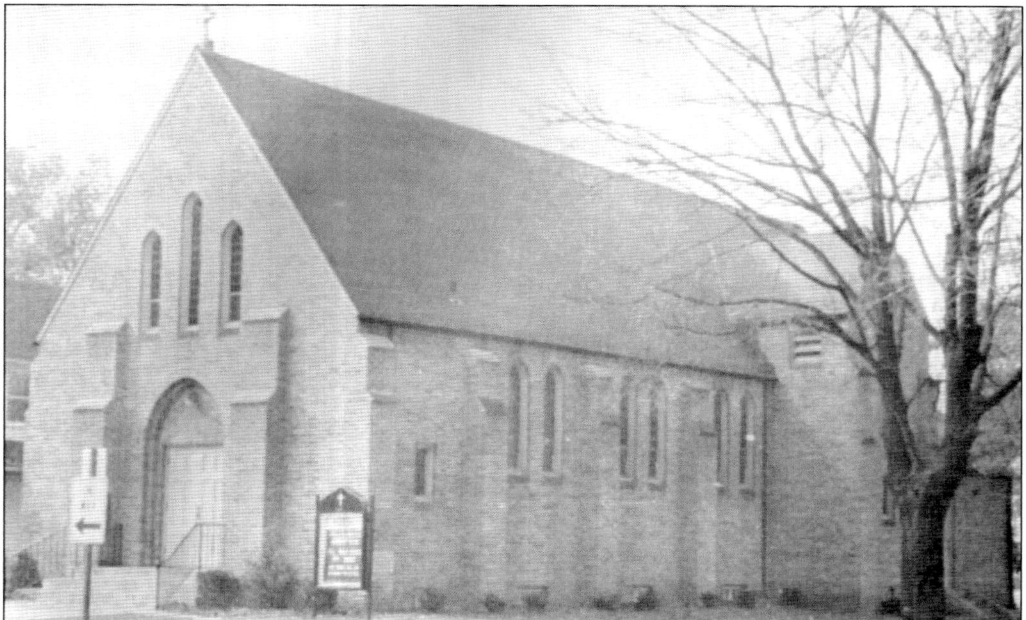

The Gothic Revival–style St. John Lutheran Church was built in 1940 on the southwest corner of Fourth and Jefferson Street. A German Lutheran brick school and wooden church were built in 1873 with a $1,000 mortgage. The church was sold by sheriff's auction in 1887. In 1936, Lutherans bought their old church back to use for their parsonage. The parsonage was moved in 1976, when the new addition to the 1940 church was built.

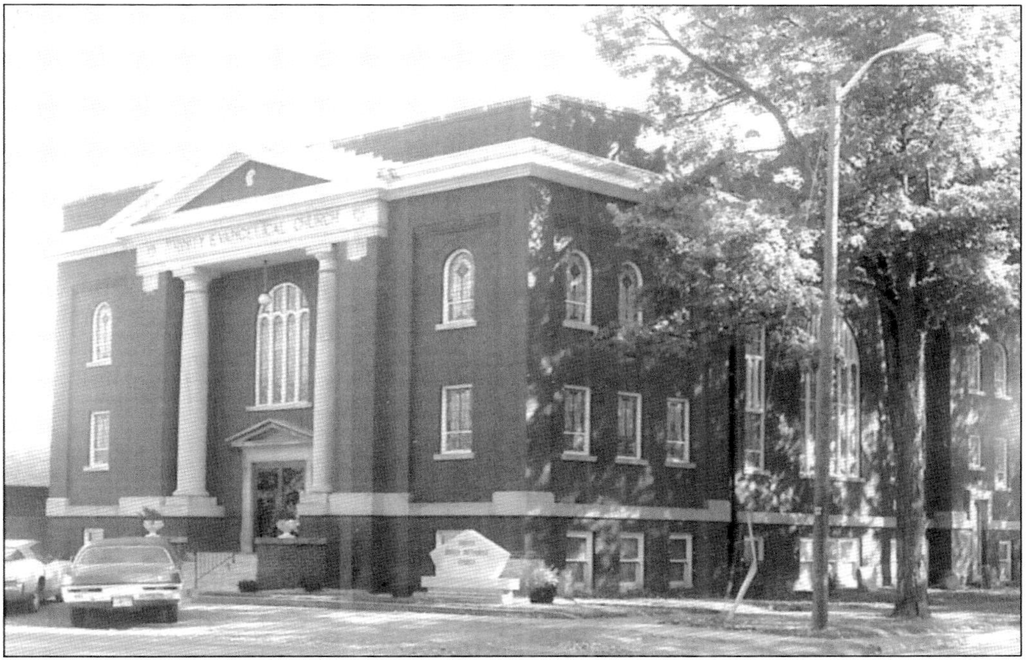

Trinity Church, located at 801 Jefferson Street, was built in 1916 in the neoclassical style. It merged with St. Paul's Evangelical United Brethren Church (EUB) on the corner of Sixth and Pontiac Streets in 1959, and St. Paul's Church was sold for $15,000. In 1968, the EUB and Methodist denominations merged to form the United Methodist Church. (Courtesy of Trinity United Methodist Church.)

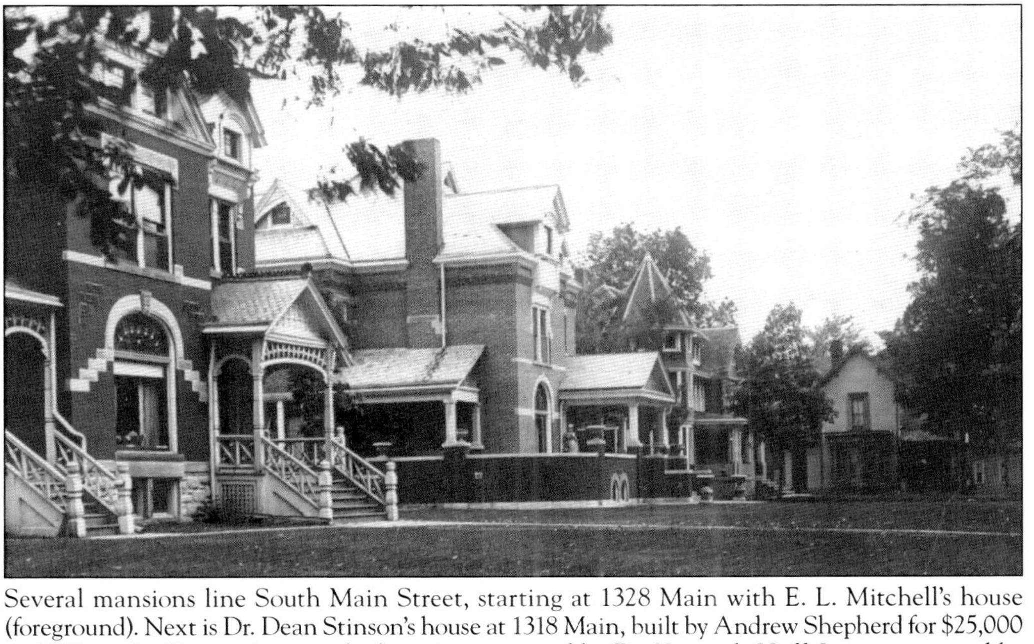

Several mansions line South Main Street, starting at 1328 Main with E. L. Mitchell's house (foreground). Next is Dr. Dean Stinson's house at 1318 Main, built by Andrew Shepherd for $25,000 in 1881 in the Queen Anne style; later it was owned by Dr. Kenneth Hoff. It is now owned by William Baldwin. The third house in this image was demolished to build the Catholic rectory.

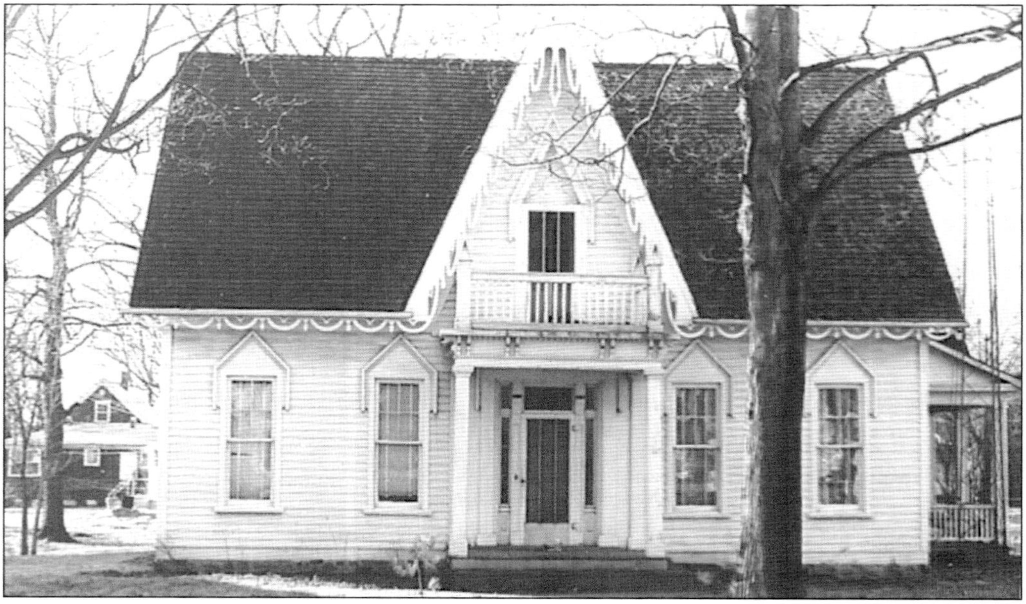

The Lyon-Jones house, at 201 West Ninth Street (also listed as 902 Jefferson Street), was built in 1854 by David Lyon, a merchant tailor. The style of architecture is Gothic Revival. The acorns in the trim were carved by hand by David Lyon. The house was pictured in *Indiana Houses of the 19th Century* in 1962. George and Hazel Jones purchased the house in 1947.

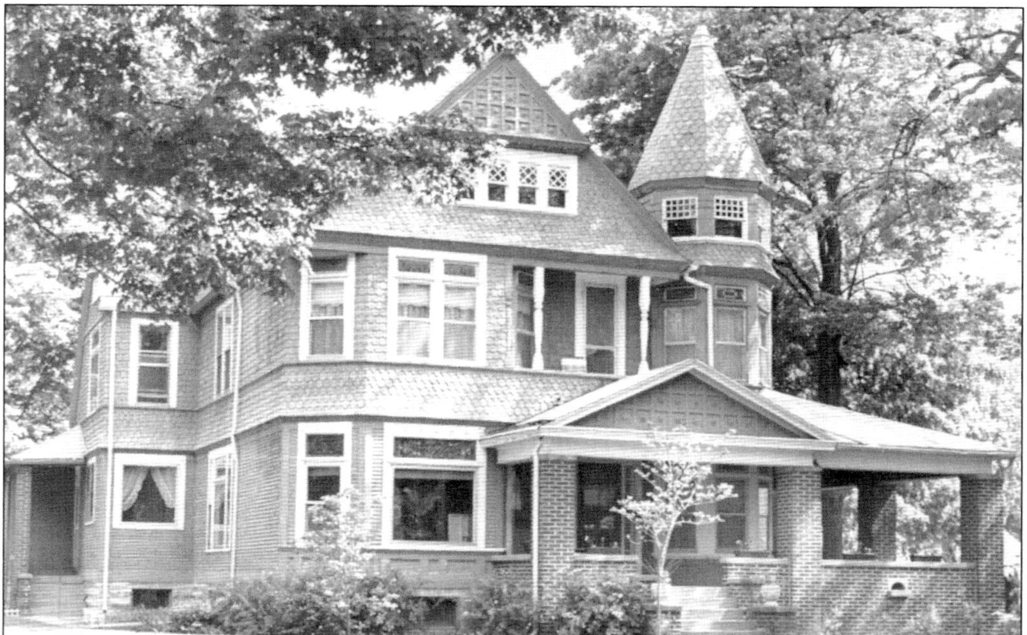

The Brackett house, 328 West Ninth Street, is a fine example of Queen Anne architecture. Listed on the National Register, the 12-room home was built from 1884 to 1886 for Lyman Brackett, who owned a lumberyard and a wholesale grocery business and was a president of the Rochester State Bank, vice president of Rochester Telephone Company, and an owner of the Arlington Hotel.

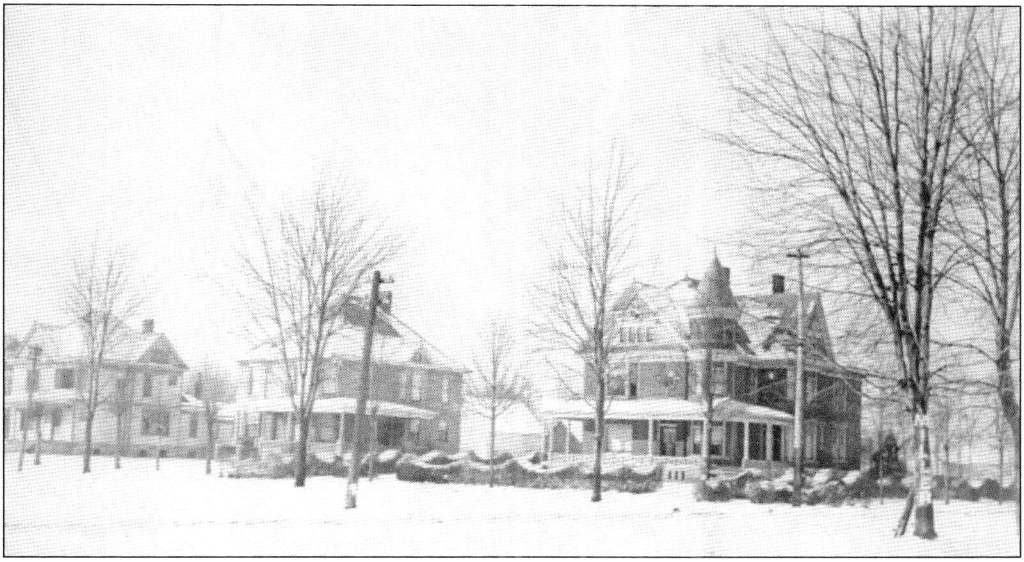

John E. Beyer built this beautiful house (right) at Pontiac and Seventh Streets in 1896. He was Rochester's first multi-millionaire, owned Rochester Electric Power, ice plant, Winona Creamery, and Winona Assembly and started Bank of Indiana. Judge Wendell Tombaugh owns the house now and has indexed and published many books of historic records and newspapers. Beyer's half-brother Harry Pfeiffer built the house on the left. (Courtesy of *Rochester Sentinel*.)

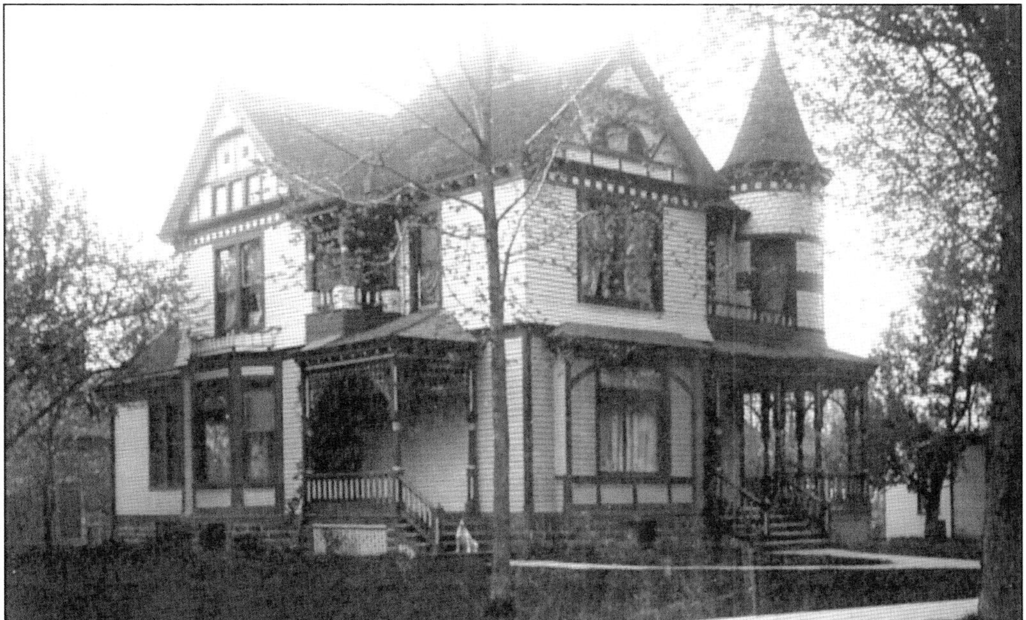

Henry Barnhart's home at 1118 South Main Street was built in 1895 in the Queen Anne style. Barnhart bought the *Rochester Sentinel* in 1885 and was one of the founders of Rochester Telephone Company in 1895. He served in the U.S. House of Representatives from 1908 to 1919. His son, Hugh Barnhart, grew up here and continued the *Rochester Sentinel* and Rochester Telephone Company. After Henry Barnhart's death in 1934, the house was used as a nursing home.

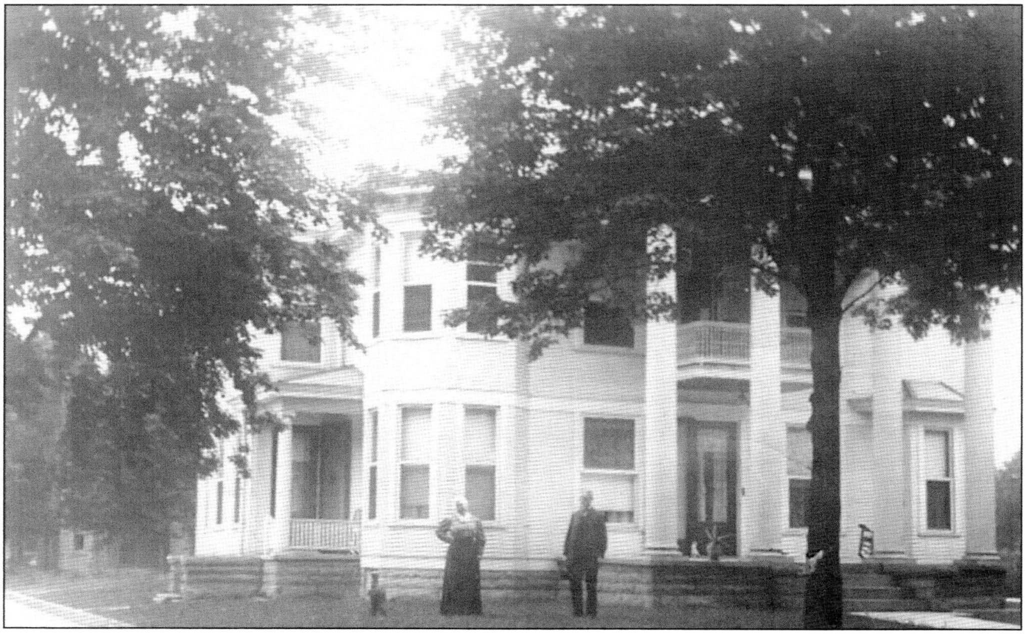

The Classical Revival Dr. O. P. Waite house at 728 Jefferson Street was also known as "Sunnyside." This picture was taken in 1907, showing Waite and his wife, Agnes Aitken. Dr. Waite built the house in 1881, when he moved to Rochester to practice medicine with Dr. Charles Spohn. Aged 92 when he died in 1934, Dr. Waite was the oldest surviving member of the Fulton County Medical Association. (Courtesy of James Heyde.)

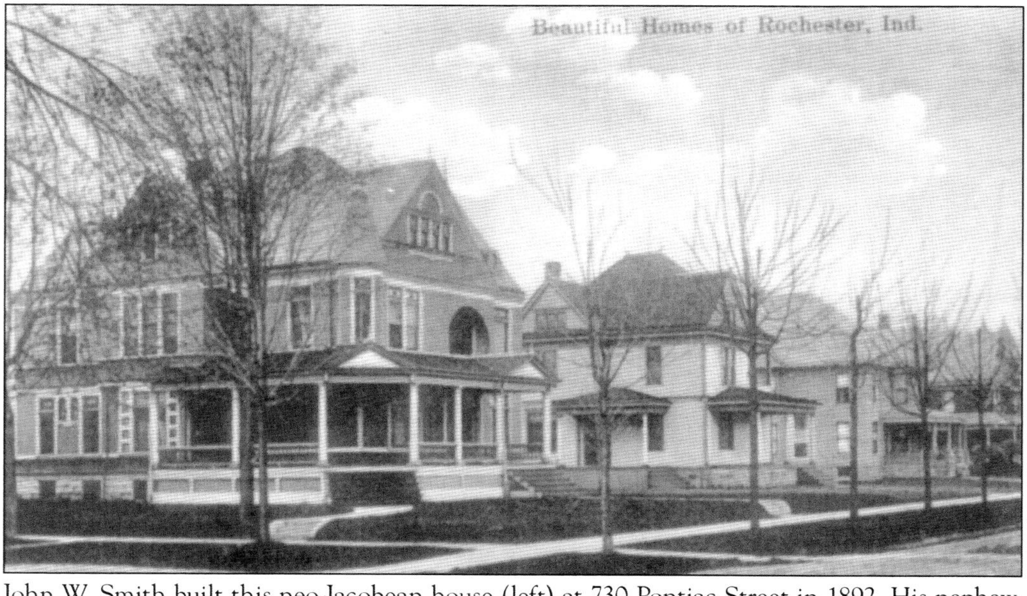

John W. Smith built this neo-Jacobean house (left) at 730 Pontiac Street in 1892. His nephew, Omar Smith, was elected Rochester's first mayor in 1910 and lived here. Omar was president of the First National Bank, as was his son, Percy Smith. The house is listed on the National Register of Historic Places as the Smith-Nicholson house, because Bobbie Nicholson owned it at the time of registration in 1978.

Eight
Famous People

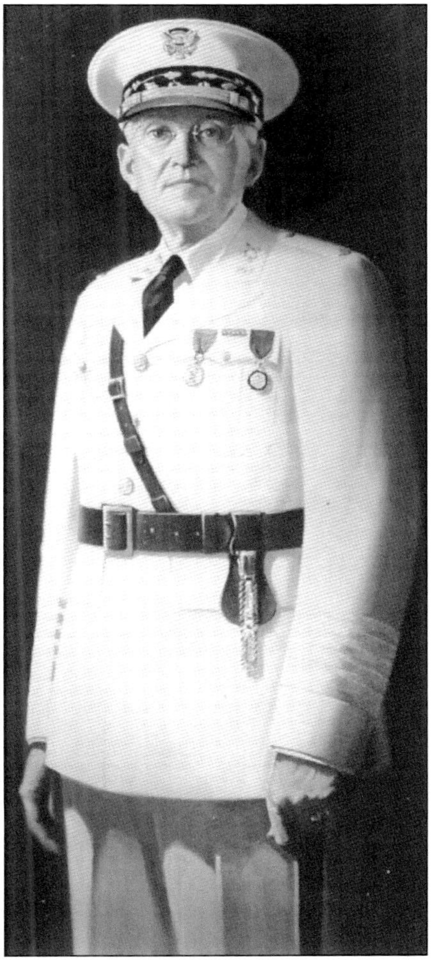

Paul Spotts Emrick, Purdue band director from 1905 to 1954, was born in Rochester in 1884 and used his memories of geese forming a V as they flew over Lake Manitou to create the first marching band forming letters in 1907. He originated the world's largest drum in 1919, illuminated formations at night in 1935, and established numerous other firsts. Emrick retired to Lake Manitou and was buried in Rochester's IOOF cemetery in 1965.

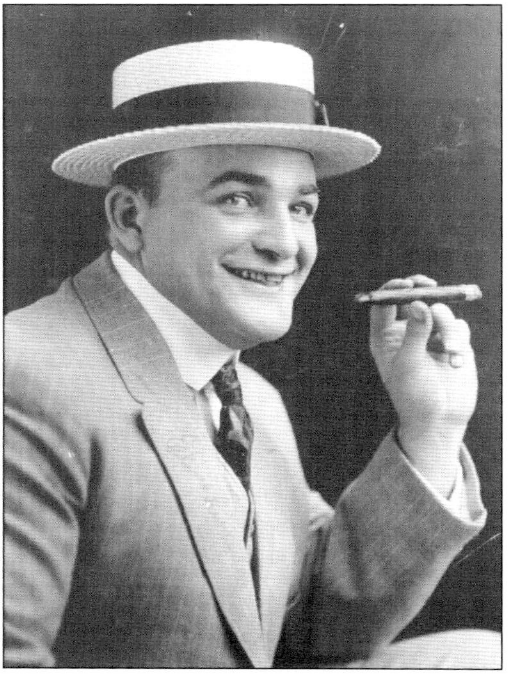

Elmo Lincoln, the most famous person ever born in Rochester, became a movie star in 1918, when he was selected to play the lead in *Tarzan of the Apes*. Elmo's real name was Otto Elmo Linkenhelt; his mother was Eldora Hunter. This photograph shows Elmo in 1912, when he first got into movies. He became so popular that movies were written especially for him, such as *Elmo the Mighty* and *Elmo the Fearless*.

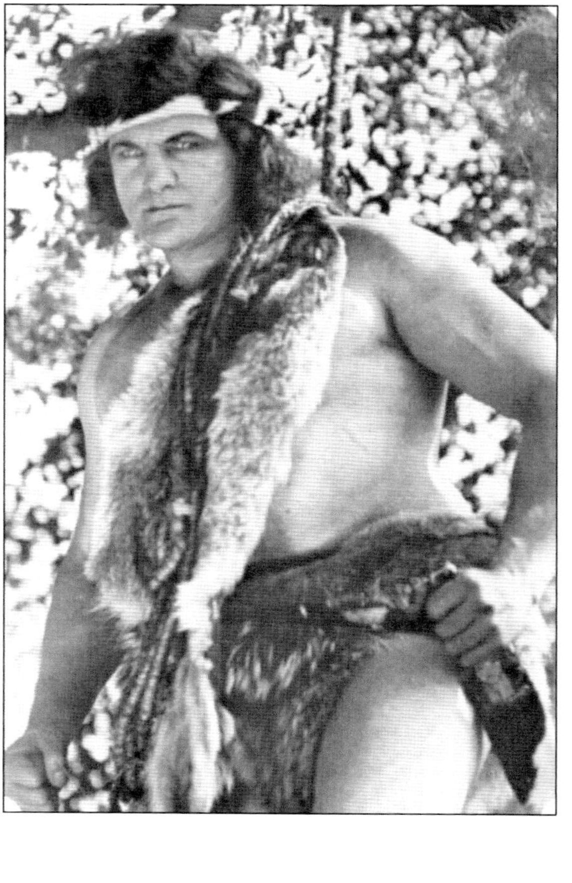

Elmo Lincoln brought Tarzan to the screen in 1918, four years after the jungle hero made his first appearance via a best-selling book by Edgar Rice Burroughs. Elmo landed the part because, according to D. W. Griffith, he had a "barrel chest that reminded the Hollywood director of an ape." Strict codes, however, soon required him to cover his chest with an animal fur.

Dr. George Hoffman (1865–1951) was a brilliant physician and a genius in diagnosis and neurology. In early 1900s, he gave speeches to medical conventions and was widely known and respected. He served as county health officer in the 1920s. He was a founder of the Farmers and Merchants Bank in 1934. He had an observatory built on top of his house, which he filled with his collections. He became famous as an Einstein-like eccentric.

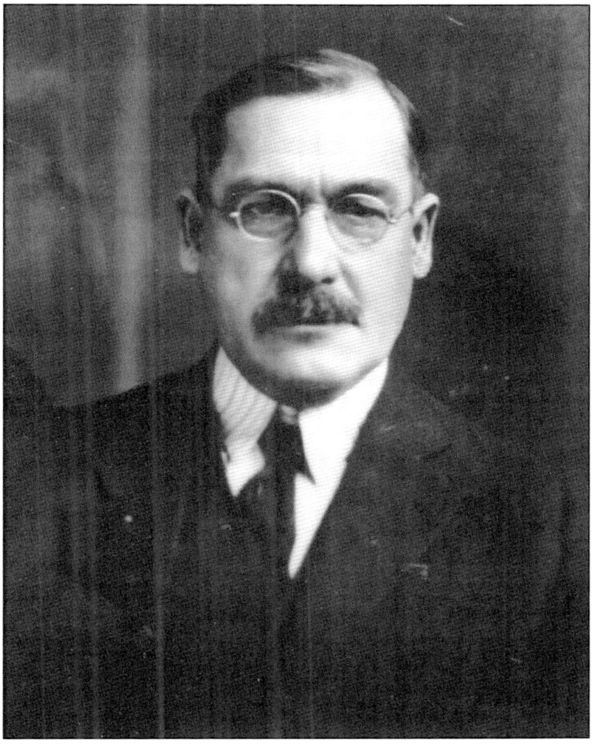

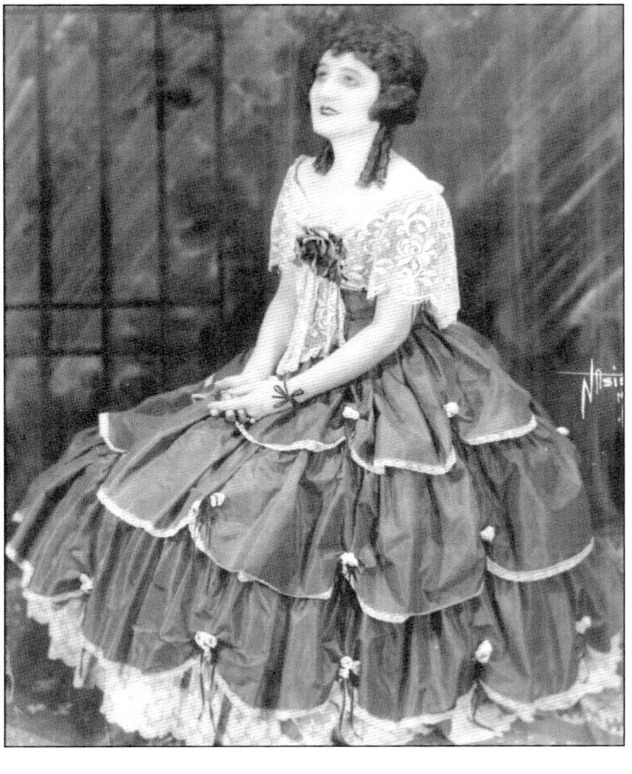

In 1923 and 1924, Freeda Sullivan (later married to Wilson and Hill) sang on the Keith Vaudeville circuit on the East Coast, Canada, and Midwest. A soprano in Otis Mitchell's Maryland Singers, she sang Stephen Foster and old time Southern tunes; her signature solo was "My Old Kentucky Home." She sang in Ohio nightclubs during the rest of Prohibition, and sang at the Grace United Methodist Church until the 1960s. Her father was the Standard Oil agent in Rochester.

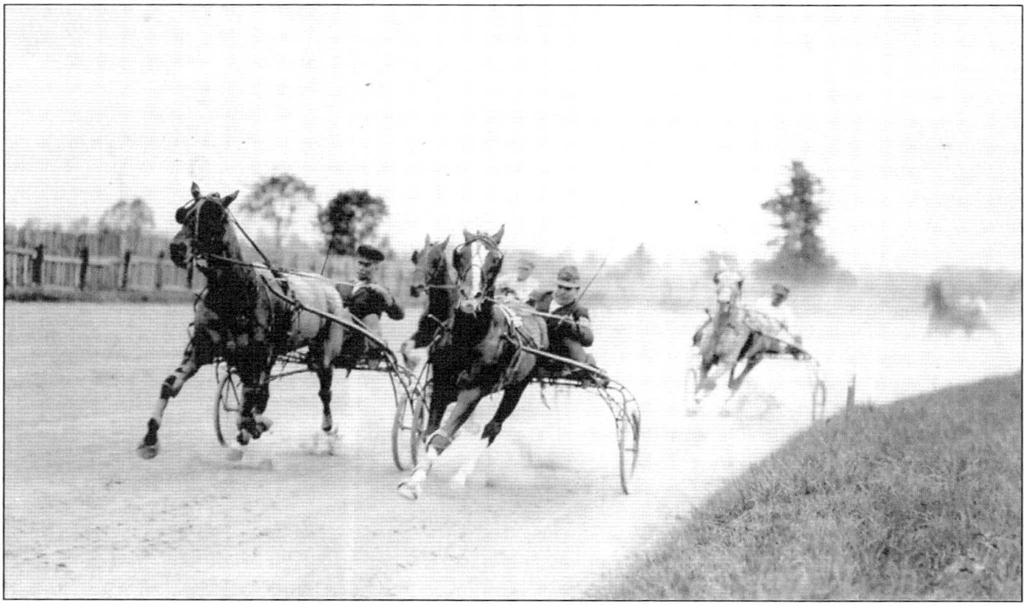

Oliver M. Powell, "The Pacing Farmer," wearing a slouch hat, pulls ahead in a sulky race. He raised and trained pacing horses at his farm south of Rochester from 1893 to 1951, setting six world records, the first in 1915 at Fulton County fairgrounds' half-mile track (now City Park). *Harness Horseman* magazine (October 1942) declared that Powell had sold more speed than any man in the United States. (Courtesy of Powell's great-granddaughter Sherri Engle Anderson.)

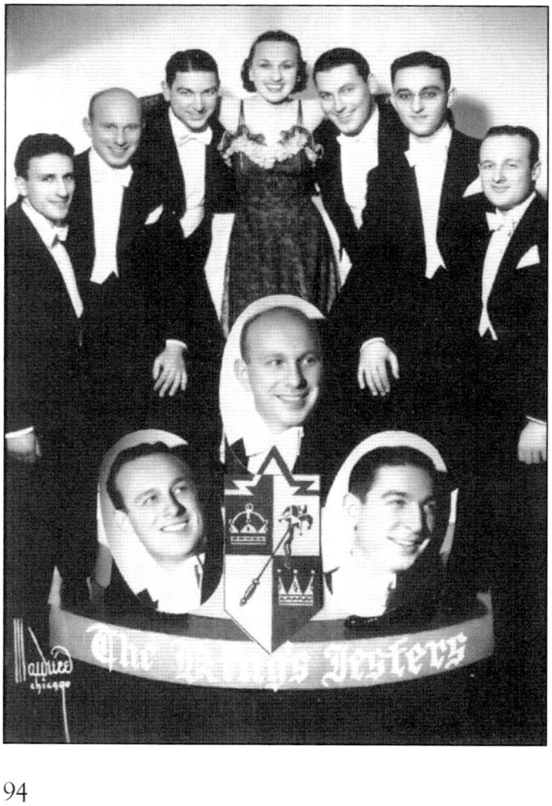

The King's Jesters (in the collage of three), George Howard, John Ravencroft, and Fritz Bastow, were schoolmates at Rochester High School before becoming singers on the radio. They also sang with others. Seen here around 1940 from left to right are Sidney Neirman, John Ravencroft, Fritz Bastow, Marjorie Whitney, Bob Casey, Jim Awad, and George Howard.

Round barn builder Charles Vallandingham "Lan" Kindig built hundreds of houses, barns, churches, and sheds with his sons until he died October 22, 1940, at age 77. He owned C. V. Kindig and Sons Construction Company and built at least 23 round barns in northern Indiana from 1910 to 1924. His sons were Oral "Hap," Cleve "Pete," and Roy. (Courtesy of Helen Kindig Notz.)

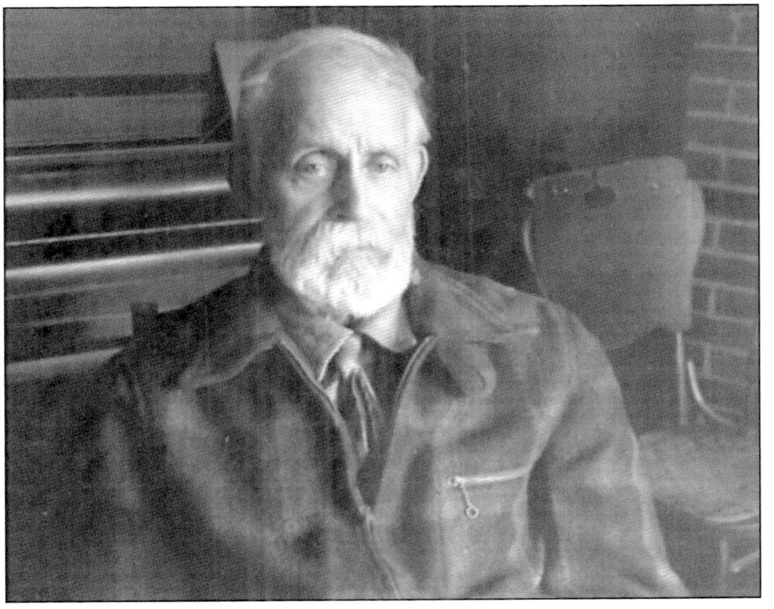

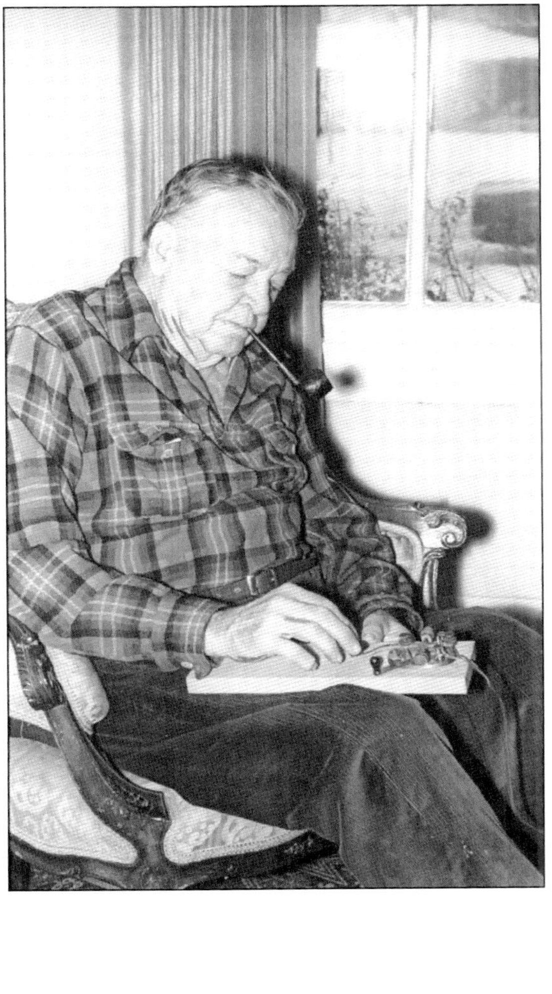

In 1903, Floyd "Jack" Mattice was the first to broadcast a ball game. He operated a telegraph to earn money for college. He was Fulton County prosecutor and later worked for the FBI. He served as counsel to two Japanese generals during the Tokyo War Trials after World War II. They were both hanged, but they gave him a Japanese robe, which is displayed in the Fulton County Museum.

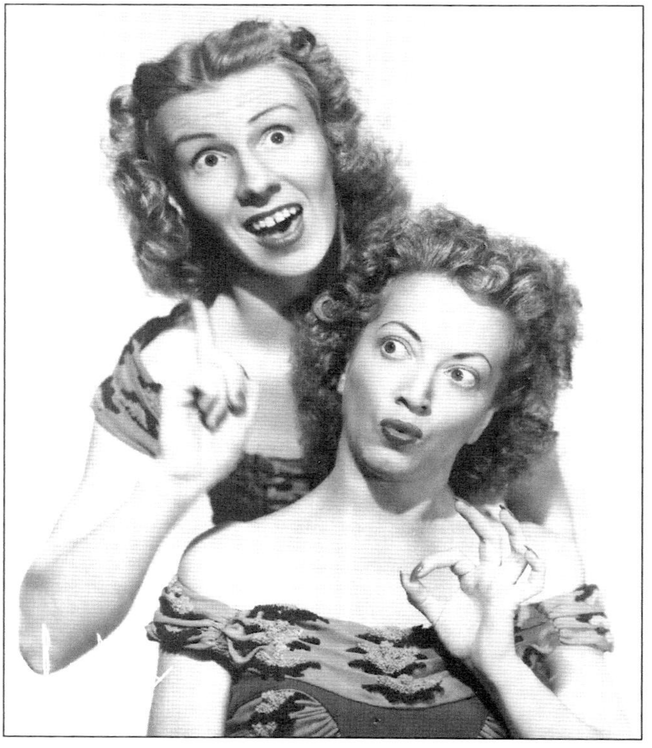

Helen "Pam" Parmalee (left) and Louise Davidson performed at USO shows during World War II. Billed as "Belles of the Brawl," they traveled to Hawaii, Guam, Japan, Korea, and the Philippines to entertain the troops. They founded the Pam and Louise Dance Studio in Rochester in 1953 and taught up to 200 students each week, giving an annual dance recital and other performances. Lou died in 1974, but Pam continued teaching dance until 1999, when she retired and closed the studio. (Courtesy of Debbie Brown Gottschalk Frost.)

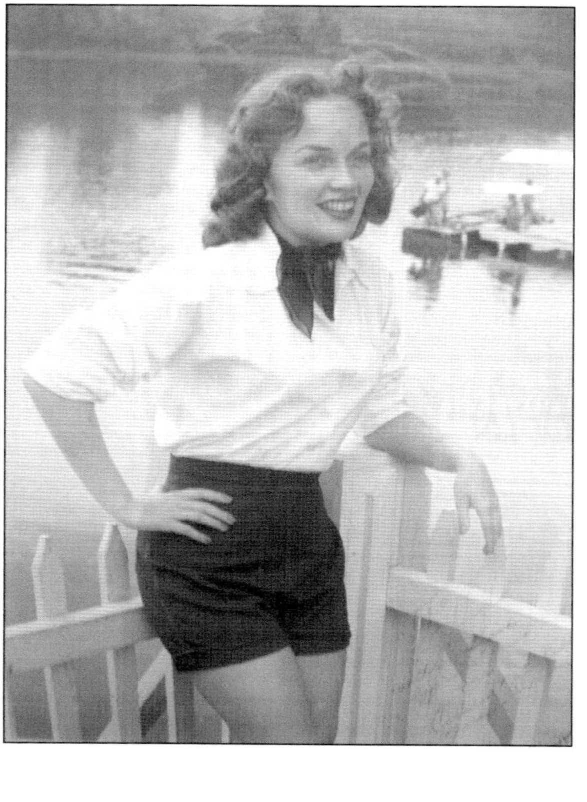

Carol Mitchell was crowned Miss Indiana on September 8, 1951, and was first runner-up for Miss America in 1952, losing by only one vote. Her talents were dancing marionettes and quickly drawn caricatures. She received a $3,000 scholarship to Indiana University. She had her own television show at Bloomington and Fort Wayne. Her parents were E. L. and Mildred Mitchell. She married H. Leslie Popp. After his death, she married Carl Bennett.

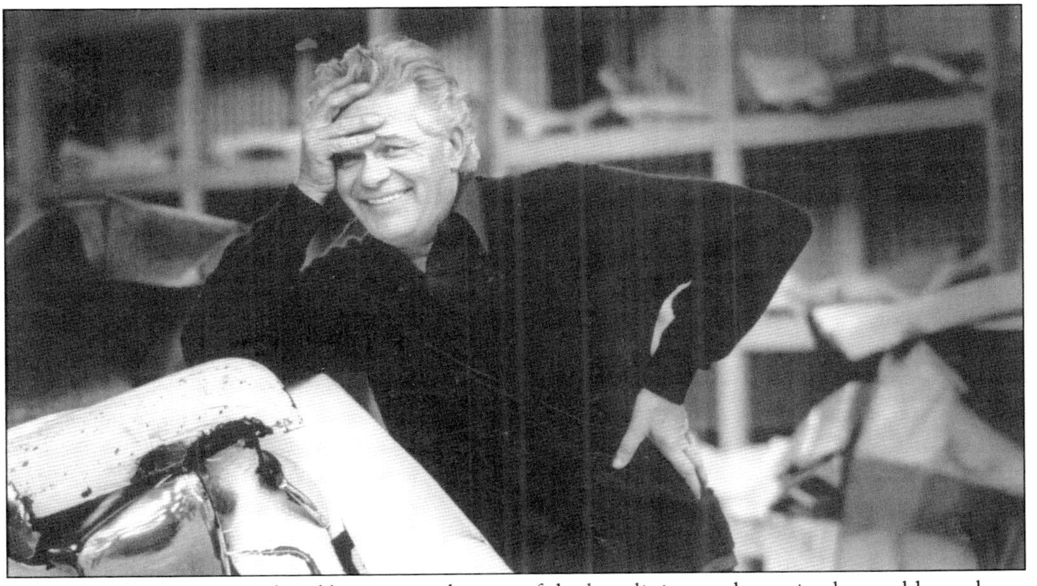

John Chamberlain, considered by many to be one of the best living sculptors in the world, was born in 1927 in Rochester, which was founded and named by his ancestor, Alexander Chamberlain, in 1835. John's parents owned Chamberlain's Tavern at 128 East Eighth Street. Most of his sculptures are made of car metal in bright colors. His art has been featured in many famous museums in New York, Chicago, and Indianapolis. (Courtesy of Pace Wildenstein.)

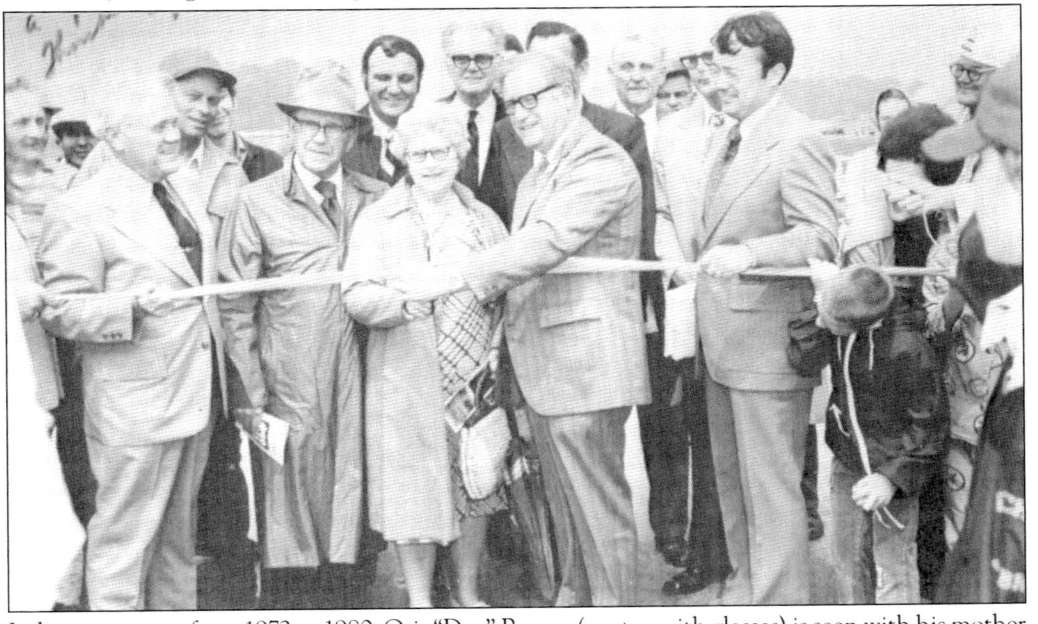

Indiana governor from 1972 to 1980, Otis "Doc" Bowen (center, with glasses) is seen with his mother cutting the ribbon to open the new U.S. 31 south of Rochester on May 25, 1975. Left of his mother is his father, Vernie Bowen. Also seen here are road builder James Heyde of McMahan-O'Connor Construction (the man with dark hair behind Bowen's mother) and mayor Wayne Hittle (behind Doc and mostly hidden). Bowen's ancestor Constant Bowen came to Fulton County in 1836. A physician, Doc was U.S. Secretary of Health from 1985 to 1988 under Pres. Ronald Reagan.

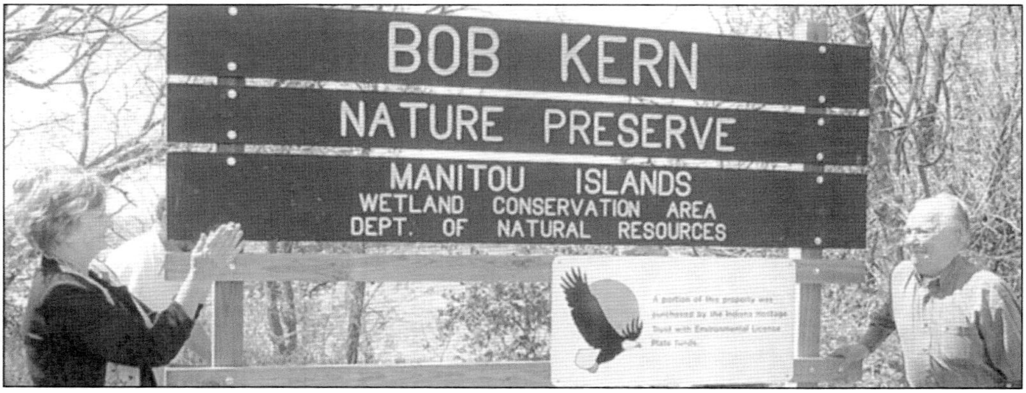

Bob Kern Nature Preserve–Manitou Islands Wetlands was dedicated in 2004 on the east side of Lake Manitou. Bob Kern (right) planted over 500,000 trees on 1,500 acres over 50 years and was the third largest grower of Christmas trees in the United States. He created 15 ponds, establishing many wildlife plantings and winning three awards for conservation. At left is Maggie Kernan, wife of Indiana governor Joe Kernan. (Courtesy of *Rochester Sentinel.*)

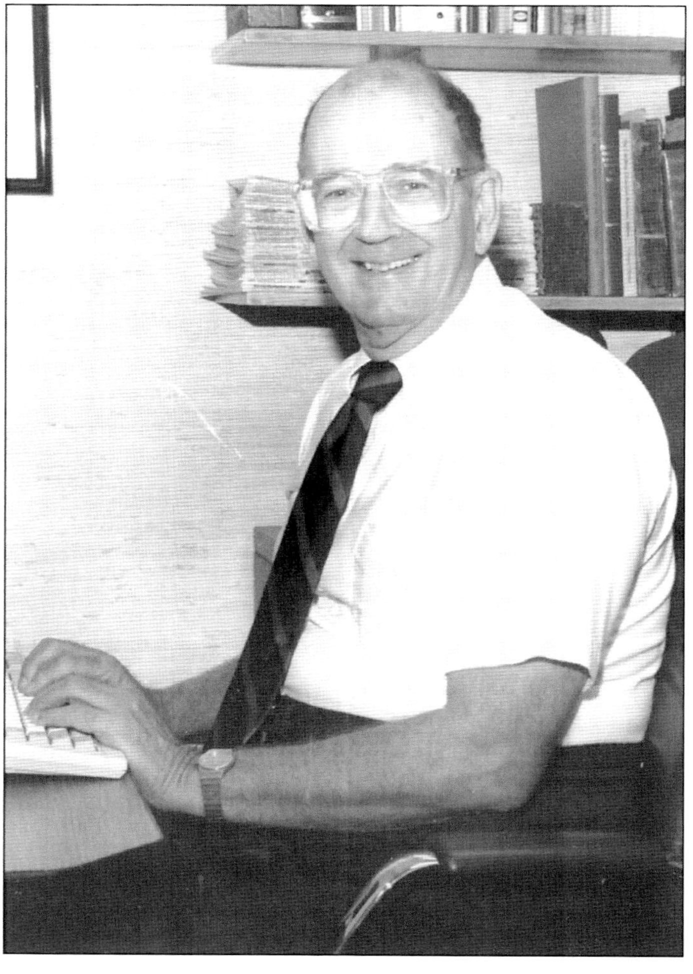

Jack K. Overmyer was editor of the *Rochester Sentinel* from 1952 to 1979 and publisher until 1994. He was founder and first president of the Fulton County Historical Society in 1963. His book *A Stupendous Effort: The 87th Indiana in the War of the Rebellion* was published in 1997 by Indiana University Press. The *Sentinel* published collections of his writings: *Reflections of a Hoosier Editor*, 1998; *Reflections Resumed*, 2002; and *Gatherings*, 2005. (Courtesy of Jack K. Overmyer.)

Nine

Circus, Fairs, and Festivals

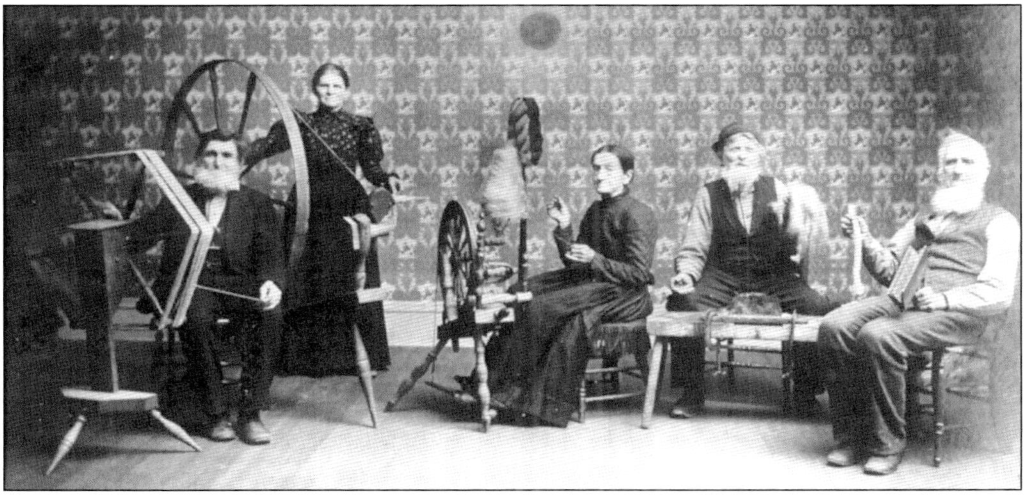

These pioneers demonstrated how to make thread at the Antique Fair held in the Armory Hall in January 1900. From left are George Moore, age 82, reeling yarn; Margaret Daugherty, 64, "walking spinning wheel" for cotton; Susannah Ault, 73, spinning flax; Henry Ault, 73, hacking flax; and Ephraim Daugherty, 91, carding wool.

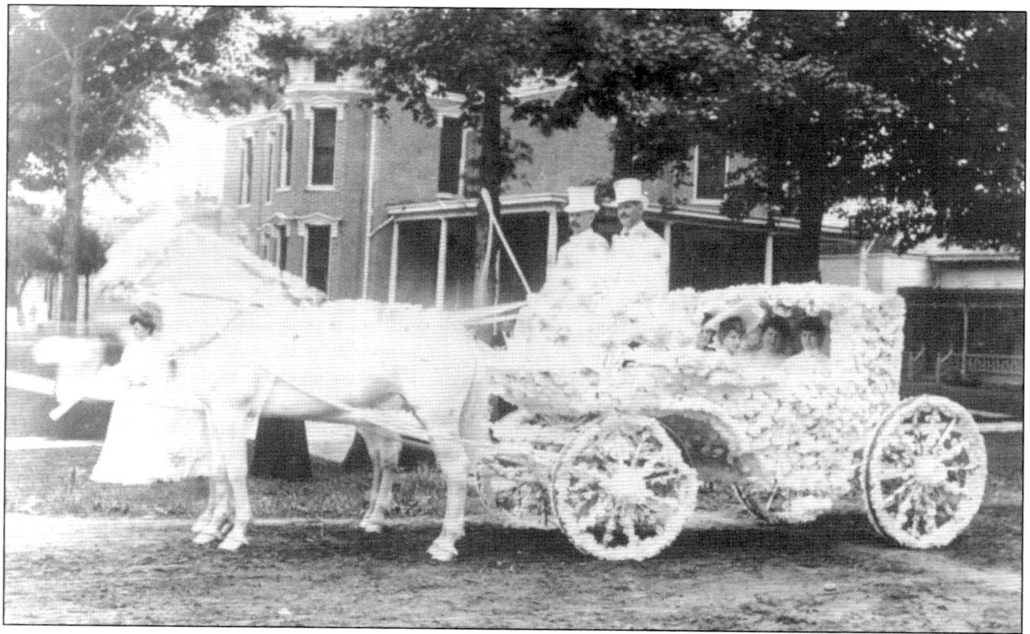

Ward and Huffer livery barn took first prize in the Blossom Parade in 1908. Horses and buggies, automobiles, and floats were decorated with flowers. Tents were erected in the street by the courthouse and rides were sold on a big tilt-a-whirl. The girls in the coach are, from left to right, Blanche (Thalman) Wile, Anna (Plank) Ensign, Daisy (Bell) Alspach, and Ray (Miller) Meyers.

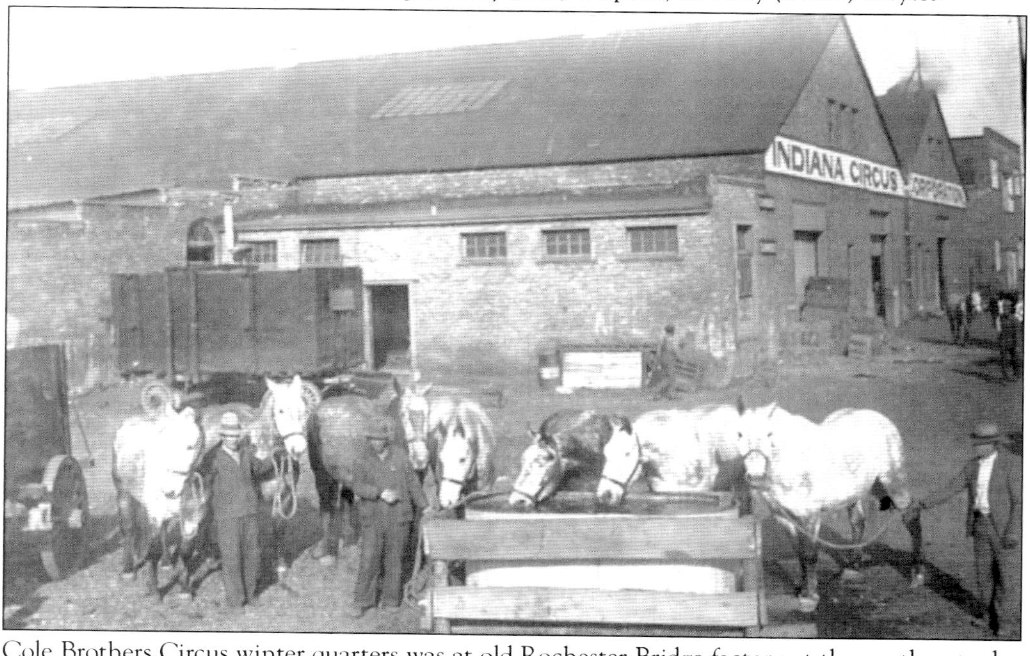

Cole Brothers Circus winter quarters was at old Rochester Bridge factory at the northeast edge of Rochester at Lucas and Erie Streets from 1934 to 1940. Many beautiful horses were trained at the circus for pulling wagons, carrying bareback trick riders, and doing tricks in the center ring. Fortunately, the horses were not at the winter quarters when it was destroyed by fire in 1940.

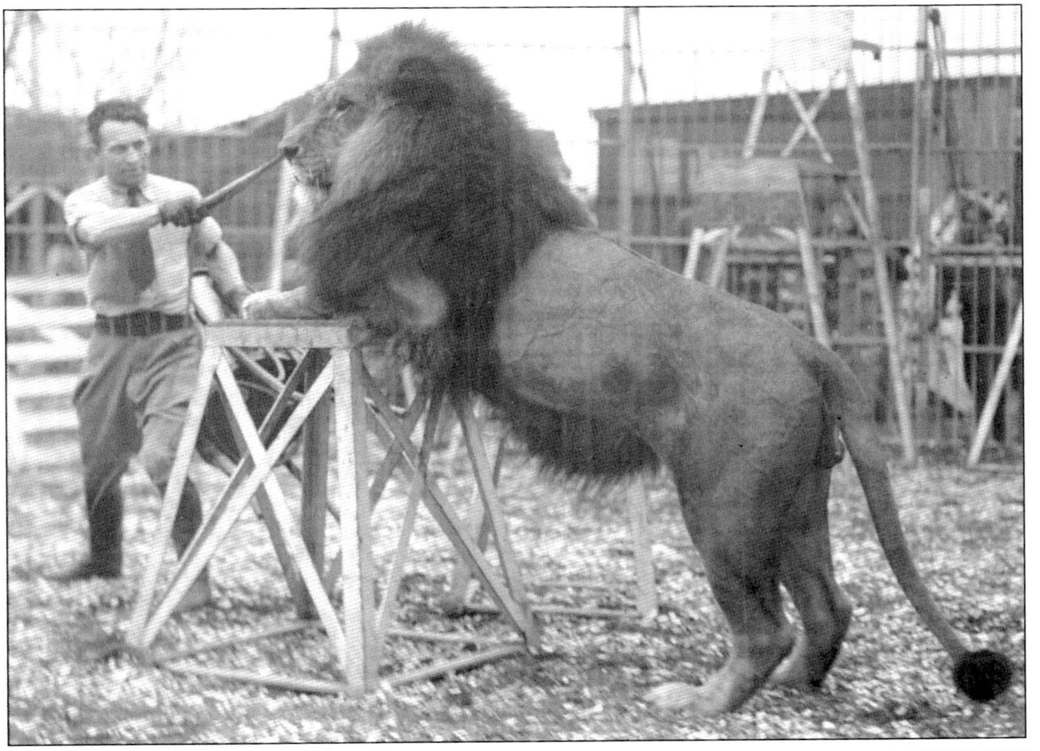

Clyde Beatty, a world-famous lion tamer, poses with his favorite lion, Nero, who saved his life once. He got his adult cats from the wilds of Africa, and they were ferocious, not like the tame cats raised by their trainers today. Several times the big cats got in fights, and one was killed during the act. Beatty lived at 531 Pontiac Street from 1935 to 1938; he also bred lions, and he trained lion cubs on his kitchen table.

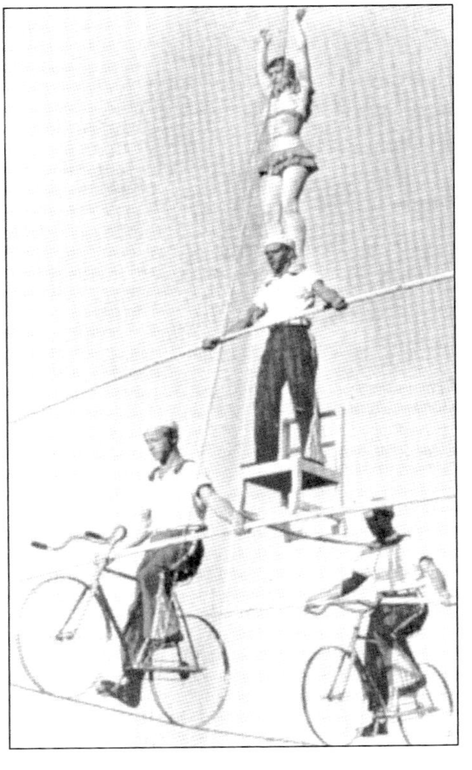

The Great Gretonas performed on high wires for the Cole Brothers Circus. Taking their name from their leader, Otto Gretona, the act included Willi and Clara Lamberti (man with wife on shoulder). The man at the back is either Franz Heinzmann or Eugene Lechler, around 1930. Heinzmann was killed from a fall from a 100-foot pole in Pueblo, Colorado, on June 20, 1950, while performing at the state fairgrounds.

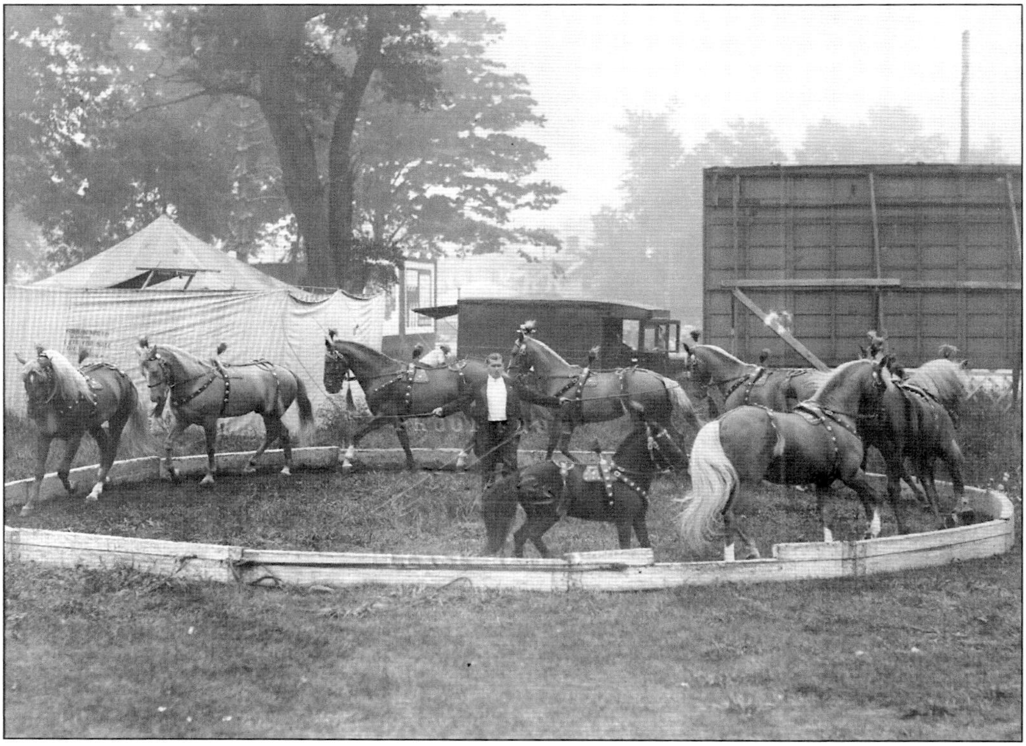

Jorgen Christiansen trained his liberty horse act, in which the horses performed "at liberty" —without reins. He also trained a carousel of 79 animals. Born in Denmark, Christianson came to America in 1923 for Ringling Brothers, then came to the Cole Brothers Circus in 1937. He moved to Fulton in 1939 and died in Rochester in 1969. He was inducted into Circus Hall of Fame in 1967. (Courtesy of *Rochester Sentinel.*)

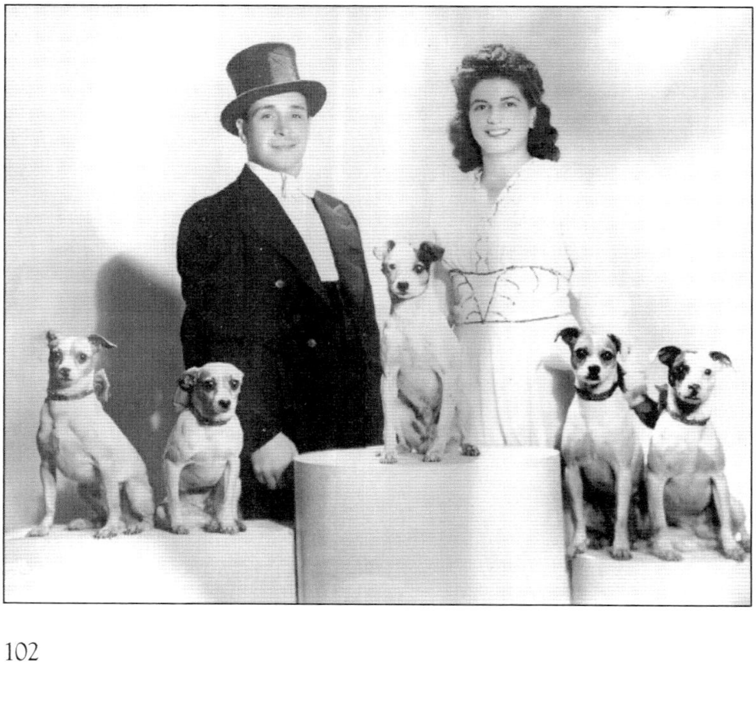

Johnny "Laddie" Zoppe and wife Sara show their fox terriers for their circus act in 1947. His nickname "Laddie" came from his unsupported ladder act. They came from Italy to perform in the Cole Brothers Circus at Rochester in 1936, bought a house north on Old 31, and lived there the rest of their lives, raising three children: Davide, Johnny, and Sonja (Loudermilk). All three performed their own circus acts.

On February 20, 1940, fire destroyed much of the circus and killed several animals. Dead animals were taken to Barts Fertilizer plant on River Road (now Olson Road). Howard Barts, who operated the fertilizer plant from 1922 to 1960, is shown with his truck and a dead elephant. He saved a tusk from the elephant, which is still in the family. (Courtesy of Howard's daughter Alice Barts Sroufe.)

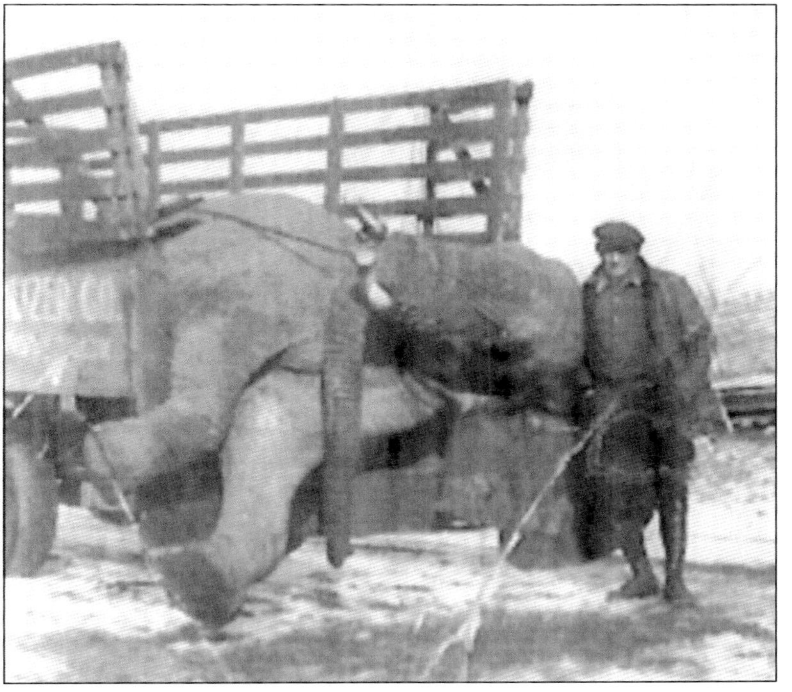

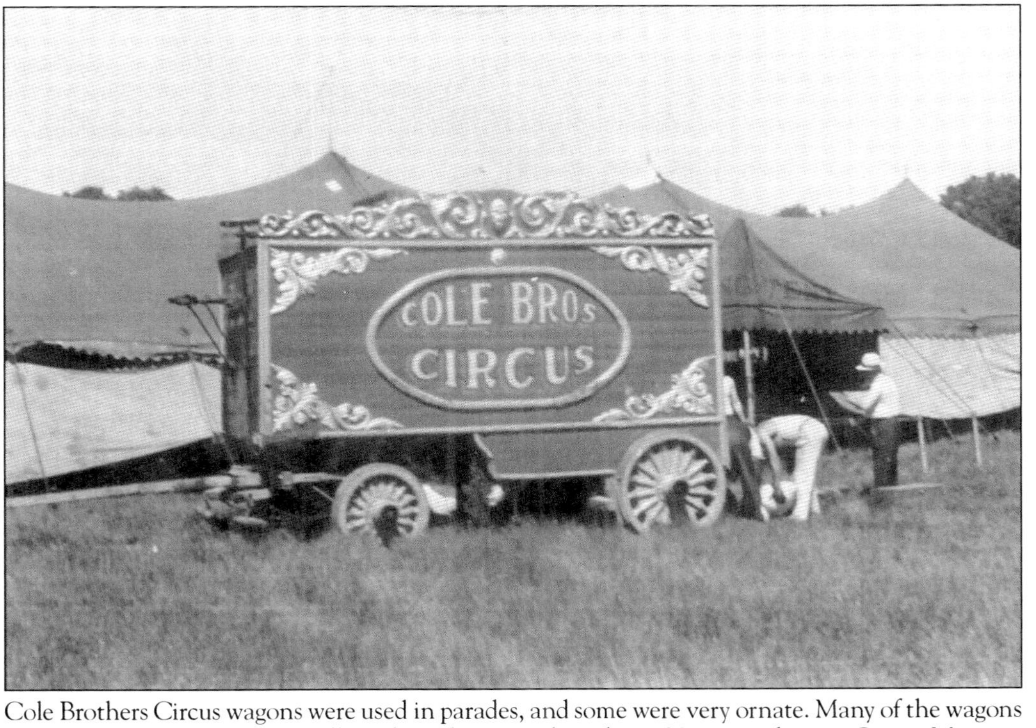

Cole Brothers Circus wagons were used in parades, and some were very ornate. Many of the wagons sat deteriorating at A. C. Bradley's farm for years, but about 20 were taken to Circus Museum at Baraboo, Wisconsin, and restored in the 1960s. They can be seen there, and postcards are available that state they are from Cole Brothers Circus at Rochester, Indiana.

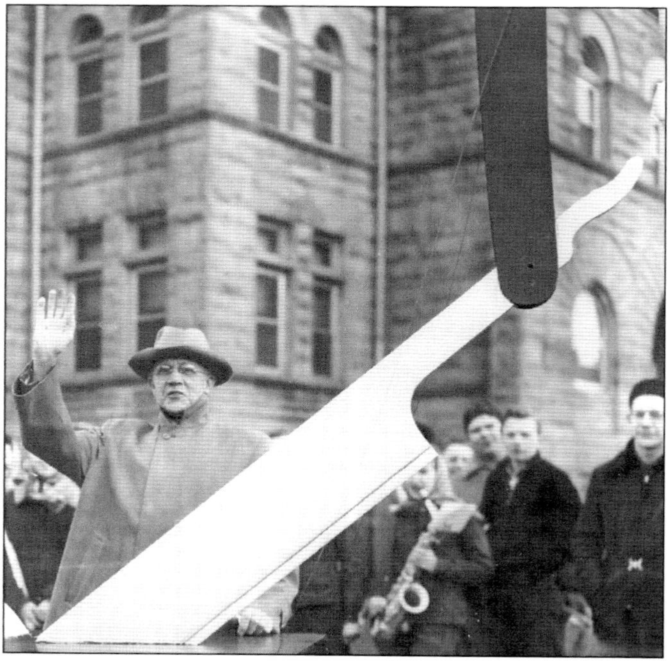

Mayor Robert Shafer buried the razor and declared the beginning of the Rochester centennial celebration in early 1953. The city's men declared themselves "Brothers of the Brush" and let their beards grow for a beard contest in July. Rochester was incorporated as a town in 1853 and as a city in 1910. (Courtesy of *Rochester Sentinel.*)

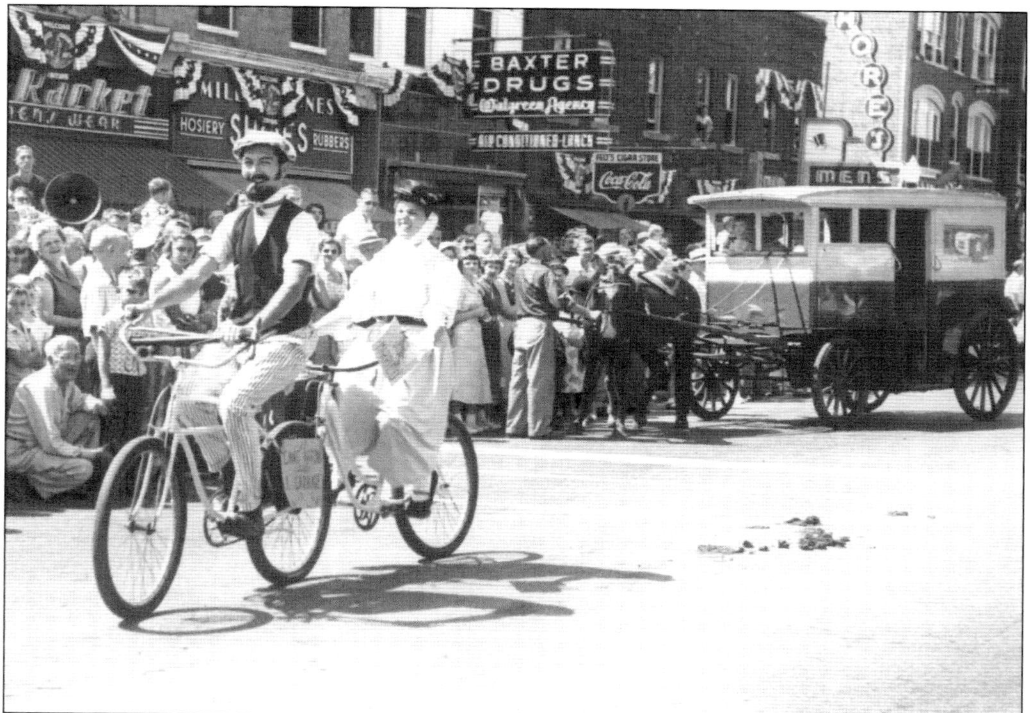

The Rochester centennial parade on July 4, 1953, featured many historic exhibits (such as this bicycle built for two), people dressed in 1853 attire, and horse-drawn buggies and wagons—even an ox team. Centennial week featured a style show, a box social, the Century on Parade pageant at the fairgrounds, a square dance, wrestling, music, pony races, a husband-calling contest, and more.

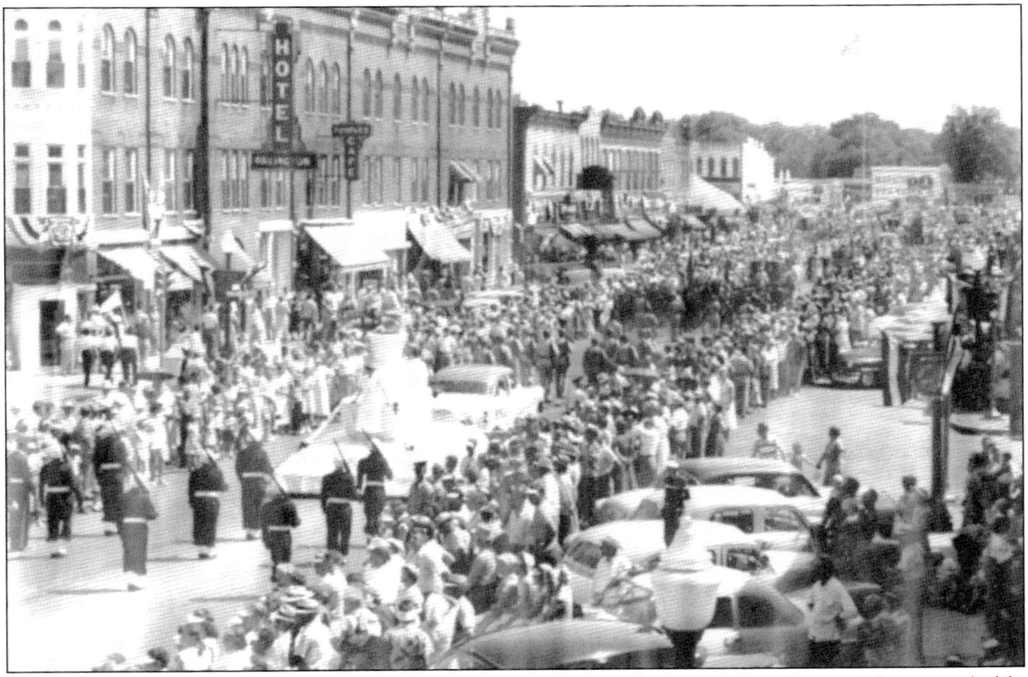

The centennial parade started at the north and traveled south down Main Street. This is probably the tail end of the parade, which began at 2:00 p.m. on a Saturday. A special edition of the *Rochester Sentinel* featured many old photographs. A Rochester centennial book was published with many interesting stories of local history.

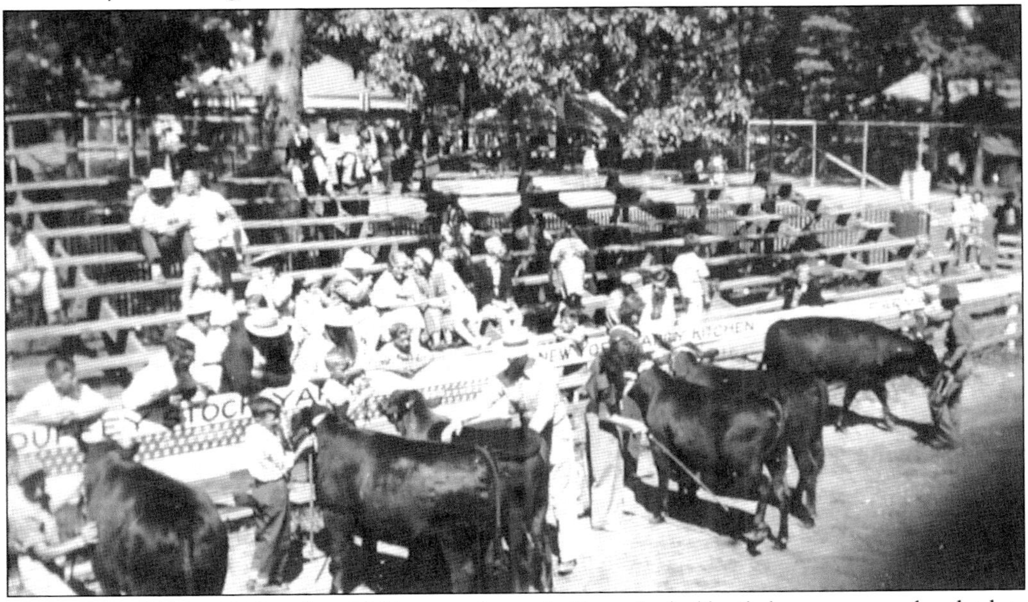

The 4-H Beef Show 1941 at the old fairgrounds was held on the half-mile horse racetrack, which is now the drive around the city park. Note the ads for Duffy Stockyards, New York Candy Kitchen, and Farmall tractors. The log cabin in the background was moved to Fulton County Historical Society grounds in 1985. Fulton County Fairs started in 1857 but changed to 4-H in 1918.

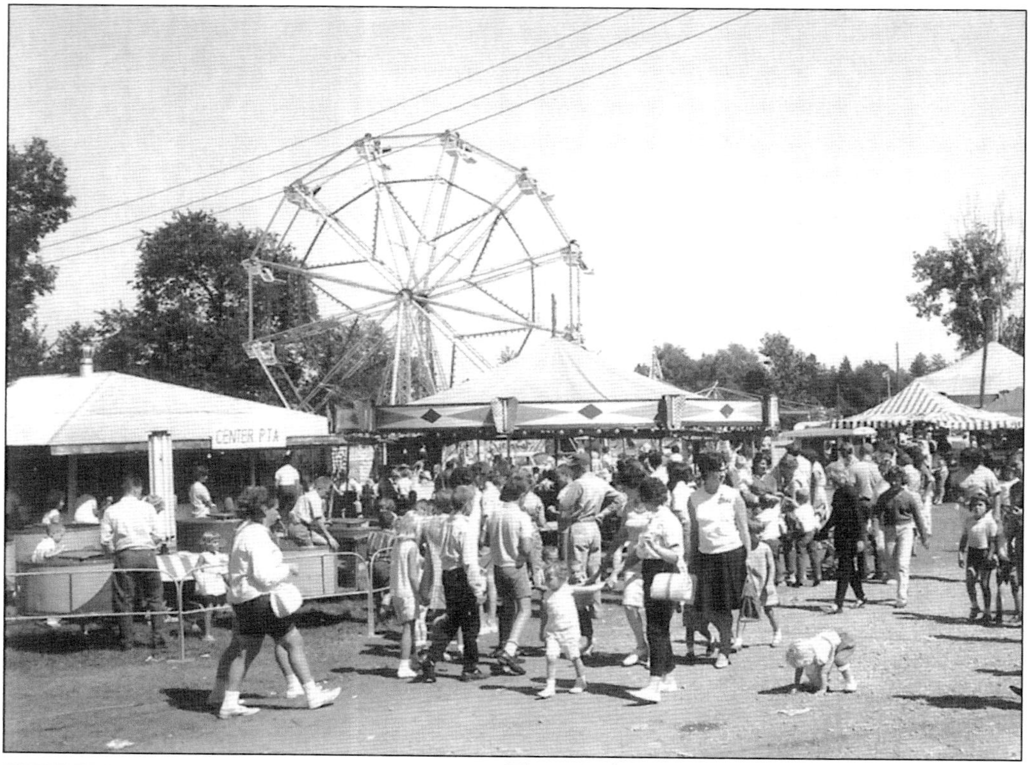

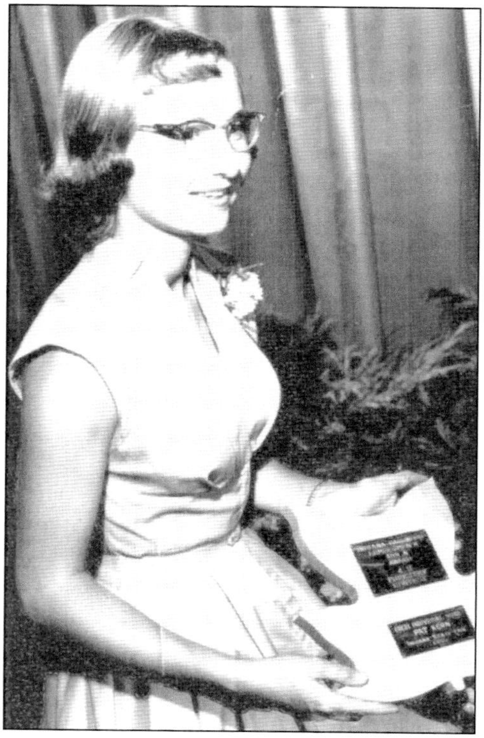

The 4-H fair in 1965 had a Ferris wheel for rides. The 4-H fair was moved to its present grounds in 1955. To raise money to purchase the land and construct buildings, the community held an auction of donated tools and items, with auctioneer Arkie the Arkansas Woodchopper of WLS Chicago radio Barn Dance fame. (Courtesy of Fulton County REMC)

Patricia Kern, daughter of Bob and Ruth Kern, won first place for forestry at the Indiana State Fair in 1955. She made a life work of botany, earning her doctorate at the University of Washington, Seattle, in 1968. She was director of the New York Botanical Garden's herbarium from 1968 to 2000, when she retired. She and her husband, Noel Holmgren, authored several books on botany. (Courtesy of her sister Shirley Kern Needham.)

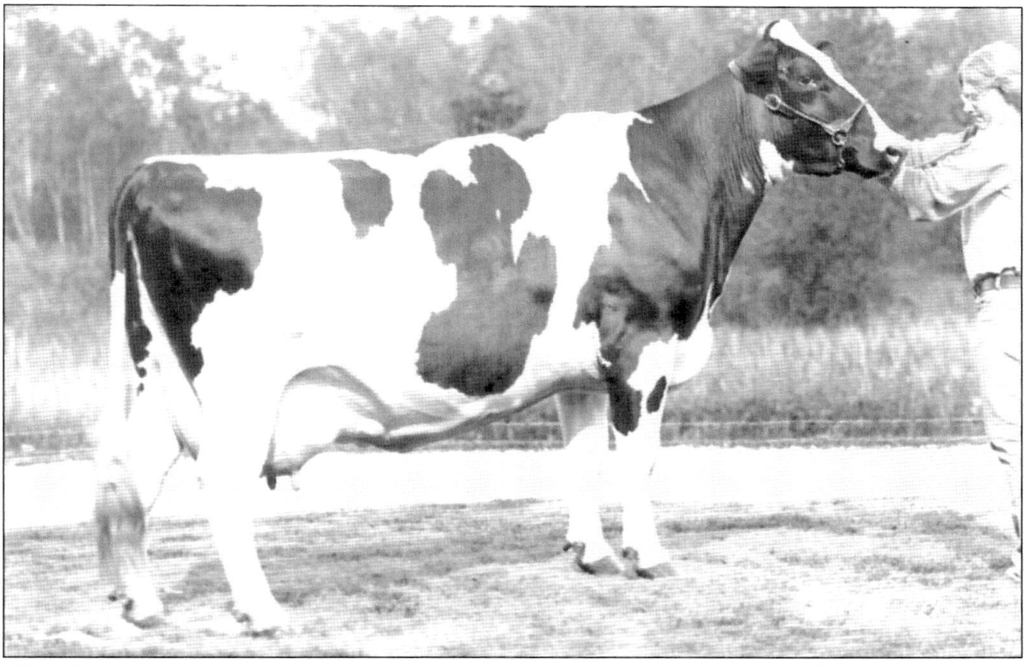

Ellen the cow was in the *Guinness Book of World Records* as the world's top milk producer, a record that stood from 1975 to 1992. A registered Holstein, Ellen was owned by Harold and Norma Beecher and their eight children. She was the 4-H project of their son Stan (in photograph). She produced 55,661 pounds of milk in one year. People came from all over the world to see her. Semen from her bull calves was sold, thus increasing milk production in many countries.

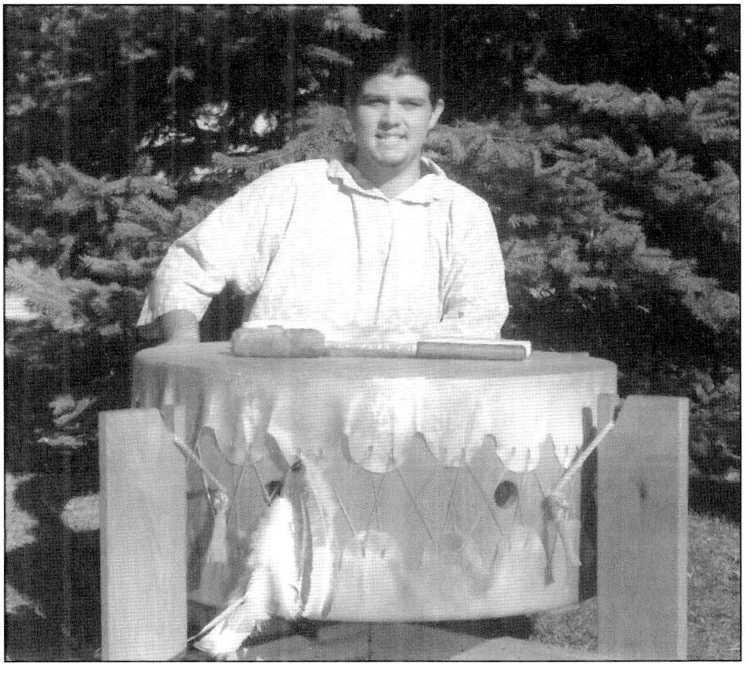

Jeremy Flook displays his American Indian drum and drum sticks, which won Grand Champion for Other Crafts and Sweepstakes Award at the 2009 Indiana State Fair. The drum reflects his Cherokee and Potawatomi heritage, which he learned from his grandparents, Joan and Roy McClellan, and great-grandparents, Edna and Chet Carpenter. He made the shell of wood and the heads and lacing of elk hide. (Courtesy of his mother, Kathleen McClellan Flook.)

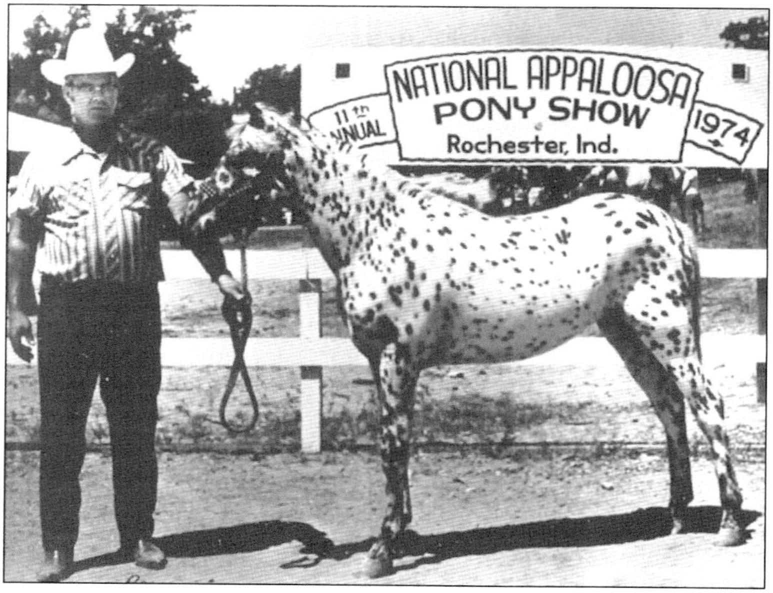

Robert Smith, Ray Smiley, and Don Smiley founded National Appaloosa Pony, Inc. (NAPI), in 1963 in Rochester. Don Smiley, shown here in 1974, raised Appaloosa ponies on his farm on what is now Dogwood Drive. At the NAPI shows, Don's daughter Beth showed her pony, Manitou Squaw. Robert's daughter Glendon Smith showed her pony, Tippecanoe Jake.

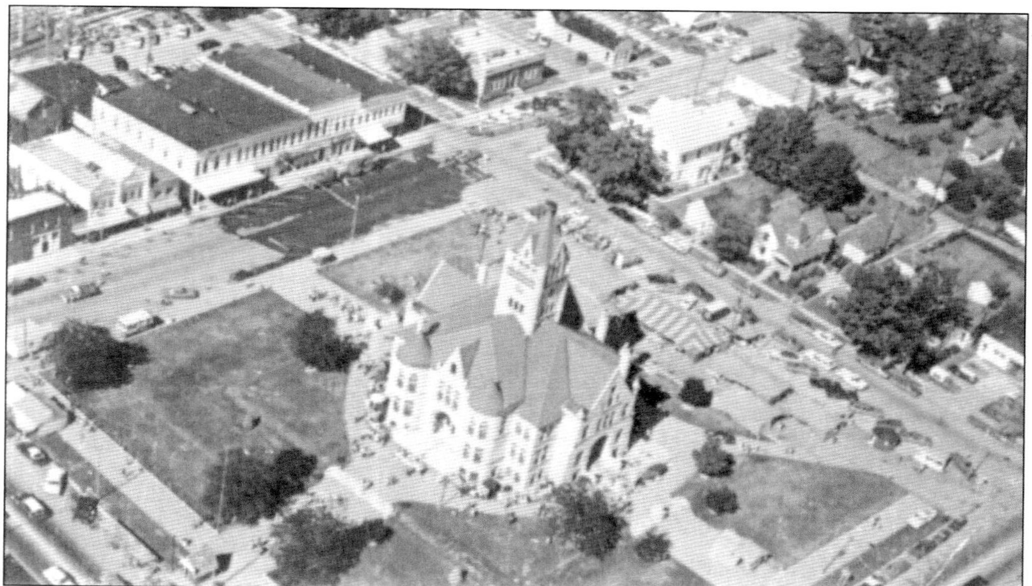

The Round Barn Festival was started in 1971 as an art show. This aerial view shows artists' exhibits around the courthouse sidewalks and tents on Eighth Street and on the courthouse's east side parking lot. The festival has grown and now occupies Main Street from Ninth through Sixth Streets, as well as east and west on Eighth Street and the whole courthouse square.

Frances Pfeiffer, chairman of the Round Barn Festival (RBF), and her husband, Forest, drive a 1912 Lincoln truck in the 1978 parade. In the back of the truck are flight bags of Western Saddle Club of Rochester, England, who came to perform at the RBF. The truck was donated to the Fulton County Historical Society by Carl Zartman in 1973. Hot weather caused RBF to switch its parade to twilight.

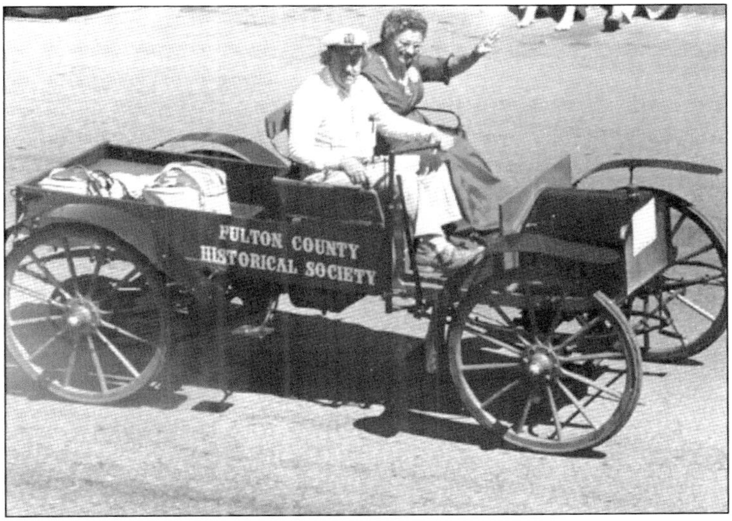

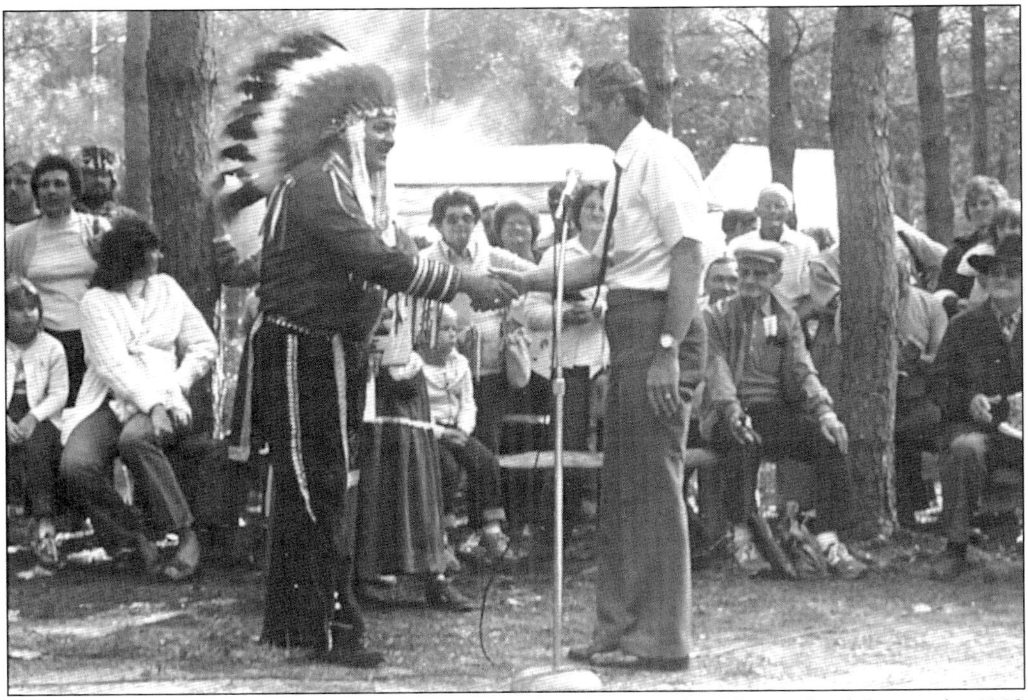

Rochester mayor Don Cook welcomes Frank Wano, Potawatomi hereditary chief, during the 1983 Trail of Courage, held for nine years in Bob Kern's pine woods on Tippecanoe River and U.S. 31. Cook presented the chief with a key to the city. Wano was among a delegation of Citizen Band Potawatomi from Shawnee, Oklahoma. He was a descendant of Chief Shipshewano, who was on the Trail of Death forced removal in 1838.

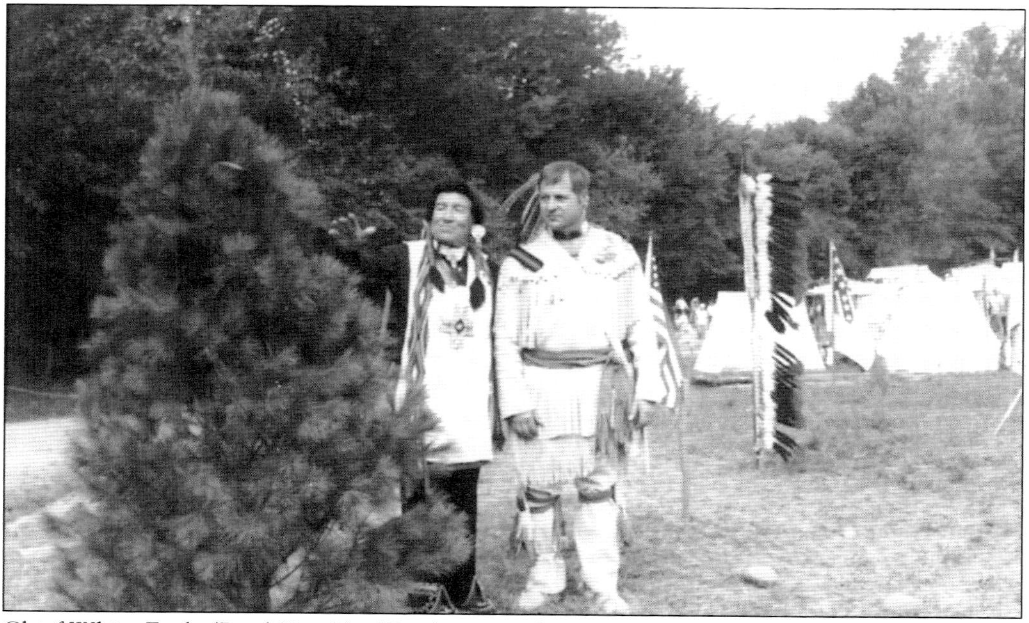

Chief White Eagle (Basil Heath) of Rochester and Ron Hall (right) conducted the Great Peace Tree ceremony at the Trail of Courage Living History Festival in 1988. Bob Kern donated the white pine tree, which was planted on top of two crossed tomahawks to symbolize putting aside the instruments of war or "burying the hatchet," an ancient Iroquois ceremony. Actual peace tree roots with tomahawks have been discovered in Indiana.

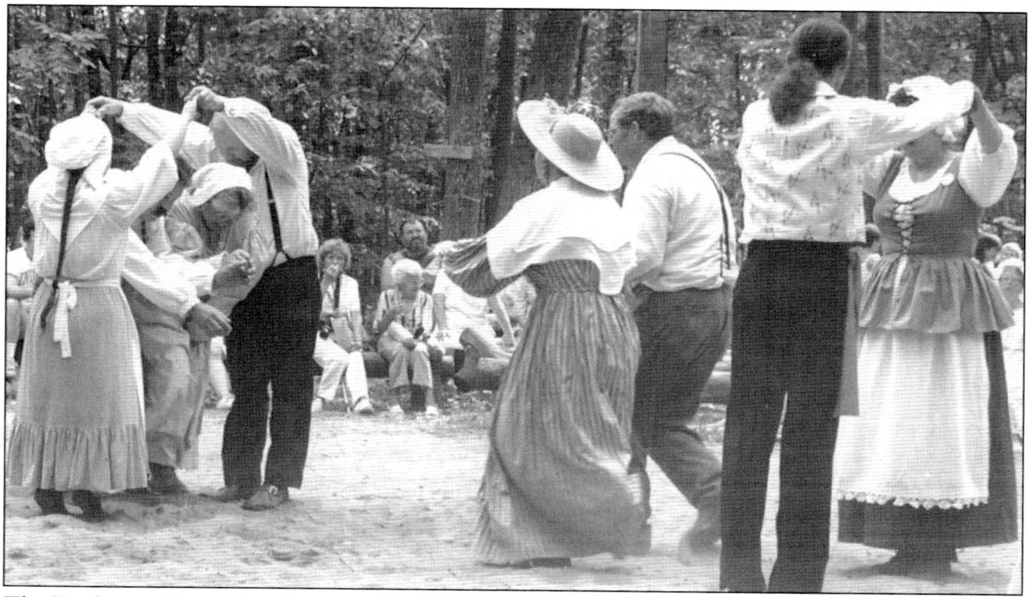

The Rochester Heymakers historic dance troupe performed at 1988's Trail of Courage. Rochester's Jean Clements, the dance teacher, dances at right with Tippecanoe's Melvin Fretz. The middle couple is Plymouth's Jennifer Laffoon and Rochester's Bill Willard. At left, Gloria Baloy of Mishawaka and Raymond "Doc" Clements of Twelve Mile form London Bridge for Winamac's Christine and Bob Smith to go under.

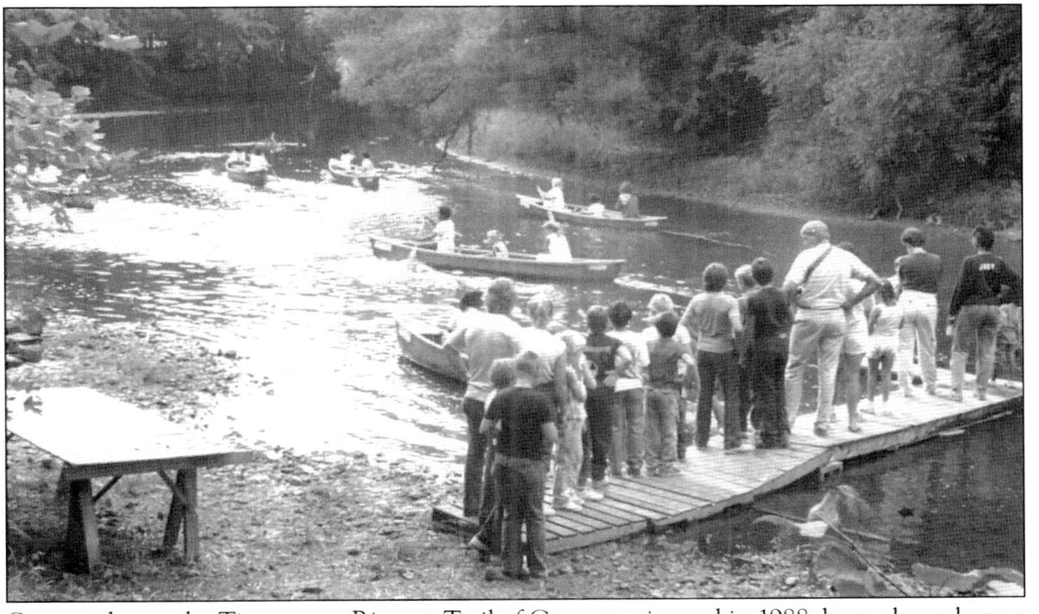

Canoe rides on the Tippecanoe River at Trail of Courage, pictured in 1988, have always been a big hit with the public. Germany Bridge Campgrounds owner Paul Bardsley brought the canoes. Bardsley retired in 1997 and sold his campground and canoes, but canoe rides continue at the Trail of Courage with different sponsors.

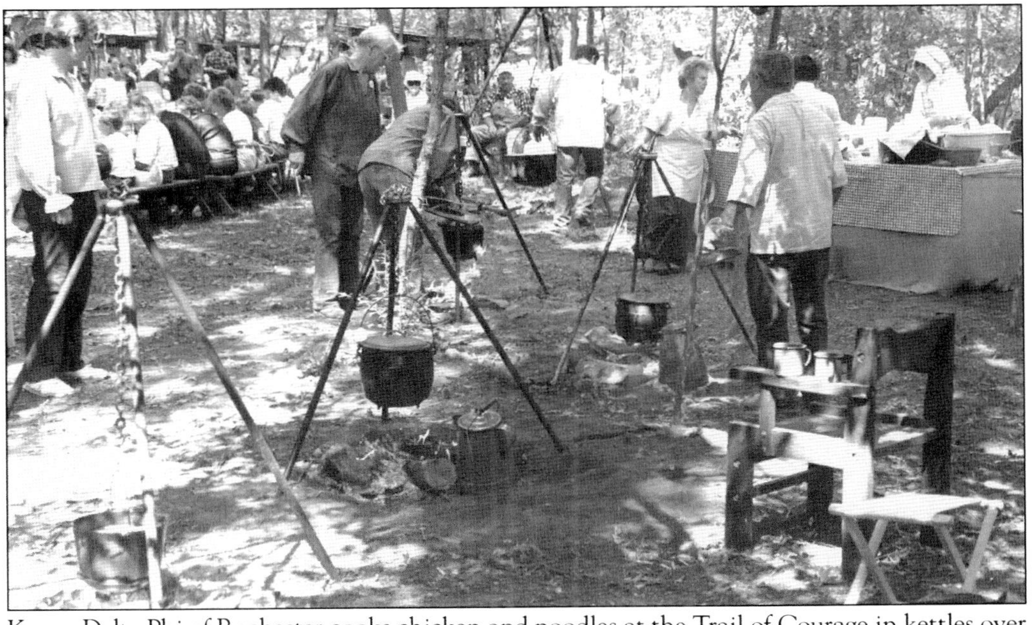

Kappa Delta Phi of Rochester cooks chicken and noodles at the Trail of Courage in kettles over wood fires in 1988. This has been a perennial favorite ever since. All foods at this pre-1840 living history festival are cooked over wood fires. Many are cooked in big iron kettles. Volunteers in period clothing learn to cook as their ancestors did to preserve historic skills and earn money for their group's project.

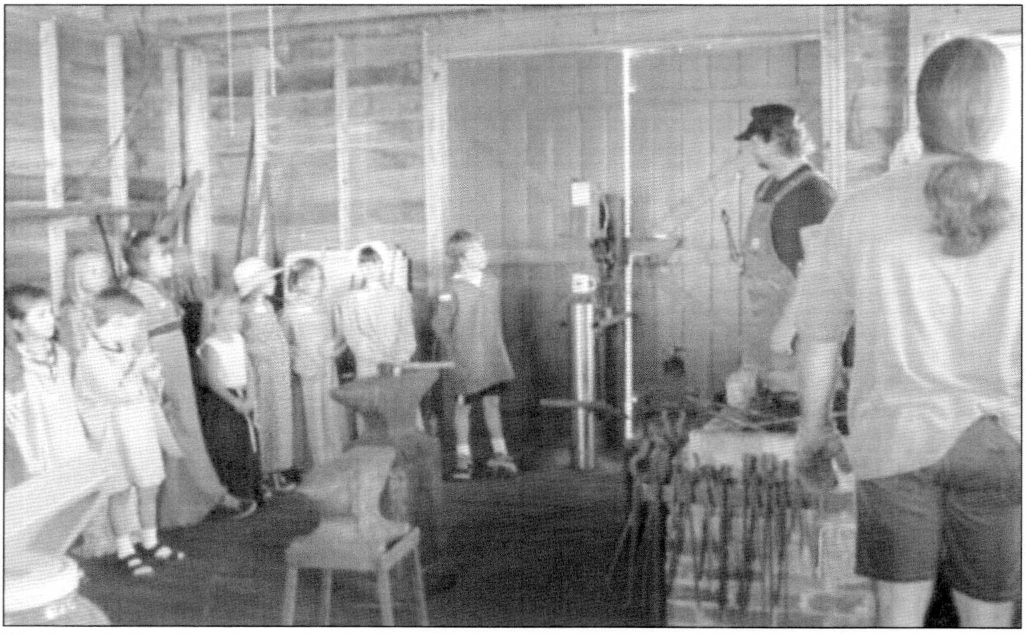

Blacksmith Ray Boardman demonstrated ironworking in 2001 on the forge in the Sutton-Terock Memorial Blacksmith Shop, built by the Indiana Blacksmithing Association in 1997. The replica shop is located south of the Round Barn Museum in the Living History Village called Loyal, Indiana. Loyal is named for a real village west of the museum, originally called Germany but renamed during World War I.

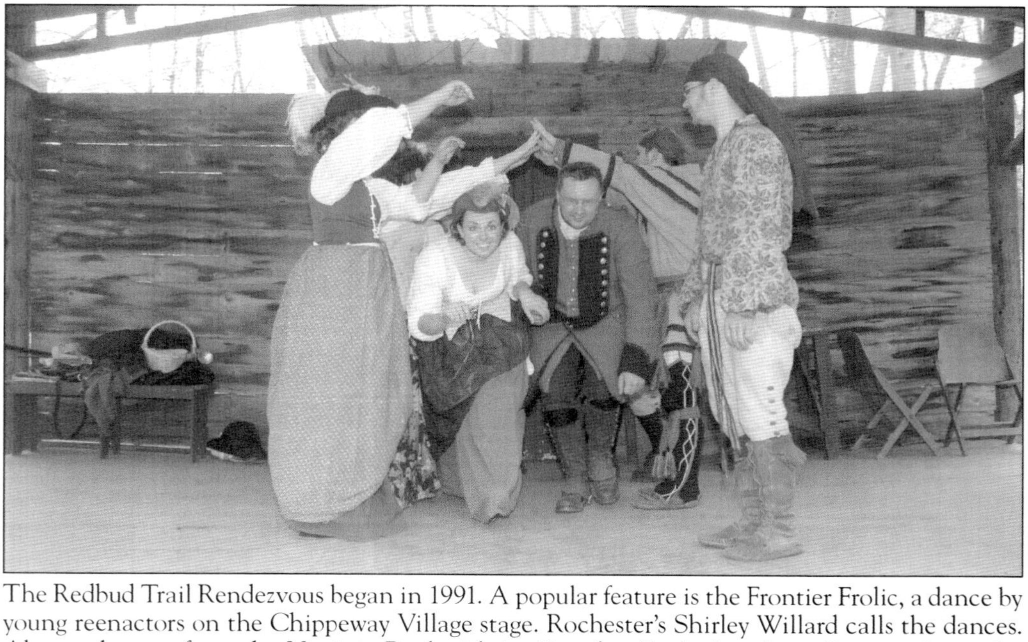

The Redbud Trail Rendezvous began in 1991. A popular feature is the Frontier Frolic, a dance by young reenactors on the Chippeway Village stage. Rochester's Shirley Willard calls the dances. Above, they perform the Virginia Reel with its "London Bridge" ending. Coming down the center are Kali Edwards of Watervliet, Michigan, and Rochester's Kevin Kennedy. (Courtesy of *Rochester Sentinel*.)

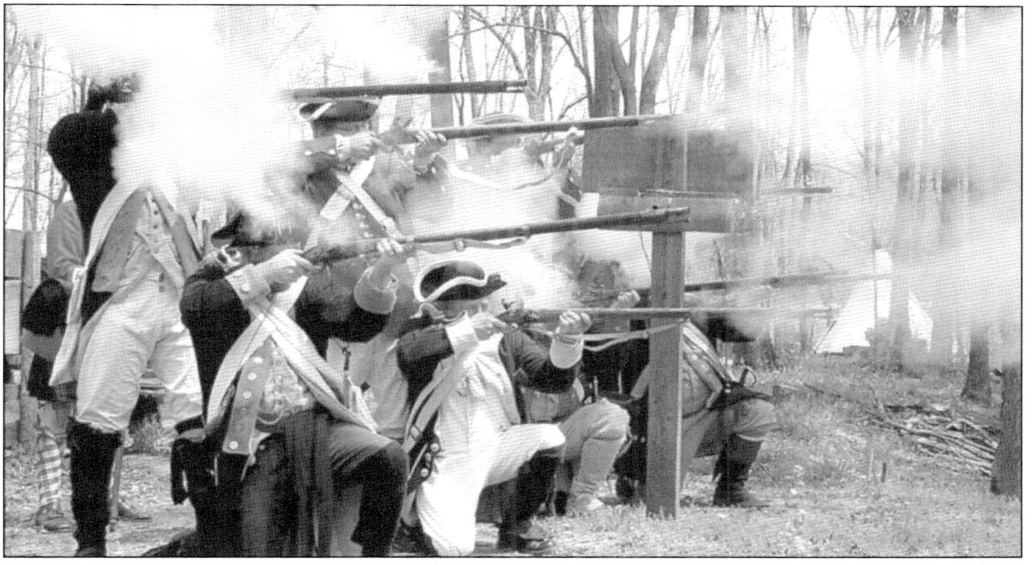

Revolutionary War reenactors shoot at the shooting range made of gravel hauled by the Fulton County Highway Department. Like the Trail of Courage, the Redbud Trail Rendezvous celebrates frontier Indiana. Both have historic camps from the French and Indian War, voyageurs, War of 1812, Plains Indians, and Woodland Indians. Rendezvous events feature pre-1840 trade goods spread out on Hudson's Bay blankets and traditional skills and crafts such as spinning, basketry, flintnapping, sewing, and blacksmithing.

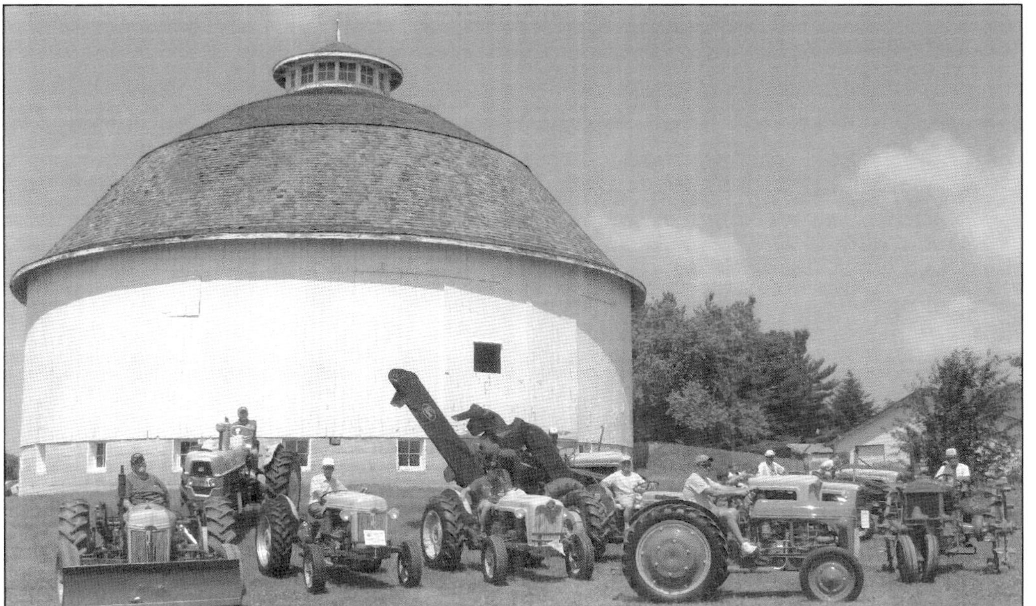

The Round Barn Museum provides a backdrop for antique Ford tractors during the Fulton County Historical Power Association show, held June 19–21, 2009. The featured local business was Jim Streator's Ford New Holland Sales. Began in 2003, the show has tractor and horse pulls, John Henry tug-of-war contests, exhibits of hit-and-miss engines, steam engines, a 1915 sawmill, model railroads, and other action-filled entertainment.

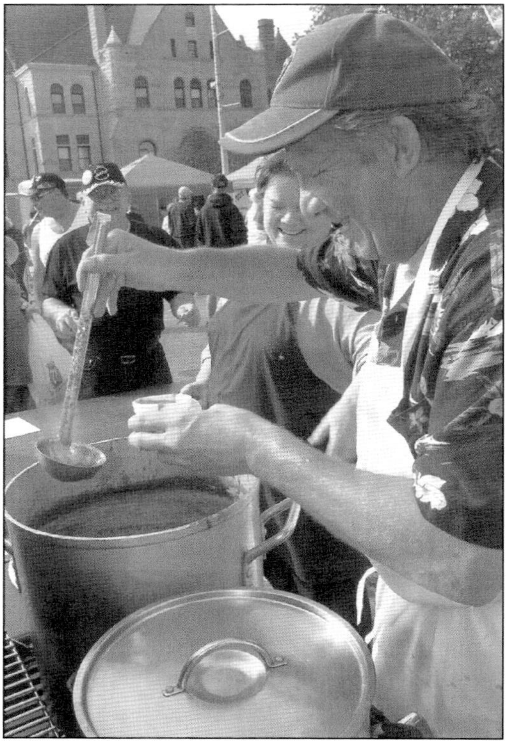

The Chili Cook Off, sponsored by the chamber of commerce each October, was established in 1992. Shown here in 2008, Norman McGwinn, owner of the Dug Out, dips his chili. Local businesses sign up to enter teams of volunteer cooks. The Dug Out had been the Brass Rail, then Manitou Bar and Grill. The name was changed to the Dug Out when Ed Fansler bought it in 1981. (Courtesy of Mike Kenny, *Rochester Sentinel* photographer.)

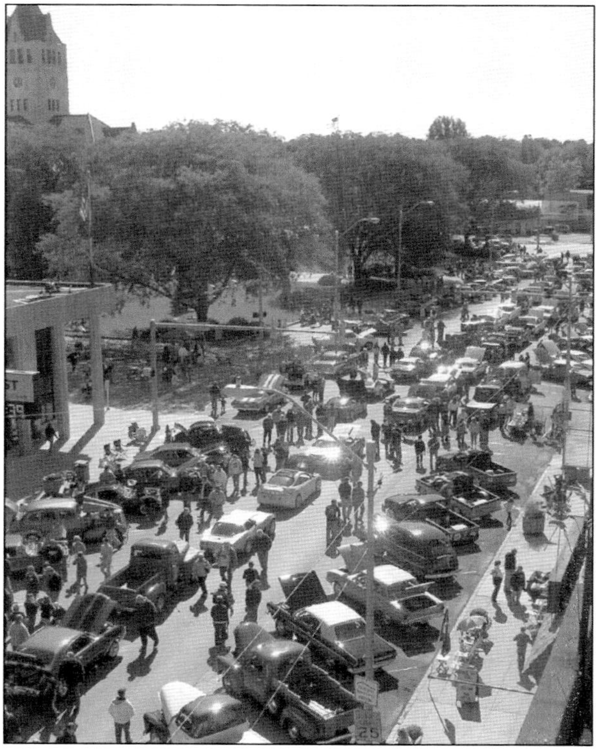

The Red Hot Car Show filled Main Street on October 10, 2009. *Sentinel* photographer Mike Kenny took this photograph from the top of Bailey's Hardware at 712–714 Main Street. Sponsored by the Rochester–Lake Manitou Chamber of Commerce, the Red Hot Car Show began in 1996. Held with the Chili Cook Off the second weekend of October, it draws a big crowd. (Courtesy of Mike Kenny, *Rochester Sentinel* photographer.)

Ten

Recreation and Clubs

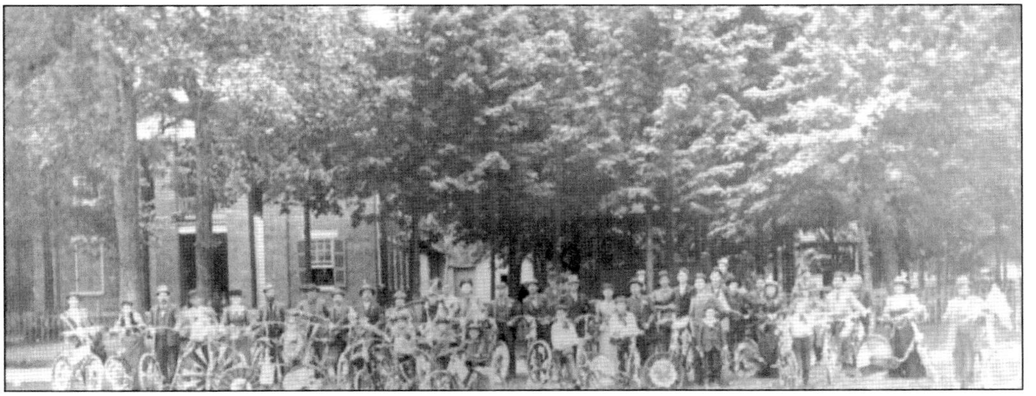

Rochester Cycle Club met for rides to the lake, river, and other interesting places. Pictured here on Memorial Day, 1892, in front to the old courthouse and its big trees, some of the people are the Frank Terrys, the William Zellers, LeRoy Meyers, Henry Myer Jr., Al Myers, Jim Terry, Albert Bitters, Delmond Ward, Oz Davis, Abel Bowers, George Adams, Herman Tetzlaff, Jacob Crim, and Harry Bitters, age seven (right).

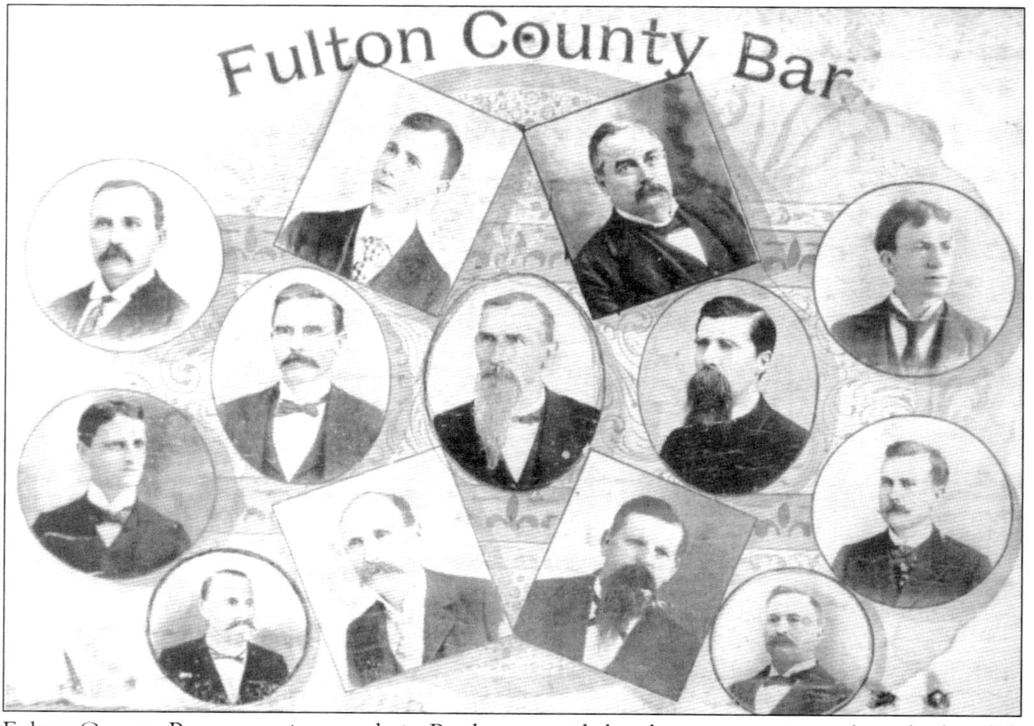

Fulton County Bar was a cigar made in Rochester, with local attorneys pictured on the box lid. Attorneys are Bernetha, Baker, Montgomery, Myers, Essick, Conner, Campbell, Metzler, Bibler, Holman, Rowley, Wagoner, and Stephenson. In 1909, Rochester made a million cigars each year in six cigar factories and smoked half that many more. Rochester men spent $50,000 for homemade cigars and about $25,000 for out-of-town brands.

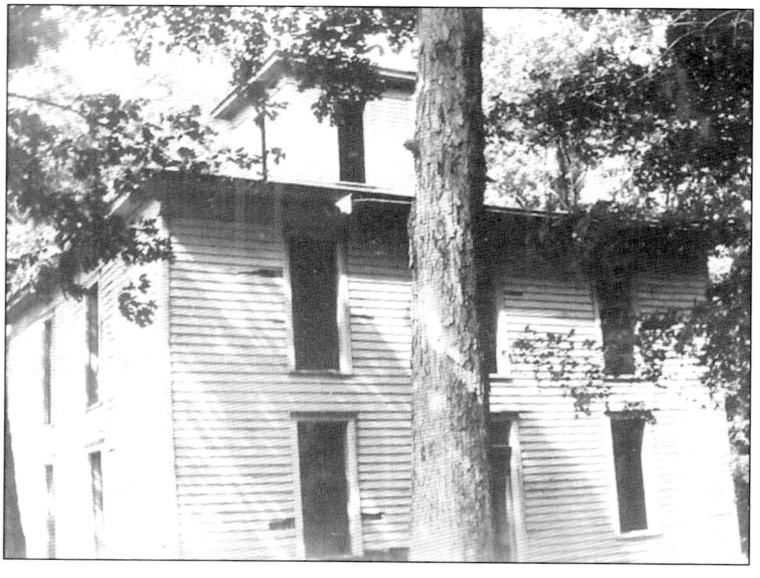

The Mineral Wells Hotel (Feece's Flowing Well and Sanitarium) southeast of Rochester was a spa for relaxation and cures by soaking in mineral water. Founded in 1890 by Rev. Billy Feece, it drew people from as far away as California and New York to take the waters until it closed in 1922. On Sundays, evangelistic services were held in a wooded grove. (Courtesy of Joe Wildermuth.)

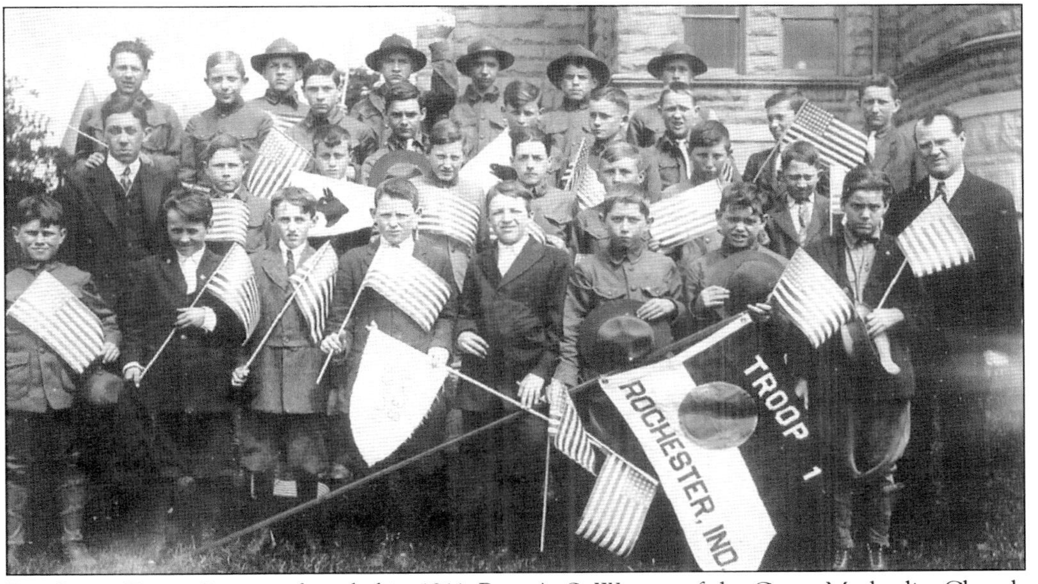

Boy Scout Troop One was founded in 1911. Rev. A. S. Warner of the Grace Methodist Church was the first Scoutmaster. They had summer camps along the Tippecanoe River. In 1914, they hiked to Michigan City and took the boat to Chicago. When Three Rivers Council (TRC) began, this troop became Troop 19. TRC merged with other councils in 1973, and Rochester's became Troop 219. John Jones is Scoutmaster.

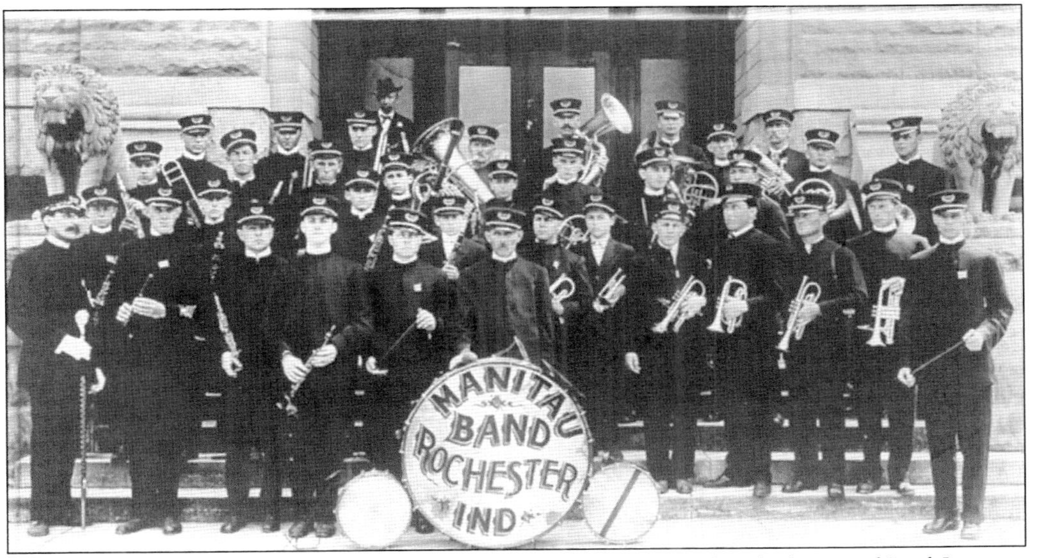

Manitau Band poses in front of the courthouse in early 1900s under the baton of Prof. Lamont Davidson (left front), who taught music at Rochester College and operated a music conservatory here. This was a marching and concert band that gave concerts at the courthouse every week in the summer. The cost of the each band uniform, consisting of coat, cap, and pants, was $11. (Courtesy of *Rochester Sentinel*.)

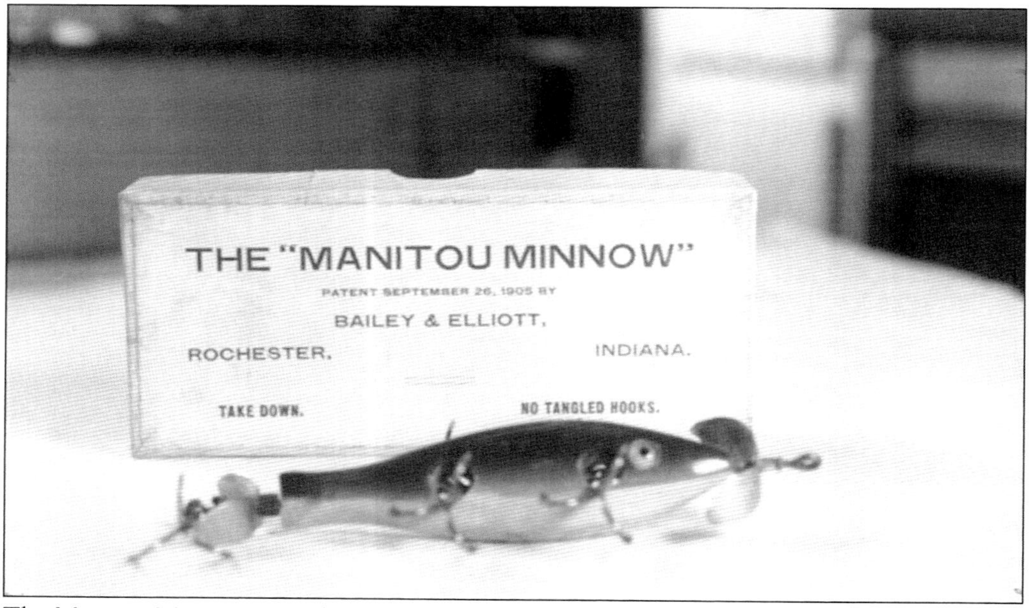

The Manitou Minnow was a bait made and patented on September 26, 1905, by Simon Bailey and George Elliott of Rochester. Elliott and Bailey had a hardware store in the 700 block of Main Street on the west side, then moved to the present location of Bailey's Hardware at 712–714 Main Street. Makers of the Dowagiac Minnow threatened to sue, so Bailey and Elliott stopped making them. This scarce antique bait is very valuable today.

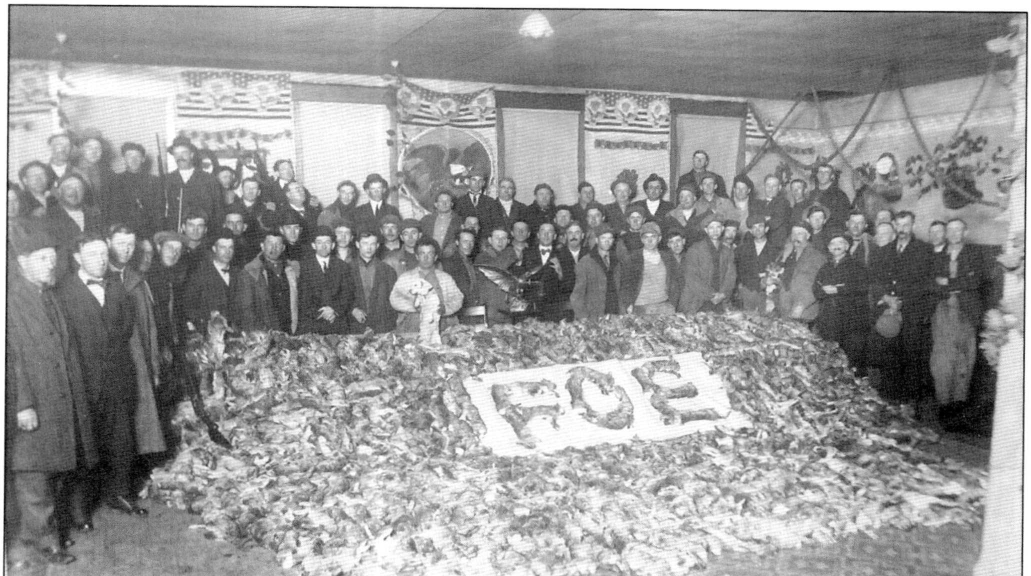

The Eagles lodge displayed the catch from its fifth annual rabbit hunt on November 25, 1915, for a free community dinner at its hall above Zimmerman Brothers Furniture Store at 619 Main Street. The lodge was founded in 1904, six years after the national organization was established in Seattle. Harry Sayger was secretary for 39 years, until his death in 1998. The Eagles built a new lodge hall in 1997 at 1081 East Fourth Street and have 802 members.

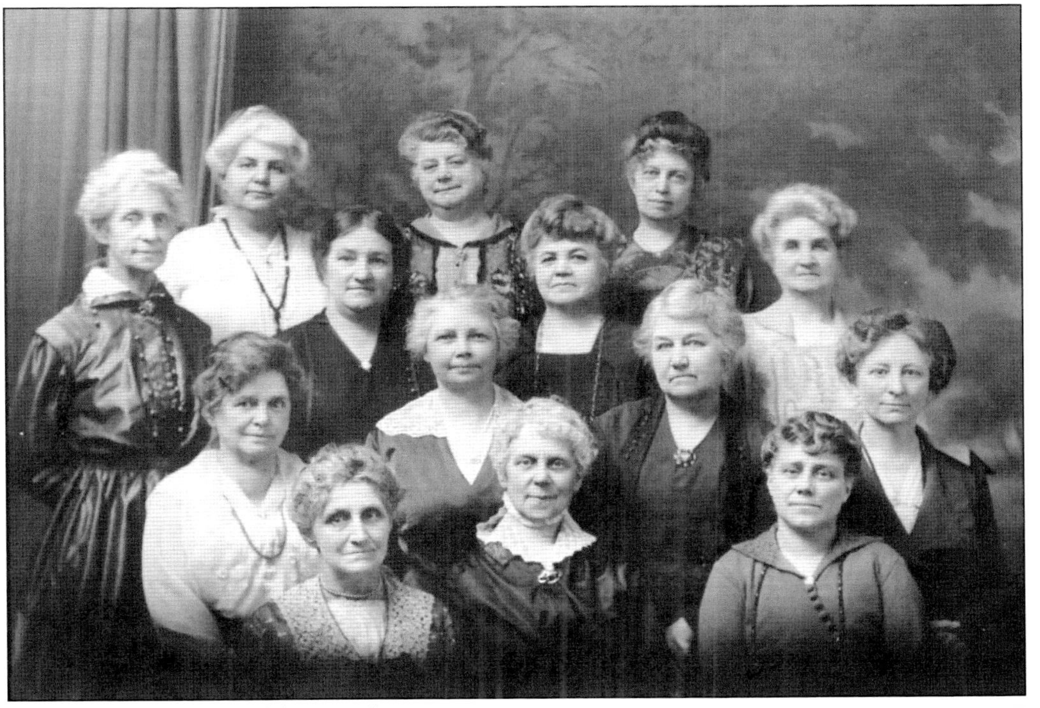

The Manitou chapter of the Daughters of the American Revolution began in 1908. Members were Mary Brackett Plank, Alwilda Dillon Barnhart, Rose Keith Gould, Mary Clayton Sisson, Sara Merriam Brackett, Mahala Troutman Myers, Cynthia Schuler Townsend, Estella Mitchell True, Elizabeth Stanton Sterner, Ellen Robbins Rannells Barr, Catherine Rannells Brackett, Estella Lyon Reiter, Emma Sterner Rannells, and Leila Copeland Smith. The Manitou chapter of the DAR celebrated its 100th anniversary in 2008.

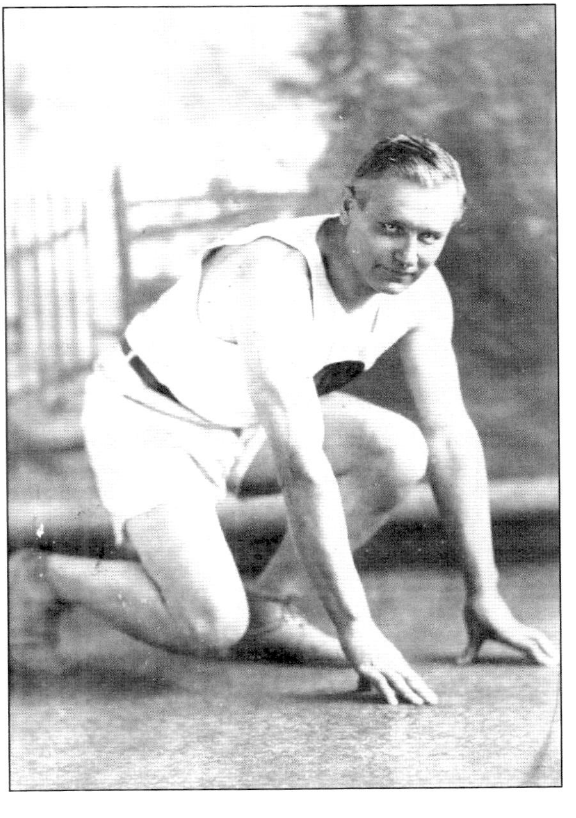

Mitchell Baker was one of the world's best long-distance runners and competed in many meets and some Olympic games. He won a 1920 marathon and was presented a large trophy that is at the Fulton County Museum today. Baker attended Rochester College and Purdue University and became an attorney. He lived at Lake Manitou and was buried at the Shelton Cemetery in 1943.

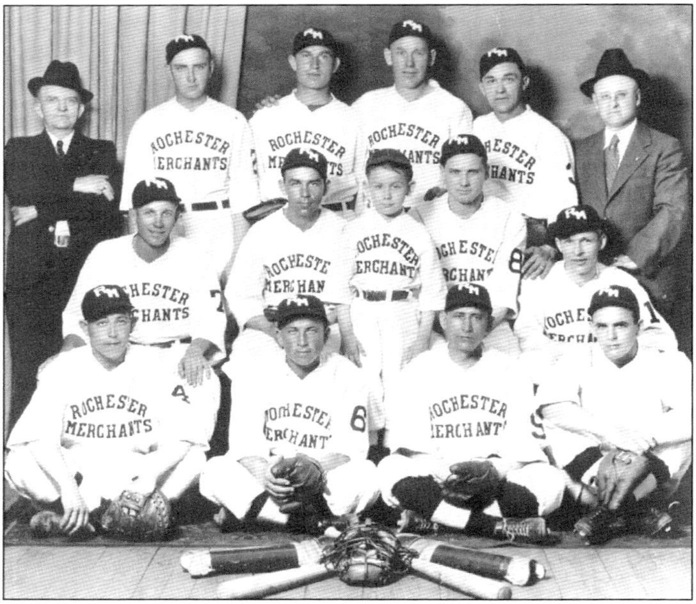

Rochester merchants sponsored this baseball team in 1935. They played other semi-pro teams across northern Indiana. From left to right are (first row) Clyde Lyle, Forest "Frosty" Skidmore, Albert "Pop" Skidmore, and Phil Hartung; (second row) Tony Smith, Hank Skidmore, Bud Smith (bat boy), Charles Smith, and Roy Haggerty; (third row) Alf Carter (secretary-treasurer), Joe Woodcox, Vic Skidmore, George Smith, Jack Wilson, and Jess Shelton (manager). (Courtesy of *Rochester Sentinel*.)

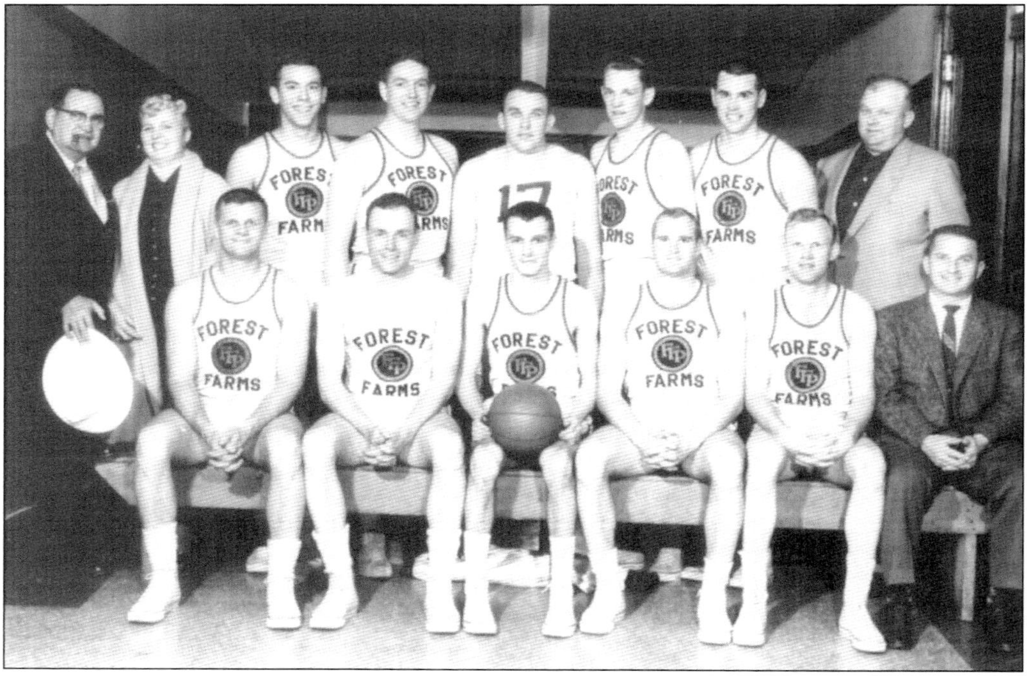

Bob Moore's hog feed business, Forest Farms, sponsored Buttermilk Bob's basketball teams in the 1950s. Pictured here from left to right are (first row) Ralph Pederson, John Stauffer, Paul Buzzard, Phil McCarter, Bill Schroer, and coach Wayne Smith; (second row) Bob Moore and wife Belle, Bud Lantz, John Nelson, Tom Miller, Forrest Jackson, Carl McNulty, and scorekeeper Gerald Knauff. Moore would treat them to steak dinners after they played and included their wives and girlfriends. (Courtesy of Dave Burkett.)

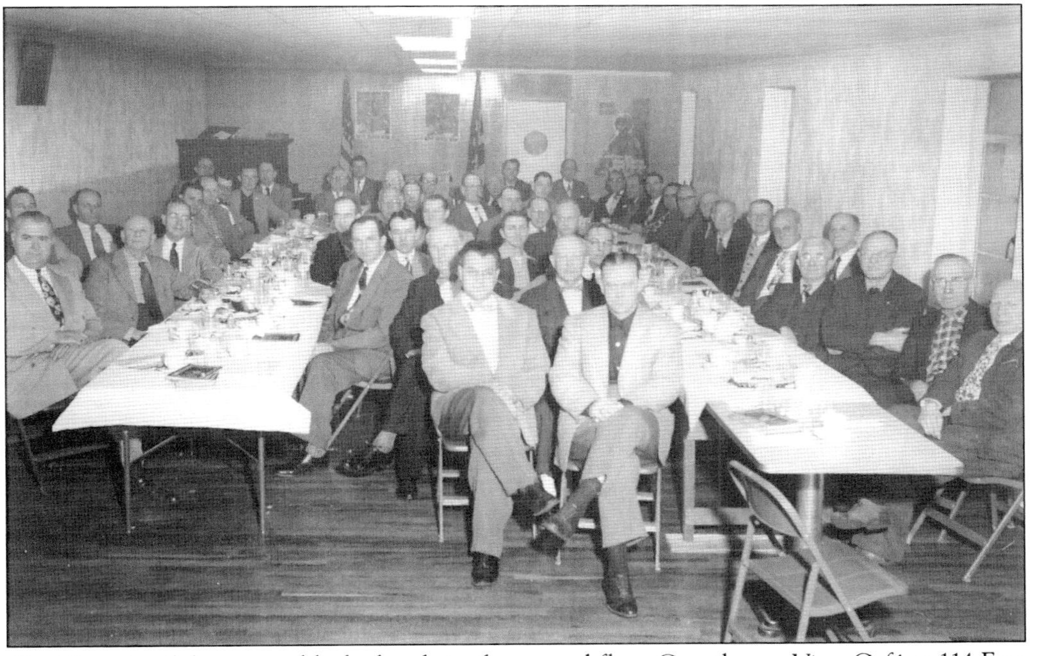

The Kiwanis Club met weekly for lunch in the second-floor Courthouse View Café at 114 East Eighth Street. Shown above in 1955, the Rochester Kiwanis Club began in 1929 with a banquet at the Fairview Hotel. It served as a chamber of commerce until the present chamber of commerce was established in 1948. (Courtesy of Vi Seiwert, Kiwanis secretary/treasurer.)

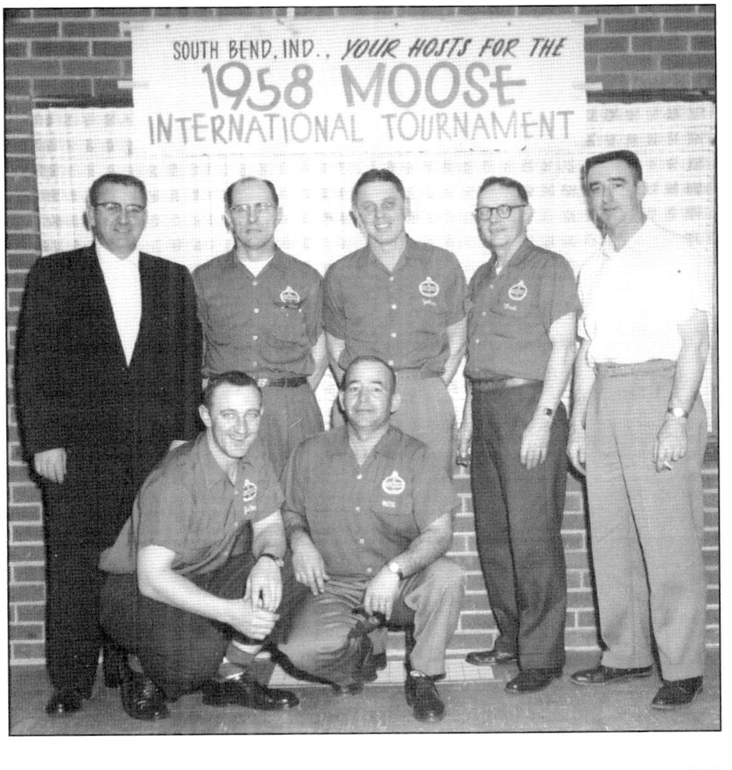

In 1958, Rochester Moose members participated in the Moose International Bowling Tournament in South Bend. Seen here from left to right are (first row) Bob Jackson and Bill Skidmore; (second row) Jacob Miller, William Kurz, John Vernon, Fred McKee, and Ed Richard. No one remembers if they won or not, but they had a lot of fun. (Courtesy of Louise Skidmore Vernon.)

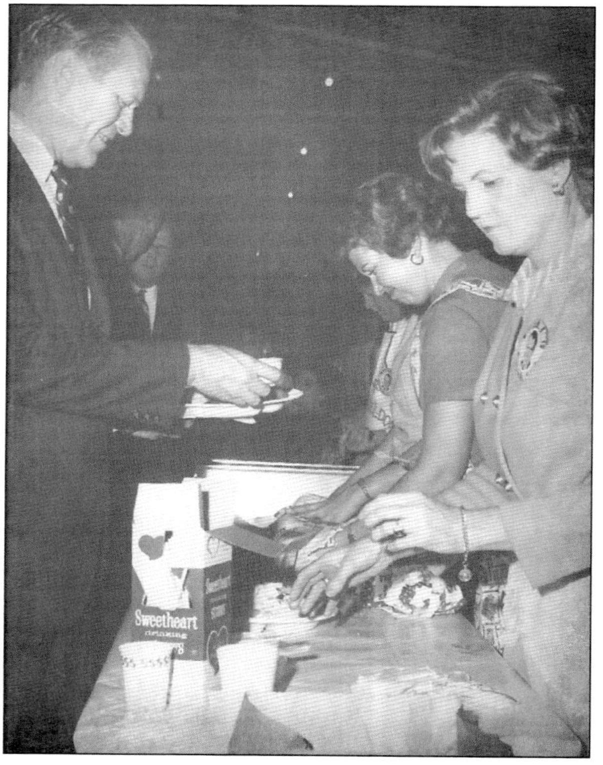

Future president Gerald Ford attended a local fish fry sponsored by the Republicans in 1966. Fish fries by the famous Akron Jonah Club, founded in 1938, provided a means for groups to earn money. Ernie Hiatt, a member, bought the Jonah Club's equipment when they disbanded in 1978 and still cooks fish. Ford became president when Richard Nixon resigned on August 9, 1974. (Courtesy of James Heyde.)

The Fulton County Players produced one or two plays a year between 1965 and 1988. In 1976, they produced *Cabaret* from November 18 to 20 on the RHS auditorium stage. From left to right, the Kit Kat Klub Girls were (first row) Sandy Parker, Ruth Mercer, and Sue Zartman; (second row) Judy Teel, Kathi Barnett, Jody Schnarel, Susie McGwire, and Sandy VandenBossche. The theatrical group was reborn as Act II in 2004. (Courtesy of Judy Teel Green.)

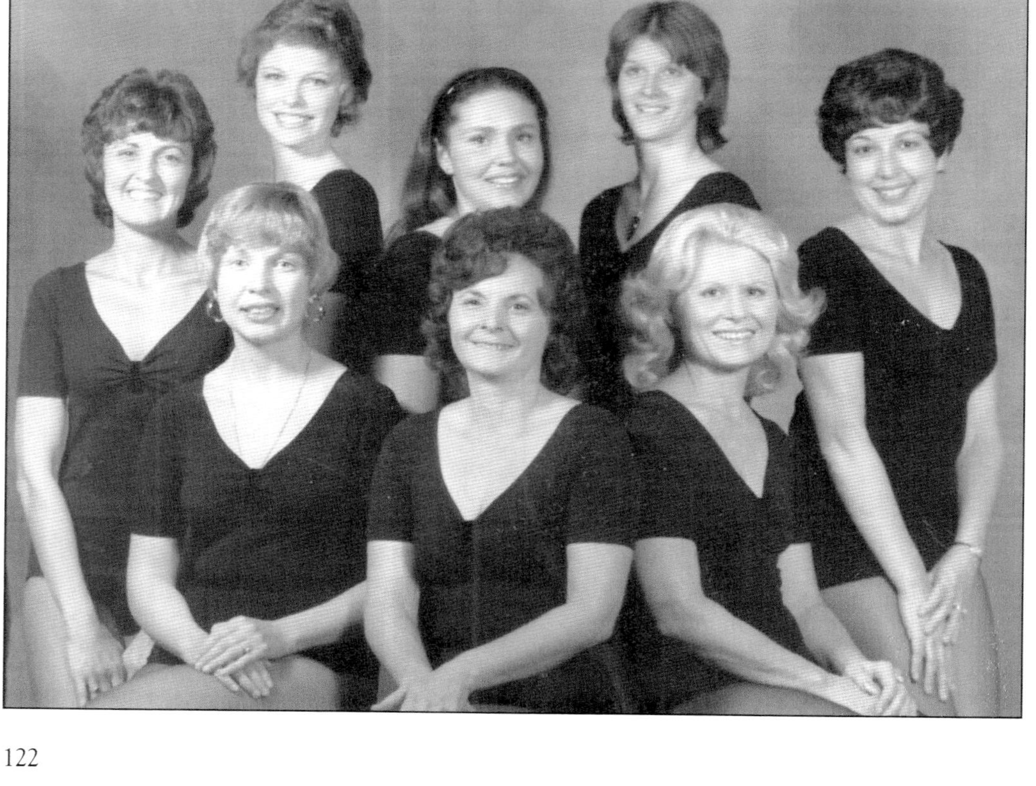

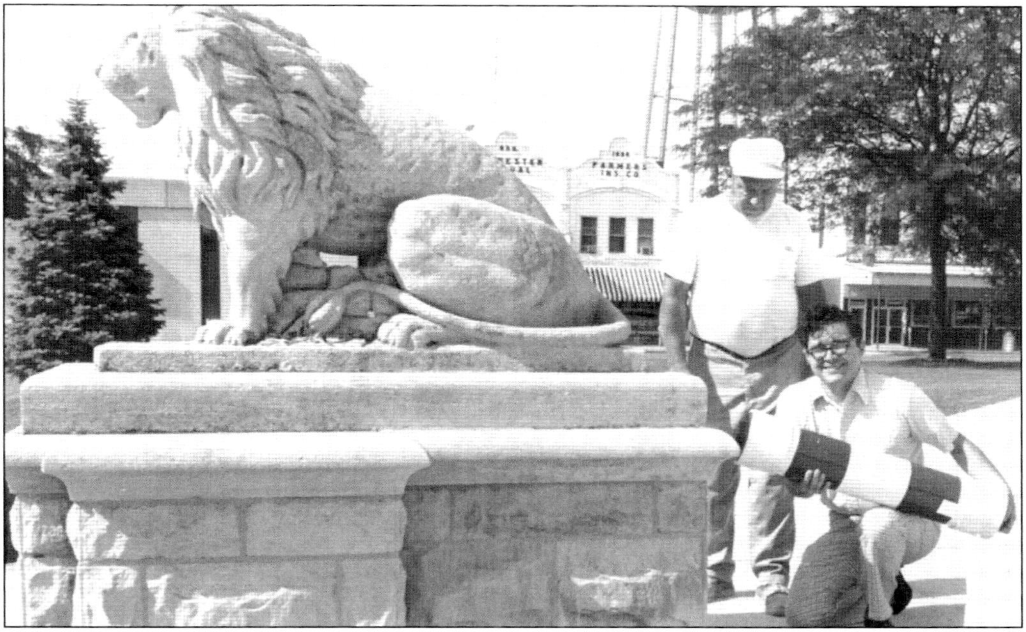

Douglas Morton holds the county bicentennial time capsule, prepared by the Rotary Club, while John Wagoner, bricklayer, stands ready to cement it into an opening under the lion on the west side of the courthouse on July 4, 1978. The polyvinyl chloride tube was crammed with articles representing current lifestyles in the county by a committee headed by Dr. P. J. Bohm. The capsule is to be opened July 4, 2078.

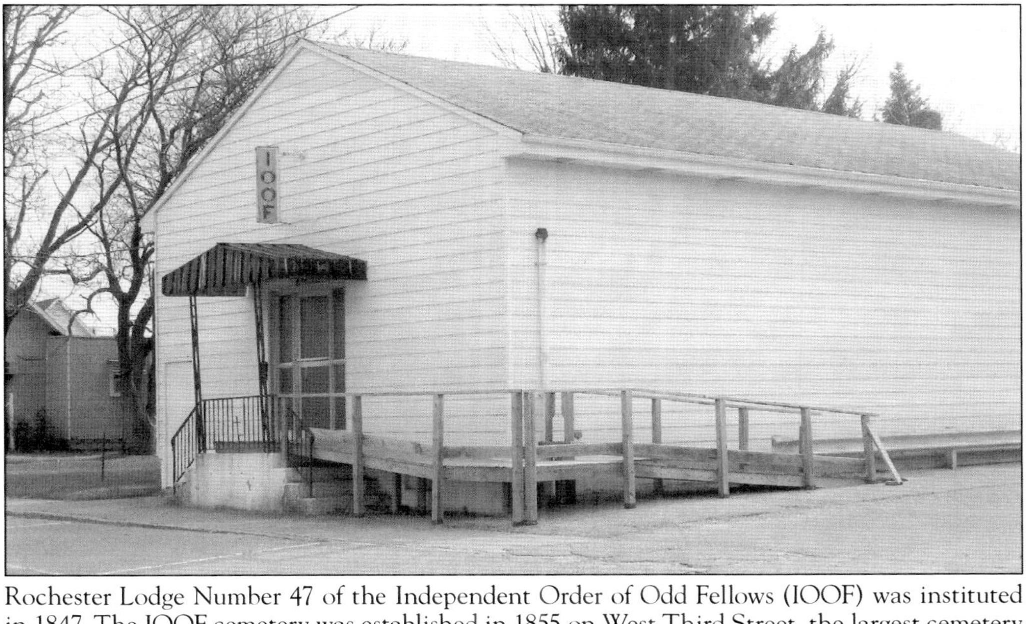

Rochester Lodge Number 47 of the Independent Order of Odd Fellows (IOOF) was instituted in 1847. The IOOF cemetery was established in 1855 on West Third Street, the largest cemetery in Fulton County. The group built its lodge at Main and Ninth Streets in 1870 with a meeting room on the second floor. It bought the Nazarene church at 217 East Seventh Street in 1965 and moved there (above). Rebekkahs use the kitchen downstairs for their annual suppers.

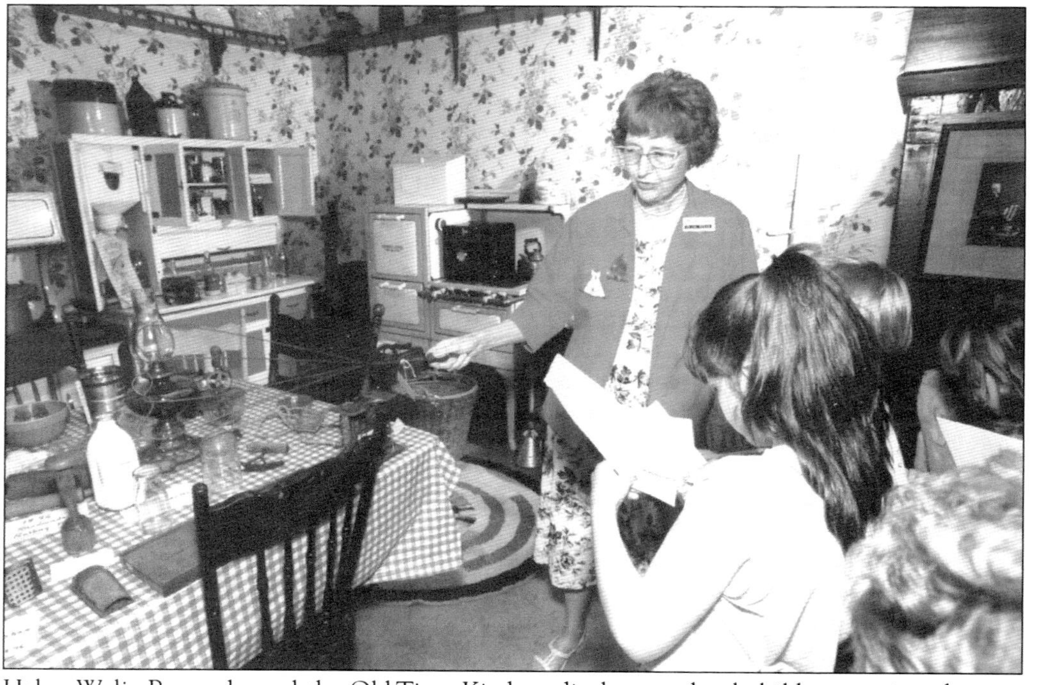

Helen Wylie Reese showed the Old-Time Kitchen display to school children touring the new Fulton County Museum in 1990. The students are filling in a treasure hunt with four pages of questions. Many volunteers served as guides for the school tours of the museum, round barn, and living history village called Loyal, Indiana.

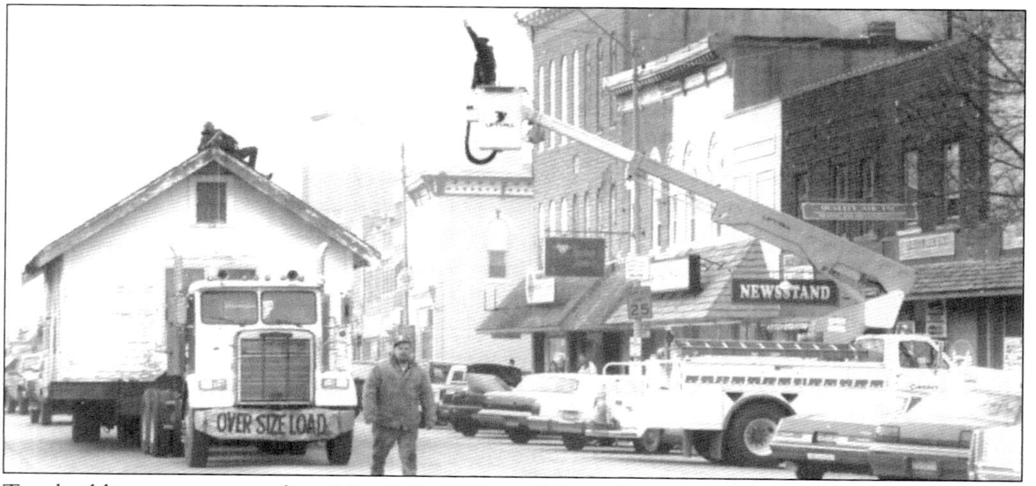

Two buildings were moved on March 2, 1998, to Fulton County Historical Society grounds. A 1910 house from 126 West Ninth Street became a 1920s General Store thanks to Rochester Telephone Company and the Solid Waste District. The former fish hatchery office (above) became an Old-Time Doctors and Dentists office thanks to Dr. Winfield S. Shafer's granddaughters, Barbara Shafer Leaverton and Elizabeth Shafer Strauss. (Courtesy of Mike Kenny, *Rochester Sentinel* photographer.)

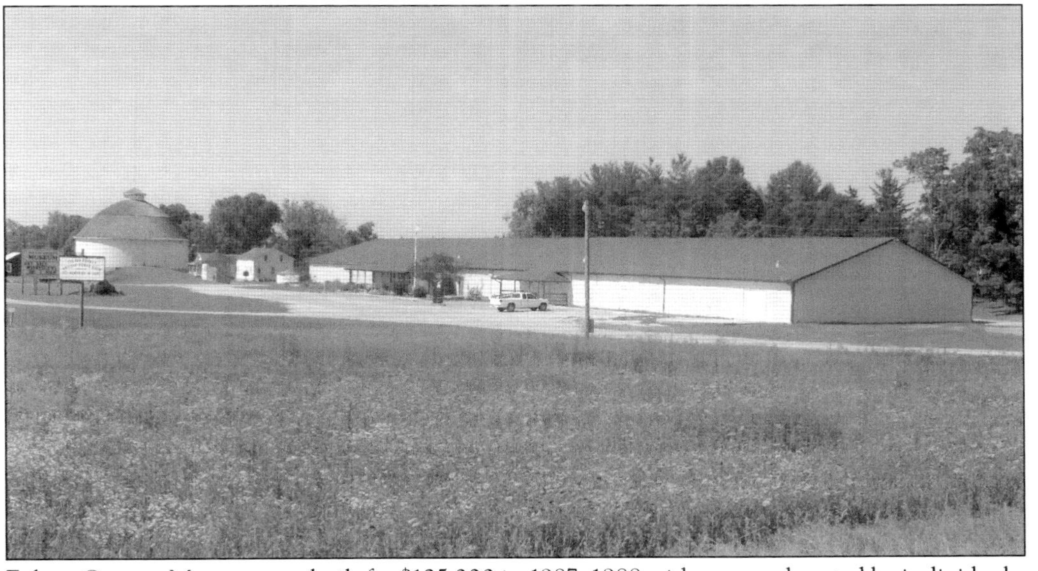

Fulton County Museum was built for $125,000 in 1987–1988 with money donated by individuals, businesses, and groups. The Leedy-Partridge-Paxton round barn was moved and restored from tornado damage in 1990–1991. The Polke house was moved in 1993. A 40-foot addition and Tetzlaff Reference Room, thanks to Ruth and Alice Tetzlaff estate, was added in 2001. Richland Center Memorial Hall added 100 feet in 2008 thanks to Richland Township.

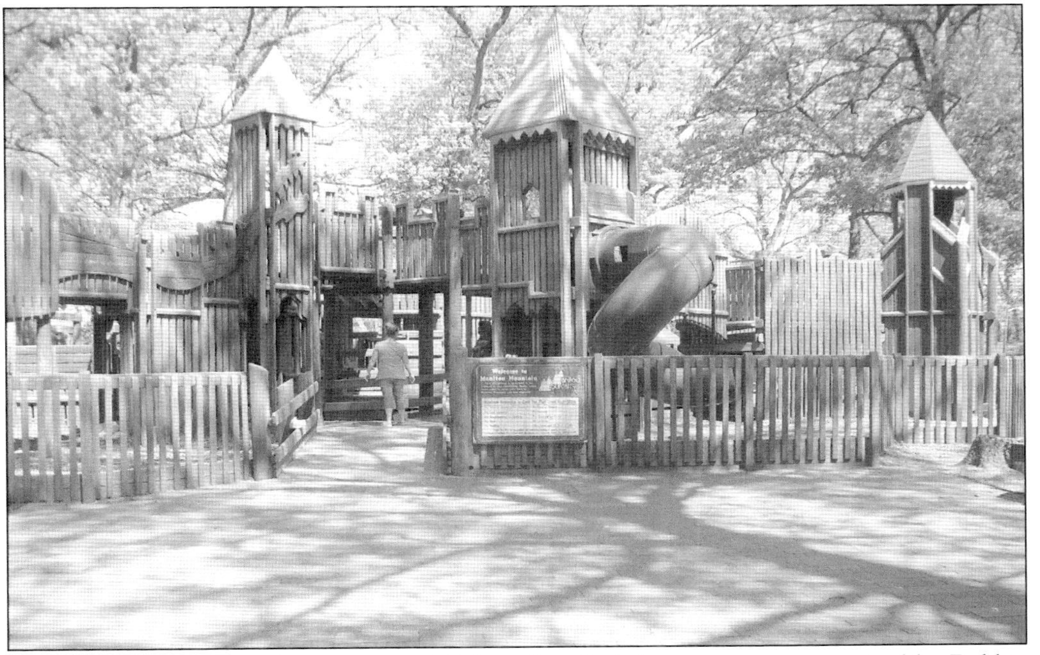

Manitou Mountain was built in June 1998 in City Park by volunteers, organized by Debbie Veenstra, Alison Heyde, and Brenda Downs of the chamber of commerce. Fund-raising brought in $100,000 to pay Leather and Associates, Inc., to provide materials and directions to the hundreds of volunteers. Even children ages five and up helped by soaping the screws and scrubbing tires. Jobs included day care for the workers, providing meals and snacks, and construction.

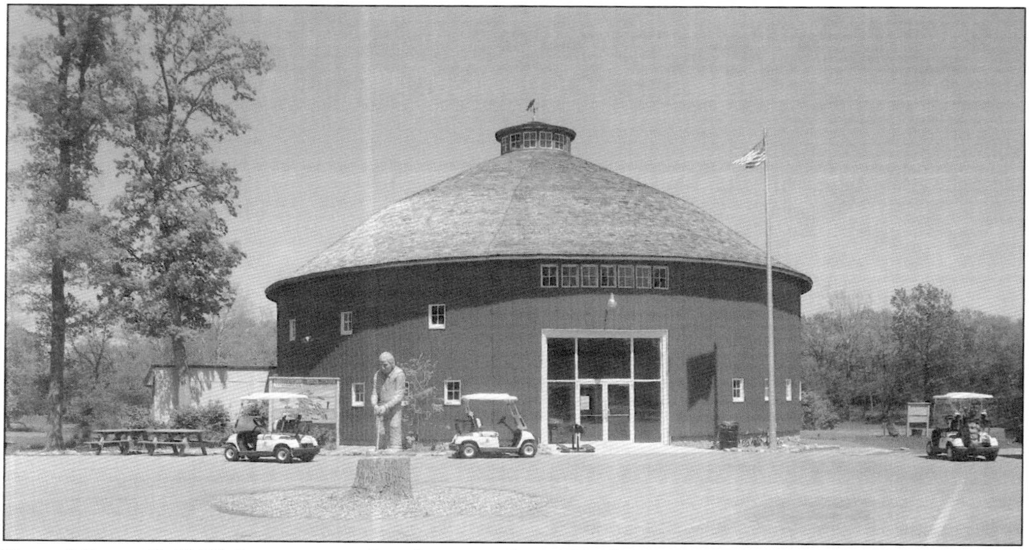

Round Barn Golf Club was moved and restored in 2001 by Amos Schwartz Construction, paid by a grant from Eli Lilly Foundation of $131,000. It was the John Gerig round barn near Akron. Rochester Homes employees and volunteers did the interior. It became the pro shop, which opened in 2005 at Mill Creek Golf Course on East Ninth Street, part of Lakeview Park. The park had been the federal fish hatchery.

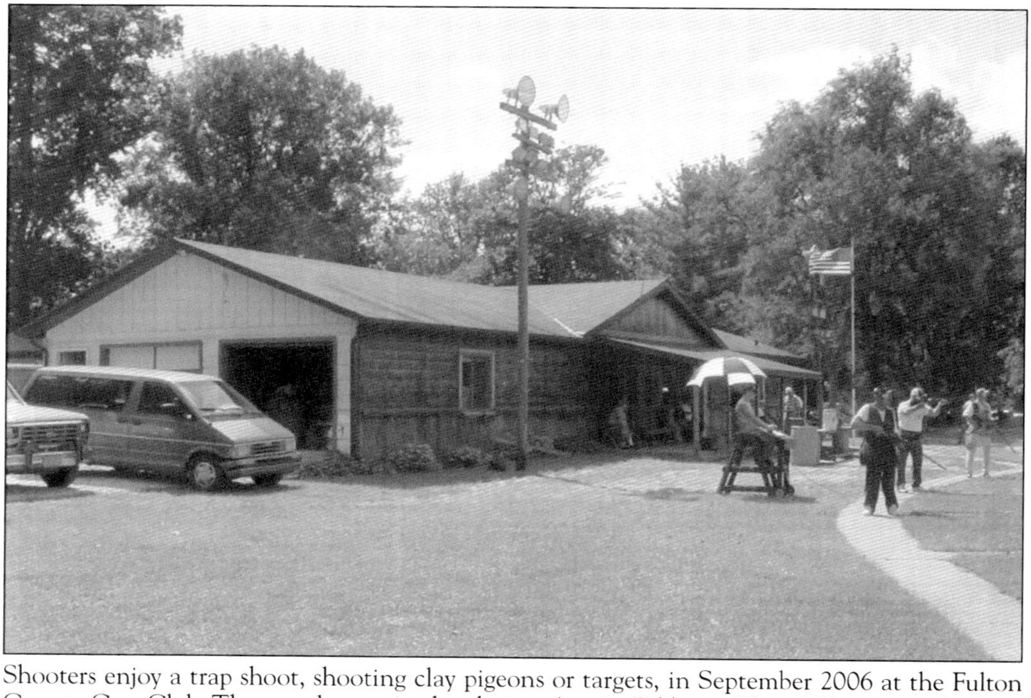

Shooters enjoy a trap shoot, shooting clay pigeons or targets, in September 2006 at the Fulton County Gun Club. The scorekeeper in the chair is Austin Gibbons. The clubhouse was built in 1976 and 1977. The property was donated by A. C. Bradley to the Izaak Walton League in 1920s. They withdrew from the national organization and incorporated as Fulton County Conservation Club in 1957. (Courtesy of Don Barker.)

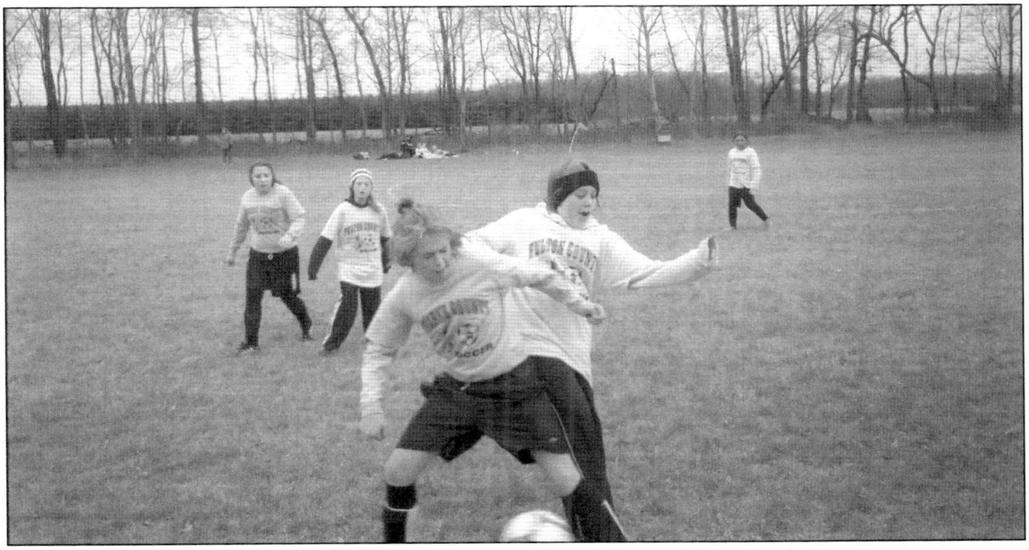

Soccer matches and girls' softball tournaments are held at the Brent Blacketor Memorial Sports Complex, located on East Fourth Street on 25 acres donated by Brent's mother, Mabel Blacketor, in 1998. The Fulton County Soccer Association was formed in 1995. Two teams of Fulton County girls play soccer above. (Courtesy of Linda Scott.)

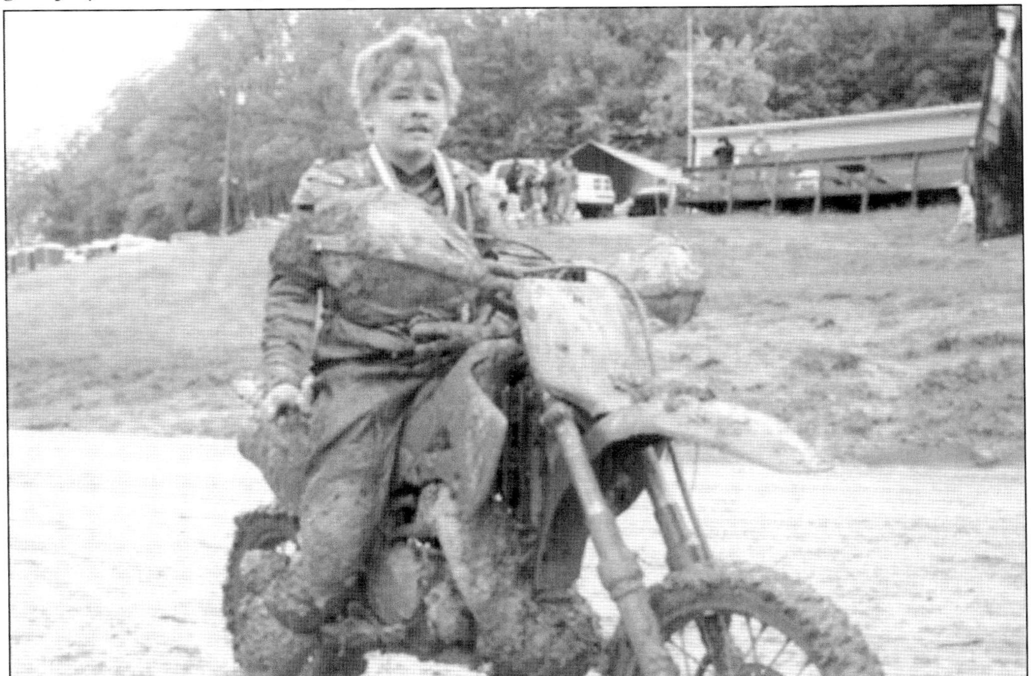

Zachray DuBois was the 2003 and 2004 Indiana State Hare Scramble Champion of the American Motorcycle Association (AMA) 50cc Auto Mixed Class. He was the 2007 Indiana State Hare Scramble Champion of the AMA 65cc Class. In 2008, he raced the GNCC (Grand National Cross Country), a 10-state national series, winning in Florida, Kentucky, Ohio, New York, and Indiana. He ended the series in second place for ages 11 and 12. (Courtesy of GNCC.)

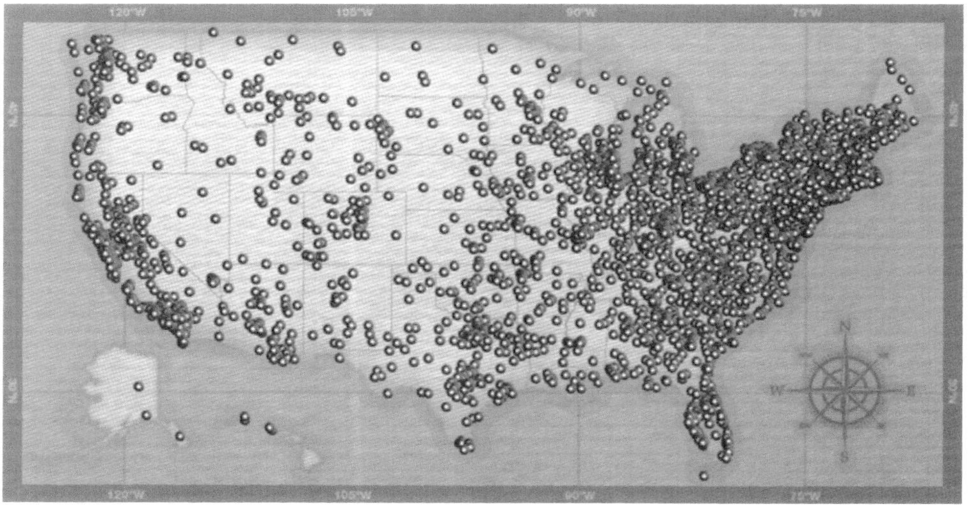